KOI

A FIREFLY BOOK

Published by Firefly Books Ltd. 2015

First printing

Publisher Cataloging-in-Publication Data (U.S.)

Brewster, Bernice.
    Koi : a complete guide to their care and color varieties / Bernice Brewster ; Steve Hickling ; Keith Holmes ; Nick Fletcher ; Mick Martin ; Tony Pitham.
[256] pages : color photographs ; cm.
Includes bibliographical references and index.
Summary: "Expert advice on keeping koi in top-quality condition and a complete directory of their magnificent color varieties" – Provided by publisher.
ISBN-13: 978-1-77085-519-9 (pbk.)
1. Koi. 2. Koi – Handbooks, manuals, etc. 3. Koi – Varieties. I. Title.
639.3/7483 dc23 SF458 K64 B74 2015

Library and Archives Canada Cataloguing in Publication

Brewster, Bernice, author
    Koi : a complete guide to their care and color varieties / Bernice Brewster, Steve Hickling, Keith Holmes, Nick Fletcher, Mick Martin, Tony Pitham.
Includes bibliographical references and index.
ISBN 978-1-77085-519-9 (pbk.)
    1. Koi—Handbooks, manuals, etc. 2. Koi. 3. Koi—Varieties.
I. Title.
SF458.K64B74 2015   639.3'7483   C2015-903118-4

Published in the United States by
Firefly Books (U.S.) Inc.
P.O. Box 1338, Ellicott Station
Buffalo, New York 14205

Published in Canada by
Firefly Books Ltd.
50 Staples Avenue, Unit 1
Richmond Hill, Ontario L4B 0A7

Printed and bound in China by 1010 Printing

Originally published by Interpet Publishing
Vincent Lane, Dorking, Surrey,
RH4 3YX, UK.

Credits
Compiled: Ideas into Print,
Claydon, Suffolk IP6 0AB, UK
Designers: Stuart Watkinson
and Philip Clucas MSIAD
Computer graphics: Phil Holmes
and Stuart Watkinson
Koi variety photographs: Nishikigoi
International (Nigel Caddock); Andrew McGill;
Kinsai Publisher Co. Ltd., Tokyo, (Shunzo Baba)
Text adviser varieties section: Kate McGill
Consultant for this edition: Bernice Brewster
Production management: Consortium,
Poslingford, Suffolk CO10 8RA, UK.

KOI

A Complete Guide to their Care and Color Varieties

Bernice Brewster, Steve Hickling, Keith Holmes,
Nick Fletcher, Mick Martin and Tony Pitham

FIREFLY BOOKS

Authors

Bernice Brewster runs an aquatic consultancy, with a major interest in the koi hobby. She writes for koi magazines and contributes papers to scientific and veterinary journals on fish husbandry. Bernice has written the chapters on Water Quality, and Feeding Koi and contributed to Physiology and Health Care.

Steve Hickling is a leading authority on koi. At World of Koi in Kent, UK, Steve and his team built a reputation for constructing state-of-the-art koi ponds, incorporating filtration systems that are now available worldwide. Steve has contributed chapters on Filtration, and Designing and Building a Koi Pond.

Keith Holmes is manager of Koi Water Barn in Kent, UK. Koi health has always been an area of particular interest for him and his practical experience, combined with the advice and guidance of numerous experts, have made a major contribution to the Physiology and Health Care chapter.

Nick Fletcher, former editor of the UK aquatic monthly *Practical Fishkeeping*, still regularly contributes articles to this and other fish-related publications. He has kept koi for 30 years and is actively involved in his local koi club. Nick has contributed the chapters on Buying Koi, Showing Koi, and the koi varieties section.

Mick Martin has been an avid koi-keeper for more than 20 years, gaining invaluable practical experience of koi husbandry through breeding his own koi, visiting Japan and buying high-grade koi on behalf of World of Koi. He has contributed the chapters on Breeding Koi and Koi-keeping — the Enduring Hobby.

Tony Pitham is the owner of Koi Water Barn in Kent, UK and is one of the most respected koi dealers working in Japan. He has judged and photographed the prestigious All Japan Shinkokai show and supplied many show-winning koi.

CONSULTANTS
Dr. Peter Burgess is a fish health consultant and university lecturer, specializing in ornamental fish. He holds degrees in parasitology, microbiology and fish biology, and was awarded a PhD for research on whitespot disease in tropical marine fish.

Dr. Paula Reynolds is an aquatic pathobiologist and proprietor of Lincolnshire Fish Health Laboratories and Research Centre. As well as offering a fish health service, her center carries out health screening on koi from around the world.

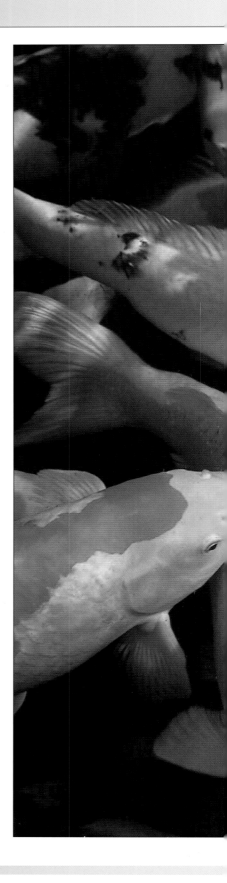

Contents

Part One

Part Two

Introduction

Koi-keeping is a hobby that generates obsession. Your starting point may be modest, but over the years, as your knowledge and understanding of these magnificent fish and their environment grows, you will find more and more to absorb you. And then you will be hooked.

The popularity of keeping koi has grown worldwide, spawning new clubs, shows and specialist magazines and consequently more and more koi-keepers. As a result, manufacturers are investing time and money in developing new foods, remedies, pumps, filtration systems and all manner of technical wizardry, which can only be a good thing for you, the hobbyist.

The hobby has changed tremendously over the past 20 years and this book reflects current thinking and the latest technical advances. The first part explores all the practical aspects of keeping koi, from understanding water quality and the filtration systems that maintain it, to the decisions, difficulties and triumphs of designing and building a koi pond in your own garden. Computer graphics reveal the working principles of the latest equipment in stunning clarity. This part of the book also features chapters on the physiology and health care of koi, how to feed them properly and how to buy good-quality stock in the first place. The section closes with expert insights into the world of showing and breeding koi — providing an introduction to yet more exciting and rewarding aspects of the hobby.

Why are koi called "koi"? Where did they come from? How has an international hobby grown up from naturally occurring color changes in carp kept as food fish? This is the subject of the first chapter in this part of the book and where our fascinating journey of discovery begins.

Koi-keeping — the enduring hobby

Who would have thought that the rather ordinary black common carp (Cyprinus carpio) found in waters throughout Europe for centuries could have undergone such a transformation on the other side of the world? In just two centuries, the breeding of koi for the serious enthusiast and the hobbyist alike has become an international industry. Koi husbandry has expanded beyond all bounds in the home of Nishikigoi (brocaded carp) — Japan. This is how the fairy tale story unfolded and became part of the Nishikigoi folklore.

Where did koi come from?

It is widely accepted that common carp were transported from Eurasia to the Far East more than 2,000 years ago and to Japan via China and Korea, where they were bred as a source of food. Carp are a very hardy breed of fish and could withstand the trauma of transportation by land and sea to far-off lands. There is evidence that the common carp, *Cyprinus carpio*, finally made it to Japan about 1,000 years ago.

But why were carp kept in captivity in those early years? It seems that Japanese farmers kept carp in mud ponds to supplement their daily diet of rice and vegetables. It is said they kept them in the paddy fields in which they grew their rice, but it seems more likely they were kept in the reservoir ponds above the paddy fields. Once any species is kept in a restricted breeding ground, sooner or later it will produce a mutation. In the case of carp, over hundreds of years these mutations caused external differences, including a

pronounced color change. The mutant fish were prized by the farmers and kept out of interest, instead of becoming food for the table. When these fine color irregularities were found, the farmers began producing "colored carp" as a hobby. This apparently occurred between 1840 and 1844, long after the early years of carp farming. From such humble beginnings, the keeping of Nishikigoi had started. Although koi are now bred throughout the world, only koi born and bred in Japan are true Nishikigoi.

The development of koi breeding

There are two distinct periods in the history of koi, the first being pre-1800. There is little documentary evidence about this era, since many of the references to koi actually concern wild carp. The ancient Chinese and Japanese illustrations on silk showed koi, but without any bright

Right: *A stylized, 19th century picture of a carp with a bogbean plant by Sadatora. Koi were often depicted in works of art, indicating their importance in Japanese culture.*

Above: *This Ai Goromo was voted best in the Koromo class at the All Japan Show 2001. Koromo means "cloaked" or "robed." Matsunosuke first established this variety in about 1950 in Niigata.*

Below: *A mountain scene typical of the area around Niigata, with a terraced mud pond in the distance. Originally, the ponds were used for topping up the rice paddy fields and held carp to supplement the diet.*

Above: *The indoor koi pool at the Nishikigoi Information Centre, Ojiya. Displays promote the history of koi-keeping, whereas the gardens feature traditional and modern pond designs.*

colors. In fact, there is little evidence of colored koi before the early 1800s. At that time, Nishikigoi were kept as a prized possession by the noblemen of the time — the forerunners of today's hobbyists!

It is widely accepted that the true colored koi originated in Japan from the Niigata prefecture (similar to a small county) during the early 1800s. Nishikigoi originated in the villages of Takerawa, Higashiyama, Ota, Taneuhara and Kamagashima. Today, some of these villages have been enveloped by the expansion of the city of Ojiya, the "home" of Nishikigoi. In fact, there is a wonderful Nishikigoi Information Centre given over to the history of koi in the center of the city. Niigata is located on the west coast of Honshu Island, a 2-hour bullet train ride from the capital, Tokyo. Niigata is revered throughout the world as being the best area for breeding koi.

The origin of the name koi

The name "koi" dates back to about 500 BC, when it was first mentioned and recorded to describe a wild carp presented by King Shoko of Ro to Confucius on the birth of his first son. The Japanese word for carp is *koi*, which was later used to describe all carp, both the wild and the more recent, colored varieties. There appears to be no documentary evidence to show when the word "koi" was first used just to describe the modern-day colored carp. Over the years, colored carp have been given many different names. When colored koi were first exported to the West, they were mainly red or red-and-white. In the early days they were known as flower carp (Hanagoi), brocaded carp (Nishikigoi), fancy carp (Moyoogoi) or even colored and colorful carp. Today, we tend to call them koi carp. In Japan they were originally called Hirogoi or Irogoi, meaning colored carp, but later they became known just as goi or koi. The preferred name in Japan for all single or multicolored carp is Nishikigoi, from the Japanese word *nishiki*, used to describe an expensive cloth of many colors imported from the Indian subcontinent into Japan and China, hence Nishikigoi – "carp of many colors." Nishikigoi are held in such high esteem that they are recognized as the national fish of Japan.

Some people say this is due to the quality of the mountain waters, whereas others claim the secret lies in the mud ponds that naturally contain montmorillionite clay, which is rich in vitamins and minerals. Whatever the reason, or as a result of the combination of both qualities, Niigata attracted the most famous names in koi breeding to the area.

There is no record of what was the first koi mutation, but it is thought to have been a red carp called "Hoo-kazuki," possibly from a mutant black carp. From this original red carp mutation the first white koi was produced. These were subsequently crossbred, resulting in the first red-and-white carp, originally called "Hara-aka," meaning red belly. The red-and-white carp is the oldest and still by far the most popular colored variety in Japan. It was not until much later, in about 1890, that it was officially recognized and named Kohaku. However, it is accepted that the Kohaku line was only stabilized in Niigata in about 1930.

Although red-and-white koi were the most talked about mutation, other colored carp were being developed. It was not long before the true all-black "Magoi" was produced from the original two strains of wild carp: one brown/black, the other a blue/black. From this early mutation came the first known true blue koi, the Asagi, meaning "light blue." Much later, an Asagi Sanke was crossed with a Doitsu mirror carp and the first Shusui (meaning "autumn water") was bred. A Shusui is said to represent the reflections of red autumn leaves floating against a pure blue sky.

Right: A wonderful Nidan Kohaku, "Nidan" meaning it has a two-stepped hi (red) pattern. The deep red is perfectly balanced over a pure snow-white body. The Kohaku is probably the most popular variety of koi in Japan today and also one of the oldest, dating back to the early 1890s.

The emergence of fishkeeping

Since the 1800s, there has been a massive expansion in the koi industry throughout the world. The Industrial Revolution in the Western world resulted in significantly better roads, transport and communication, and an increased awareness of other nations across the world. With the spread of this knowledge, public zoos and aquariums displaying wildlife from the other side of the globe became very popular. As a result, people tried to recreate these habitats in their own homes and gardens, and fishkeeping began in earnest.

During this early time, before the science of genetics had been developed, breeders gained important knowledge of how to maintain these unusual colors and improve on them.

But even now, with strong bloodlines going back over many years, it is still difficult to predict the resultant brood from a successful spawning.

Then followed what is known as the third mutation of early Nishikigoi. These are the Bekko varieties, comprising three types: Shiro Bekko (white fish with black spots — known as a tortoiseshell pattern); Aka Bekko (red fish with black spots) and Ki Bekko (yellow fish with black spots). The Bekko varieties do not produce natural metallic scales, apart from those bred with Gin-Rin (reflective silver) scales, unlike the similar Utsurimono varieties (black koi with white, red or yellow markings). These original mutations became the founders of all the colorful koi to be bred later, with the exception of the Ogon variety (single-colored metallic koi) that was developed many years later.

One further color combination played a tremendous part in the history of Nishikigoi. A tricolored koi (white with red and black markings) called a Taisho Sanshoku, later to be referred to as just Sanke, was developed during the Meji era (1868–1912). No one knows who actually bred the first Taisho Sanke, but it was first exhibited in 1915, when the fish was about 15 years old.

Further developments

At the turn of the 20th century, koi-keeping became a very popular hobby within Japan. Another change in direction was to have an even greater impact on the breeding of future koi; mirror carp were introduced into Japan from Germany. Their large shiny, uniform scales — five to six times larger than normal — proved very popular and the fish became known as Doitsu (Japanese for *Deutsch*, meaning "German"). The Doitsu had a much heavier, deeper and shorter body and was thought to be a hardier species than its Japanese counterpart, the Magoi.

As a result of more modern breeding methods, two kinds of Doitsu koi were perfected. Leather back carp (Kawagoi) had few or no scales, whereas the mirror carp (Kamamigoi) displayed large symmetrical scales along its back, either side of the dorsal fin. Some mirror carp displayed scales along their lateral line as well, and these are sometimes referred to as striped carp (Yoroigoi). Other varieties produced scales in irregular patterns reminiscent of ancient Japanese armor. The first successful crosses between the German carp and the Japanese carp were made in 1904. All varieties were to be known as Doitsu Nishikigoi. These modern varieties contributed greatly to the expansion of Nishikigoi throughout the world. This breeding finally provided the last part of the jigsaw — the Ogon.

Above: *An Asagi with the typical uniform blue-gray scaling. This distinct reticulation is synonymous with the variety. The Asagi was one of the first Nishikigoi produced as a result of a mutation from a Magoi some 160 years ago.*

Right: *It is said that a good Taisho Sanke will support an excellent Kohaku pattern beneath smaller, well-placed patches of sumi (black). The Sanke, as it is more familiarly known, is another old variety, first exhibited in 1915.*

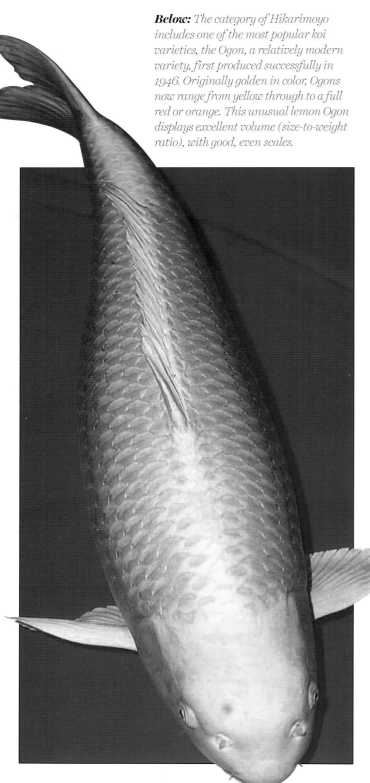

Below: *The category of Hikarimoyo includes one of the most popular koi varieties, the Ogon, a relatively modern variety, first produced successfully in 1946. Originally golden in color, Ogons now range from yellow through to a full red or orange. This unusual lemon Ogon displays excellent volume (size-to-weight ratio), with good, even scales.*

Following on from the Taisho Sanke came the Showa Sanshoku Sanke (later called Showa), and along with it the end of the Taisho era. In 1927, the Showa Sanke made its debut, primarily a black koi with patches of red and white, unlike the Taisho Sanke, which is a white koi with patches of red and black.

In the early 1920s, a wild carp with golden scales was crossed with a koi in a breeding program to produce the greatest amount of golden color. By 1946, the first Ogon (golden koi) was produced. The name "Ogon" initially referred only to the gold form, but today it applies to all single-color metallic koi. Ogons are included in the category Hikarimoyo (abbreviated from Hikarimoyo-Mono; Hikari meaning "shining" and mono denoting a single color). The exception to this category is the Matsuba Ogon. Although this koi variety is predominantly one color, its scalation is enhanced with black edging to the scales. This produces the famous "pinecone" pattern, so popular with hobbyists.

To put koi breeding into perspective, it is only very recently that modern varieties, such as Matsuba Ogon (1960s), Gin Matsuba (Platinum Ogon), Purachina (1965), Gin-Rin or Dia (wild silver reflective scales) varieties (early 1960s) and the Midorigoi (light green koi) in 1965, have all been developed. Thirteen colors and their numerous varieties are recognized for Nishikigoi and these are discussed in detail on pages 172–245.

Enjoying koi today

Koi-keeping enjoyed its heyday during the 1960s, when everyone in Japan appeared to keep koi. At that time there were more than 3,000 koi-breeders, but today there are just over 1,000. Koi mainly originating from Japan are now bred throughout the world, including Thailand, China, Korea, Israel, South Africa, United States and Europe. As a result, Japan has tended to raise the quality of the koi it sells and now specializes more in the superior high-grade koi we have come to expect from the "Home of Nishikigoi."

Japanese hobbyists are well catered for by the Zen Nippon Airinkai, or ZNA, the world's largest koi society, which is now accessible on the Internet. Many countries have local koi-keeping societies run by enthusiastic volunteers eager to pass on their knowledge to new-found members. There is plenty of reading matter for koi enthusiasts, with monthly and quarterly magazines available throughout the world.

Surfing the web

The Internet has become a household tool and probably most people surf the web regularly looking for information on all aspects of koi-keeping, from finding retailers to advice on water quality, filtration and health care. It is worth bearing in mind that the quality of information on some sites may be not be as good as others; sometimes the views expressed are a matter of opinion, rather than accredited fact.

Almost all the koi-keeping clubs and societies have websites and these are very informative on all matters relating to koi, as well as social activities and koi shows. Many of the koi clubs and societies also hold photographic koi shows, where members post photographs of favorite koi, which are formally judged and winners chosen. Additionally, the All Japan Koi Show, with the best Japanese koi competing, takes place at the end of January. The results appear on the

Above: *A traditional koi pond in Japan. The large moss- and lichen-covered boulders at the water's edge and the pine and juniper trees in the background are typically used to create a Japanese landscape. Note the clarity of the water.*

New varieties

New koi varieties are being produced by Japanese breeders all the time. With a greater understanding of genetics and an improved breeding program, new varieties are regularly being established. Obviously, it takes many years to perfect a new strain and ensure that it breeds true each season; only then can it be marketed as a new variety. The Pearl Scale Asagi is a good example of a recent addition. It features a reverse scale reticulation, where each scale is light blue edged with navy blue. Another development is the Kohaku/ Goshiki. This is a Doitsu fish with the classic Kohaku pattern (red on a pure white background) for 6 months. However, it gradually develops Goshiki colors, which it retains for 6 months and then reverts back to Kohaku — two fish for the price of one!

One bizarre mutation reported in the koi press was of koi carp being bred with their eyes facing up toward the surface, instead of on the side of the head. Koi are natural bottom-feeders, but because people like to hand-feed their fish, someone thought it would be an improvement if they could see their floating food quicker! Most koi-keepers would not be in favor of such mutations, but that is exactly what occurred within the fancy goldfish breeding program.

However, it is good to see that the Japanese are not just producing the classic varieties, but are constantly searching for new and exciting colors and patterns, which will benefit the hobbyist in the long run.

Internet within hours of the final judging and are certainly worth a look to admire the winning koi. Most koi retailers also make use of the Internet to advertise and offer online sales of equipment and even koi, which can be transported by courier to their destination.

For many hobbyists a trip to Japan to buy koi is only a dream. However, the Internet has made it easier to view the Japanese koi-breeders' websites, which are posted in English. Although Japan is revered as the home of Nishikigoi breeding, an Internet search shows that top-quality koi are also being bred in Europe and North America, and many breeders now rival the Japanese in the quality of koi they produce.

It is very easy to become completely focused on koi, but other websites worth searching are those concerned with aquaculture. Many of the filter systems we use on our koi ponds owe their origin to this industry. Many koi-keepers are also keen to try their hand at breeding koi themselves, and probably one of the most informative sites is the Food and Agriculture Organization of the United Nations website on carp breeding, which is a good starting point.

Your questions answered

Nothing can beat personal contact and one of the best ways of staying in touch with like-minded koi-keepers is through joining a local koi club or society. Most of these clubs and societies host regular meetings, and many of the members have plenty of experience in koi-keeping. They have themselves probably dealt with the common problems. Of course, showing koi is a common feature of most clubs and societies, and at these events there is an opportunity to see prize koi and discuss current trends with other koi hobbyists. Some of the bigger clubs stage annual conferences, inviting

A family tradition

It is widely accepted that wine producers making a fine wine from a single grapevine have good and bad years, and the same principle applies to koi spawning; one season's brood can be much better than the one produced the previous year. And, just as in fine wine production, koi breeding is often a family concern. Knowledge and experience are passed down from father to son and jealously guarded within the family. Young children and their mothers help out in the annual cull and sexing of Nishikigoi. Decades ago, some of the families were responsible for introducing completely new varieties to the world, and their descendants continue to specialize in them today.

Below: *In contrast to the traditional Japanese koi pond, raised ponds such as this are popular in the West. In Japan, the koi pond is part of a traditional-style garden, whereas in the West the pond itself tends to be the main focus of attention.*

koi for years and have built up a wealth of experience. It is worth bearing in mind, however, that with koi health problems it is very difficult for anyone to give an authoritative opinion without actually seeing the affected fish. It is well-worthwhile attaching a digital picture of the koi, as this may help to define the problem.

There are many other sites for water quality and koi health issues. Some have been designed by other koi-keepers, but a number are written by experienced aquarists and veterinarians. Contacting these sites can help with fairly minor problems, such as persistent water quality issues, especially for those koi-keepers living in fairly remote areas where local koi club or society membership is not possible.

Social networks, such as Facebook and Twitter, can also play an important role in helping koi-keepers world-wide to stay in regular contact with one another. Some of the clubs and societies may have been organized into groups on Facebook, which means taking out a membership to participate. Lastly, of course, there are services such as Skype or FaceTime that allow online long-distance discussion with fellow koi-keepers.

Above: *The scene at a Japanese fish farm, where prime koi are "bowled up" for inspection by koi dealers from around the world. There is much competition between dealers during the spring and autumn "harvests" to obtain the best deals for their customers at home.*

Below: *A typical scene at an Open Koi Show in France. The show vats in the foreground are attracting attention from visitors united in their enthusiasm for a truly international hobby.*

professional aquarists, veterinarians and other koi-keepers to give presentations. This is a valuable opportunity not just to socialize, but also to gather more information on the hobby.

Smartphones, tablets and computers have made it easy, not only to stay in touch with like-minded koi hobbyists, but also to access magazines and journals online, or to download them to these electronic devices. A number of magazines are dedicated to the hobby and most have the option of online subscription, which in many cases gives access to discussion forums. These forums can be really helpful, particularly where there is a problem either with koi health or the pond system. Many participants have been keeping

Water quality

Water — an extraordinary substance with unique properties — is essential to all living organisms. Compared with other liquids, water behaves in some very strange ways. For example, most substances shrink as they get colder, but at 3.94°C (usually rounded up to 4°C / 39°F) water expands, bursting pipes and tanks. In the pond environment, this means that at about 4°C (39°F), this denser but warmer water sinks and the least dense, colder water is at the surface, where it freezes. This is why ice floats.

The natural circulation of water

The total amount of water found throughout the world is constant, and it is continuously recycled through evaporation and precipitation in the form of rain or snow. The oceans are full of saltwater and literally give rise to the world's supply of freshwater in the form of rain and melted snow and ice. The atmosphere is rich in the greenhouse gas carbon dioxide, which is very soluble and simply dissolves into the precipitating rain, where it forms carbonic acid and thus makes the water mildly acidic. The atmosphere also contains an assortment of gaseous pollutants, such as sulfur dioxide from industrial processes and, increasingly, nitrogen oxides derived from motor vehicle exhaust fumes, which may also dissolve into rain, making it increasingly acidic.

On reaching the ground, some of the rain will simply evaporate, but the rest soaks into the surface and percolates down through the underlying soil and rocks, where it reacts with minerals and salts. The composition of the minerals and salts gives the water its chemical characteristics, and these vary according to the type of soil and rock through which it has trickled. The mineral content of this so-called groundwater can even include an assortment of metals. Granite substrates are impermeable to water, so few salts dissolve into the water as it trickles through the underground rock and it remains acidic and soft. In the areas where the

THE NATURAL WATER CYCLE

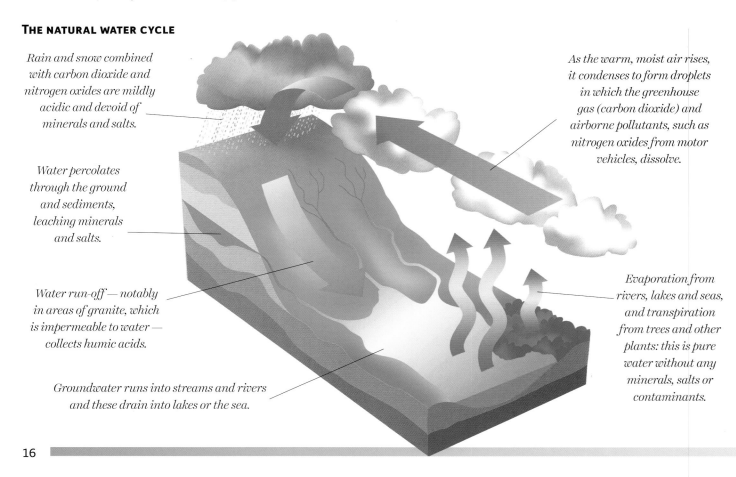

Rain and snow combined with carbon dioxide and nitrogen oxides are mildly acidic and devoid of minerals and salts.

Water percolates through the ground and sediments, leaching minerals and salts.

Water run-off — notably in areas of granite, which is impermeable to water — collects humic acids.

Groundwater runs into streams and rivers and these drain into lakes or the sea.

As the warm, moist air rises, it condenses to form droplets in which the greenhouse gas (carbon dioxide) and airborne pollutants, such as nitrogen oxides from motor vehicles, dissolve.

Evaporation from rivers, lakes and seas, and transpiration from trees and other plants: this is pure water without any minerals, salts or contaminants.

Left: Rain or snow melt water is naturally acidic, regardless of the presence of pollutants, and this causes minerals and salts to be dissolved in it as the water percolates through sediments and rocks. This means that natural bodies of water, such as the river shown here, contain a range of naturally occurring minerals and salts.

Above: Good water conditions are essential for keeping koi healthy. However, clear water does not necessarily mean it is suitable. Many dissolved pollutants, such as metals, chlorine, ammonia and nitrite, are invisible yet cause sickness or death.

water filters through chalk, limestone or gypsum, it is rich in calcium salts, which makes it alkaline and hard. Water hardness is familiar to most of us as the limescale found in kettles, pipes and on water-heating elements.

The mineral sediments through which water percolates may contribute traces of heavy metals such as aluminum, iron, lead, mercury, cadmium, zinc and bismuth. Dissolved metals can also find their way into the aquatic environment through mining, agriculture, forestry and landfill practices. Some heavy metals, such as iron or zinc, are vital for living organisms in very tiny quantities, known as "trace elements." Many, however, are very poisonous to living creatures and are particularly soluble in soft water. In hard, alkaline waters, the metal ions are "locked up" as the salts of the metals, which makes them less harmful. In soft, acidic water, the metals are present in their most damaging form and are therefore poisonous to koi. The effects of metals on koi are various and

may only affect specific organs, or the effect may be systemic, causing significant changes in all organs and tissues, which means they no longer function properly.

Agricultural activities may also influence water chemistry. For example, in unpolluted waters, nitrate is found at very low concentrations, but through the use of agricultural fertilizers, some areas may exceed recommended drinking water levels of nitrate. Groundwater may also contain residues of chemicals such as pesticides and herbicides.

Natural waters are rich in biological material, ranging from microscopic organisms to large aquatic plants and animals, including fish. The presence of plants and animals in the aquatic environment means that there are also breakdown products of solid organic material from living or dead tissues. These breakdown products include humic acid, oils, waxes, assorted hydrocarbons and fatty acids — all invisible residues that affect water quality.

Water treatment for human use

Pesticides are sometimes necessary to eradicate freshwater crustaceans and, more recently, the introduced exotic zebra and quagga mussels, which block the water systems. These molluscicides are pyrethrum derivatives and poisonous to koi. In most instances, several weeks" advance notification is given that the pipes will be treated. Following such treatment, the water in the pipes is unsuitable for water changing for about a month.

The microscopic life found in water includes bacteria, algae and single-celled organisms, technically called "protozoa." The majority of organisms found in natural waters are harmless, but some, such as the bacteria that

cause cholera or typhoid, can cause outbreaks of disease in humans. At the turn of the 20th century it was realized that adding chlorine gas as a disinfectant to drinking water reduced the incidence of waterborne disease in humans. Chlorine continues to be used as a disinfectant in mains water, and koi-keepers should be aware of its potentially harmful effects. In combination with ammonia, chlorine forms a range of substances known as "chloramines," principally monochloramine (NH_2Cl), dichloramine ($NHCl_2$) and trichloramine ($NHCl_3$), the relative quantities depending on the concentration of the parent chemicals and the pH of the water. Although chloramines have a

Below: Chlorine-based disinfectants added to drinking water are poisonous to koi. In soft water areas, the water can become contaminated with metals. And being mildly acidic, soft water causes any metals present to be in the most poisonous form.

Left: Water purifiers are commonly installed on the incoming water supply of many koi ponds. Modern purifiers can remove contaminants such as metals, in addition to chlorine and its derivatives. There are many different types available, so be sure to select the right type of water purifier based on a water report for your local area.

REVERSE OSMOSIS

In normal osmosis (right), water molecules pass across a partially permeable membrane from a dilute solution to a more concentrated one. With reverse osmosis, water pressure is used to reverse this flow of water molecules.

A partially permeable membrane allows only water molecules through.

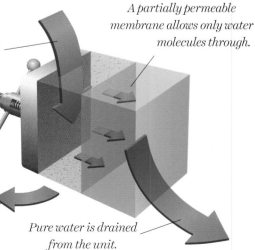

Tap water enters the reverse osmosis unit.

Mains pressure forces water through the membrane.

Leftover water can be used on the garden.

Pure water is drained from the unit.

Right: Water conditioners can remove chlorine and other harmful tap water contaminants. Many brands have a measuring device built into the container, enabling you to administer the exact dose. Mix the conditioner with pond water in a watering can and sprinkle it onto the pond surface or into the surface skimmer.

reduced disinfectant action on bacteria compared with free chlorine gas, the effect lasts longer in water, and so there has been an increasing tendency to add ammonia at the chlorination stage of water treatment.

Both monochloramines and dichloramines are toxic to fish. Chlorine and chloramines present in water are measured as "total residual chlorine." For koi, the recommended maximum continuous exposure level to total residual chlorine is 0.002 mg/l, but even at this concentration there is evidence of toxicity and effects on the gill tissue. Chlorine at concentrations of 4 mg/l will cause koi to die within 8 hours of exposure. New ponds should either have the water treated with a water conditioner, which can remove both chlorine and chloramine, or alternatively, the water filling the pond can be filtered through a water purifier.

It is not necessary to use a dechlorinator when carrying out partial water changes of up to 30 percent of the volume of the pond because the chlorine will be diluted in the system. However, if you suspect that the water authority may be flushing the mains supply, avoid water changes or be sure to add a conditioner.

Maintaining water quality for koi

Koi-keepers often say (as do all fishkeepers) that if you look after the water, the koi will look after themselves and, in many ways, there is much truth in this statement. Water quality varies according to its use; for example, drinking water is of excellent quality, but the chlorine content renders it unsuitable for fish. As we have seen, numerous factors contribute to water quality and they interact with one another, so there is no simple definition of the term. With regard to koi-keeping, water quality is almost exclusively concerned with physical and chemical characteristics such as temperature, dissolved oxygen levels, pH, the nitrogenous waste produced by the fish, alkalinity, phosphate levels, particulate organic substances and dissolved organic substances. Here, we look at these parameters in more detail.

Water temperature

Water temperature is related to weather conditions, but it is important because it affects all physical, chemical and biological processes and therefore has an effect on both koi and their pond system. For example, temperature directly influences both the solubility of oxygen and the toxicity of ammonia waste (see page 20).

Water temperature also has a profound influence on the physiology and health of koi. Increasing water temperatures cause koi to become more active, consume more food, grow, produce more ammonia as waste and spawn. Although any rise in temperature may have positive effects on koi, as the water warms, it also causes any dissolved contaminants or even treatments to become increasingly toxic to them. Decreasing temperatures cause koi to become less active, and their appetite and the efficiency of their

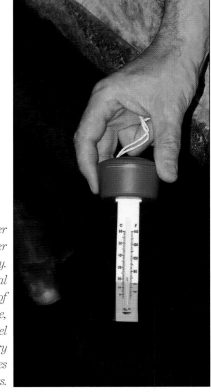

Right: Remember to monitor the water temperature routinely. There are several different types of thermometer available, from the floating model shown here to very sensitive electronic ones with remote probes.

immune system declines. However, many koi-keepers now choose to heat the pond through the colder months of the year.

Over the last 10 years or so, most koi-breeders in Japan have installed sophisticated fish houses in which koi in their first and second years are overwintered in ponds with a minimum temperature of 16°C (61°F). Keeping young koi in heated ponds through the winter means that they have never experienced cold water conditions. Therefore, in areas outside Japan that experience cold winters, it is better either to place these koi in heated pond systems or introduce them into the pond in summer when the water is warm. After feeding and growing through the summer, most of these young koi should successfully overwinter.

Dissolved oxygen levels

Oxygen is an essential requirement for koi and should be regarded as the most important water quality parameter. There are a number of factors affecting the solubility of oxygen in water, but temperature has a major effect. In cold water, when the koi are least active and their oxygen requirement is minimal, this gas is readily soluble in water, but as the water temperature increases through the spring and into the summer, the solubility declines. Heating water from 9 to 15°C (48 to 59°F) reduces the available dissolved oxygen by 13 percent. From the table showing the solubility of oxygen at a range of temperatures, you can see that in the summer, when koi are most active and their oxygen demand is greatest,

HOW TEMPERATURE AFFECTS AMMONIA TOXICITY

% free (toxic) ammonia in total ammonia

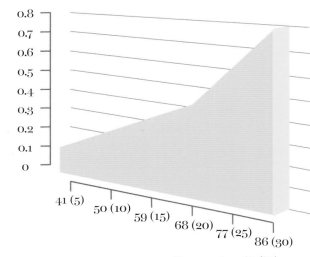

Temperature °F (°C)

HOW TEMPERATURE AFFECTS OXYGEN LEVELS

Oxygen mg/l

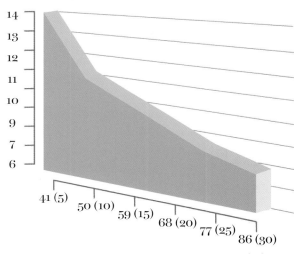

Temperature °F (°C)

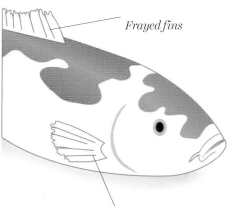

Frayed fins

Fins clamped tightly against the sides of the body.

Above: *As the water temperature rises, more of the total ammonia present changes into free ammonia, which is very poisonous to the koi.*

Koi gasping at water surface.

Above: *Oxygen solubility decreases with rising temperature. Affected koi are initially lethargic, but as oxygen level plummets they rise to the surface gasping.*

Gill cover flares as the koi tries to extract as much oxygen as possible from the water.

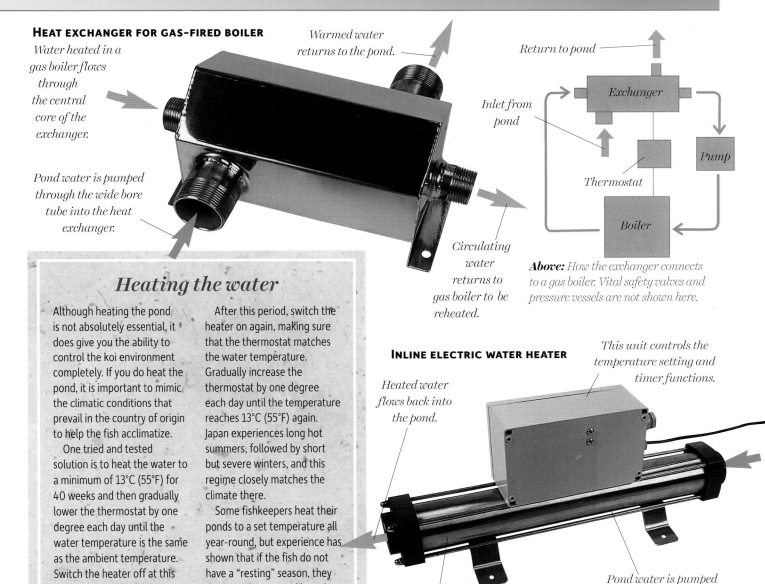

HEAT EXCHANGER FOR GAS-FIRED BOILER

Water heated in a gas boiler flows through the central core of the exchanger.

Warmed water returns to the pond.

Pond water is pumped through the wide bore tube into the heat exchanger.

Return to pond

Exchanger

Inlet from pond

Pump

Thermostat

Boiler

Circulating water returns to gas boiler to be reheated.

***Above:** How the exchanger connects to a gas boiler. Vital safety valves and pressure vessels are not shown here.*

Heating the water

Although heating the pond is not absolutely essential, it does give you the ability to control the koi environment completely. If you do heat the pond, it is important to mimic the climatic conditions that prevail in the country of origin to help the fish acclimatize.

One tried and tested solution is to heat the water to a minimum of 13°C (55°F) for 40 weeks and then gradually lower the thermostat by one degree each day until the water temperature is the same as the ambient temperature. Switch the heater off at this point and leave the fish in a "torpid" condition for 6 weeks.

After this period, switch the heater on again, making sure that the thermostat matches the water temperature. Gradually increase the thermostat by one degree each day until the temperature reaches 13°C (55°F) again. Japan experiences long hot summers, followed by short but severe winters, and this regime closely matches the climate there.

Some fishkeepers heat their ponds to a set temperature all year-round, but experience has shown that if the fish do not have a "resting" season, they do not spawn as readily and tend to hold on to the roe.

INLINE ELECTRIC WATER HEATER

This unit controls the temperature setting and timer functions.

Heated water flows back into the pond.

Pond water is pumped through the core. An arrow on the unit indicates the specified direction of flow.

Inside this stainless steel tube is an electrically heated element that warms the pond water as it passes through.

this vital gas is at a premium. The minimum dissolved oxygen concentration for healthy growth, tissue repair and reproduction in koi is 6 mg/l of water, but ideally the concentration should exceed this value. The more koi there are in the pond, the greater is the demand on the dissolved oxygen. This parameter should be viewed as the limiting factor on the number of koi that any pond can hold.

Within a koi pond there are other factors that affect the dissolved oxygen concentration. Blanketweed grows prolifically in the summer and, like all plants in the hours of daylight, these algal strands produce sugars using the energy from sunlight and carbon dioxide dissolved in the water, and liberate oxygen gas as a waste product during the process of photosynthesis. At night, respiration predominates, which

OXYGEN IN THE POND — WINTER

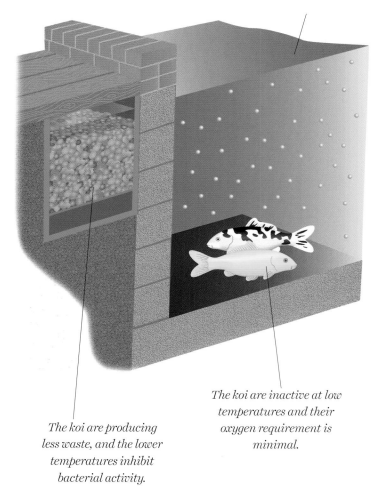

Oxygen is readily soluble in cold water.

The koi are inactive at low temperatures and their oxygen requirement is minimal.

The koi are producing less waste, and the lower temperatures inhibit bacterial activity.

OXYGEN IN THE POND — SUMMER

Less oxygen is available in the water as the temperature increases.

Blanketweed produces oxygen during the day, but consumes it at night.

At higher temperatures, the koi are increasingly active and need more oxygen.

More solid waste accumulates in the filter and this increases the demand for oxygen by the aerobic bacteria.

means that the blanketweed uses oxygen and produces carbon dioxide gas as waste.

In addition to any blanketweed growth, the bacteria and other microbes that live in the filter system consume vast amounts of oxygen by way of respiration and yet more in the oxidation of ammonia to nitrate as part of the nitrogen cycle (see the illustration on page 26) In fact, 1 g of ammonia requires 4 g of oxygen during its conversion to nitrate. The use of oxygen by the microbial flora is described as the "biological oxygen demand." Any aquatic system such as a pond will also contain a vast amount of organic material from the koi, blanketweed or other plant life, and from the

microbial population. As this material accumulates in the mechanical filtration system and breaks down, it uses oxygen and oxygen consumption increases. This is why it is important to clean this part of the filter regularly. The filter is therefore the biggest oxygen sink in a koi pond system. The filter bacteria are the most efficient at extracting oxygen from the water, followed by blanketweed and, finally, the koi can use what is left.

Many of the medications popularly used in koi ponds, such as malachite green, formalin and Leteux Meyer mix (a combination of formalin and malachite green), will strip the water of oxygen; do not use them if you suspect that the oxygen level is low. If you do need to add a medication to the pond, it is good practice to increase aeration before introducing any chemicals and to continue the aeration during the treatment.

In very cold weather, air is readily soluble in water and under certain conditions the water can become supersaturated with gas, leading to a condition known as gas bubble disease (see page 77). Although dissolved oxygen levels are elevated when water becomes supersaturated with air, it is the nitrogen content that gives rise to the symptoms of gas bubble disease. Supersaturation of water with air generally tends to occur when air under pressure is drawn into cold water. This can happen in a number of ways:

- A pipe or piece of tubing with a pinhole sucks in air and forces it into solution.
- Air diffusers in the deepest part of the pond may cause supersaturation. The pressure of water increases with depth and gases at high pressure dissolve more readily. In summer this is not a problem, as many gases are relatively insoluble in warm water, but in cold water, air readily enters solution from the air diffuser. Remedy the problem simply by raising any air diffusers to about 30 cm (12 in) below the water surface.
- Cold water already saturated with air heated in a closed, heat-exchange system becomes supersaturated as it warms up.

There are other ways in which dissolved gas levels become very high. For example, the photosynthetic activity of algal blooms can cause the water to become saturated with oxygen, and bore or well water is often saturated with nitrogen. Even air transport has been implicated as a cause of gas bubble disease in fish as a consequence of the changes in air pressure that occur during the flight.

Supersaturation of water can be detected by testing the oxygen content of the water; readings above 12 mg/l per liter are high. The gas can be seen venting at the surface of affected ponds, the water surface having the appearance of a fizzy drink as the tiny bubbles rise to the surface

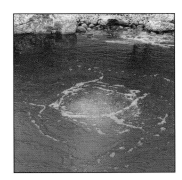

Left: In hot weather, when oxygen levels can be very low, it is vital to add extra forms of aeration, such as airstones connected to an air pump. Aerated bottom drains (here) help to add oxygen and also create a good water flow to the drain. Excessive aeration, however, can cause problems.

Above: Venturis have been traditionally used to aerate koi ponds and can be very efficient, but the delivery of air slows or stops if the pump becomes blocked by a prolific growth of blanketweed.

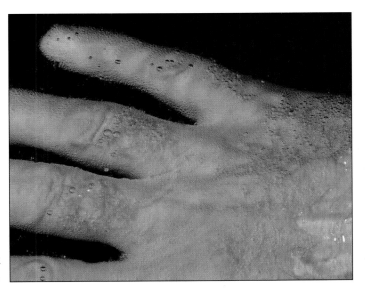

Left: If you slide your hand into some supersaturated water, it becomes coated with a layer of fine bubbles. Gas supersaturation usually occurs at low temperatures, when air readily dissolves in the cold water.

DISSOLVED OXYGEN TEST

1 Stabilize the oxygen content with the first reagent, then add eight drops of the second (shown here), forming a cloudy precipitate.

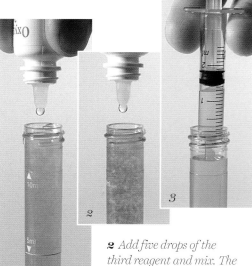

2 Add five drops of the third reagent and mix. The solution turns clear yellow.

3 Use the syringe to remove liquid down to the 10 ml mark on the test tube.

4 Pour the 10 ml of yellow solution into a small beaker for the next stage of the oxygen test.

5 Add five drops of a fourth reagent to the yellow solution in the beaker, which turns black.

6–8 Gently swirl the black solution until it is an even color. Add the final reagent a drop at a time until the black solution is colorless. Each drop added is equivalent to 0.5 mg/l of oxygen in the sample of pond water.

and burst. If you dip your hand into supersaturated water, it becomes coated in tiny bubbles.

It is important to identify the cause of supersaturation and rectify the problem. The affected water should be splashed and vigorously agitated to vent off the excess air. Oxygen levels can be monitored using simple test kits or electronic meters. Most of the meters available require frequent recalibration to ensure an accurate reading.

The pH value of water

The pH value of water is a measure of its acidity or alkalinity. The pH scale runs from 0 to 14: pH 0–6.99 is acid; pH 7.0 is regarded as neutral, and pH 7.01–14 is alkaline. Acid substances include strong battery acids with a pH of 0–1; lemon juice about pH 2; orange juice pH 4 and milk pH 6.0. Distilled or deionized water has a pH of 7 and is neutral, with no salts or minerals dissolved in it. Familiar alkaline substances include egg white, pH 8; antacid digestive remedies, pH 10; agricultural lime (calcium oxide), pH 13 and caustic soda (sodium hydroxide), pH 14. The extremes (pH 0–1 and 13–14) are the most corrosive.

Essentially, the pH is a measure of the hydrogen ions in a solution or substance and is based on a logarithmic scale, which means that each change in one pH unit reflects a 10-fold increase or decrease. This is one reason why it is important to make any pH adjustments slowly, otherwise they can have quite profound consequences on koi physiology. In the koi pond there is also a close relationship between pH and alkalinity (see page 28).

For optimum health, koi have a preferred pH range of 6.5 to 8.5. The pH of the koi pond is not a fixed value, however, and can fluctuate throughout a 24-hour period.

One of the most important reasons for monitoring the pH of the water is that in conjunction with temperature, increasing pH causes ammonia to become increasingly more poisonous to koi.

Ammonia, nitrite and nitrate

Koi produce nitrogenous waste in two forms: ammonia and urea. Ammonia — NH_3 — is the

BROAD RANGE PH TEST

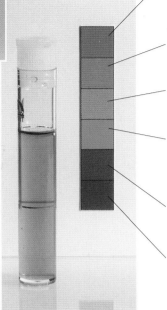

Above: *It is vital to test the pH of the water routinely, as this affects the toxicity of ammonia. The ideal pH range for the koi pond is between 6.5 and 8.5, so a broad range test kit is ideal. Here, a small tablet is mixed with 10 ml of pond water and the color compared to a chart.*

pH 4 *Too acidic — koi unwell, not feeding. Hard water: increase pH by water changes. Soft water: partial water changes, add marble chippings, oyster shell or chalk-based minerals/clays.*

pH 5 *pH still too low — koi will be lethargic. Increase pH as described above.*

pH 6.5 *Preferred pH range is 6.5–8.5, but even at this level, it could be increased.*

pH 7 *Pure or distilled water is pH 7, but unlikely to be achieved in the koi pond. Distilled water is devoid of minerals/salts.*

pH 8.5 *Top value recommended for koi. Does not cause them any major problems.*

pH 9 *In planted ponds, or those affected by algae blooms, pH can rise above 9 to about 11 during the day, but causes few welfare or health problems.*

HIGH RANGE PH TEST

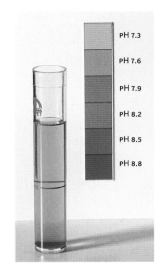

PH 7.3
PH 7.6
PH 7.9
PH 8.2
PH 8.5
PH 8.8

Above: *You can use test kits for low range and high range pH values for greater accuracy. Here the result shows a pH of 8.2.*

main form of waste and is excreted through the gills. Urea — $CO(NH_2)_2$ – is shed in small quantities in the form of dilute urine and is broken down through microbial activity into ammonia. All the ammonia produced as waste is oxidized by beneficial, oxygen-loving bacteria to nitrite (NO_2) and then to nitrate (NO_3). These conversions are essential steps of the "nitrogen cycle."

Ammonia is extremely poisonous to koi, causing changes to the gills and affecting the chemical composition of the blood (see page 78). When dissolved in water, ammonia exists in two forms: free ammonia (NH_3) and ionized ammonia (NH_4^+). Free ammonia is the most poisonous form and its relative concentration (as a proportion of total ammonia) increases in alkaline water and with rising water temperature. In mildly acidic conditions, however, more of the total ammonia will be in the ionized form. The maximum recommended continuous exposure level for free ammonia is 0.02 mg/l of water. The test kits available for monitoring ammonia levels measure the total ammonia concentration, including both free and ionised ammonia.

Activated charcoal and ion-exchange resins such as zeolite can be used to reduce the concentration of ammonia in the

FREE AND IONIZED AMMONIA

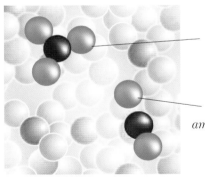

Free ammonia (NH_3) consists of one atom of nitrogen and three of hydrogen.

The nitrogen atom of ammonia attracts a hydrogen atom from water (H_2O).

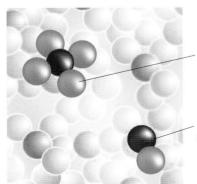

The hydrogen atom attaches to the nitrogen atom, conferring a positive charge on the newly created ammonium ion (NH_4^+).

Without one hydrogen atom, the water molecule becomes a negatively charged hydroxyl ion (OH^-).

HOW THE NITROGEN CYCLE WORKS

Water returning to the pond from the last stage of the filtration system may still contain some nitrate. Nitrate is one of the nutrients responsible for promoting the growth of blanketweed.

Water changes are an important aspect of pond management, especially if ammonia or nitrite are polluting the pond. Regular water changes can also help to reduce nitrate concentration in the water.

By adding an oxygen atom into each molecule, aerobic bacteria (Nitrobacter spp.) convert nitrite into nitrate (NO_3). Nitrate is the final breakdown product of ammonia in the nitrogen cycle and far less toxic than ammonia or nitrite.

Protein supplied in food is used by koi for tissue repair and maintenance, growth and reproduction. Any excess protein cannot be stored and is excreted as ammonia. The protein in any uneaten food also ends up as ammonia.

By removing the hydrogen and adding oxygen into each molecule, aerobic bacteria (Nitrosomonas spp.) convert ammonia into nitrite (NO_2). Although not as harmful as ammonia, it is still poisonous to koi.

Ammonia (NH_3) is released into the water by the gills. The small amount of urea voided in dilute urine breaks down to form ammonia. Ammonia is very poisonous to koi.

water. The ion-exchange resins work rather like a chemical trap, locking onto the ammonia and removing it from solution. However, it is important to realize that substances such as common salt (sodium chloride) added to the pond are more attractive to these resins, which will in turn release the ammonia back into the environment. Even where ion-exchange resins are used, it is very common to find ammonia still polluting the pond water, so they are not an effective substitute for partial water changes.

The secondary breakdown product of ammonia is nitrite, which is also poisonous to koi. The maximum recommended continuous exposure level for nitrite is 0.1 mg/l for soft water regions and 0.2 mg/l for hard water. Nitrite can build up in a koi pond, either because bacteria are converting ammonia at a faster rate than it can be broken down into nitrate (which is very common in new koi ponds), or because a different group of bacteria convert nitrate back into nitrite and nitrogen gas.

This latter process tends to occur when there is a problem with the filtration system that prevents adequate supplies of oxygen from reaching the bacterial populations.

It is important to monitor the water routinely for the presence of both ammonia and nitrite. Where either pollutant is present at detectable levels, undertake regular partial water changes to eliminate ammonia and nitrite from the pond. In some instances where the concentrations of ammonia and nitrite are excessively high, the toxicity can be reduced by increasing the salinity of the water through the addition of common salt, sodium chloride.

Nitrate is the final breakdown product of ammonia and the least harmful; the recommended maximum continuous exposure level is 50 mg/l above that found in the mains water supply for the area. Although nitrate is harmless to koi, it is a plant nutrient and will promote the growth of algae such as blanketweed. Nitrate rarely occurs at

AMMONIA TEST

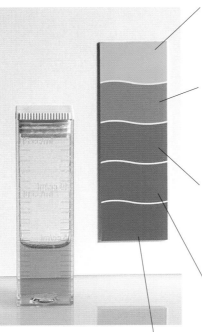

4 mg/l *A serious problem; koi will die within days. Make water changes, up to three times daily.*

2.0 mg/l *Koi feeling very unwell, often swimming through water inlet. Respiration rate increases through damage to gills and changes to body chemistry.*

1.2 mg/l *Ammonia accumulating in blood and tissues. Koi probably stop feeding. Improve conditions quickly through partial water changes.*

0.8 mg/l *Gill tissue swells and cells proliferate, leading to clubbed gills. Continue testing levels daily and make partial water changes.*

0.4 mg/l *Koi produce more mucus in response to ammonia. Monitor water and make partial water changes. Check filtration system is working well and not congested. Feed less.*

0.1 mg/l *Not harmful for a few days. Long term and especially at high temperatures and in alkaline water, this concentration exceeds recommended maximum continuous exposure levels.*

Below: *Ammonia and nitrite are very poisonous to koi. Polluted water can be crystal clear but deadly. Routine testing is the only way to ensure water is free of both.*

NITRITE TEST

Less than 0.3 mg/l *Fairly low and not a threat to koi. If nitrite values rise, monitor frequently. In the summer, a sudden increase in nitrite could indicate oxygen levels are too low.*

0.3 mg/l *In soft water, nitrite is more poisonous and this level can affect koi health; make partial water changes. In hard water, this nitrite level should be frequently monitored.*

0.8 mg/l *At this level, nitrite is harmful to koi in both soft and hard water; make regular partial water changes. Koi will show signs of irritation, rubbing and flicking on surfaces.*

1.6 mg/l *Nitrite combines with red blood pigment, affecting the ability of koi to use oxygen. Koi become lethargic and produce more mucus. Make daily water changes to reduce nitrite level.*

Over 3.0 mg/l *Nitrite pollution is now a serious problem and can kill koi. Blood vessels become relaxed and pin prick hemorrhaging occurs in gill tissue. Water change is essential.*

Below: *Where the water is soft and the alkalinity low, buffering capacity can be improved by adding oyster shells to the filter system, as shown here in a Japanese koi farm. The acidic water will erode the shells, releasing calcium carbonate into the pond.*

detectable levels in natural lakes and ponds, so it is best to control the concentration in the koi pond through partial water changes.

Water hardness

Water hardness is basically a measure of the calcium and magnesium salts present in the water, although other trace metals can contribute. Like alkalinity, the hardness of the water plays a role in acting as a buffer and often the measured values are very similar. Generally, hard water is alkaline and soft water is acidic. Soft waters are usually associated with low calcium content and other minerals necessary for koi health. Pollutants, toxic substances, including some treatments, and metals tend to be more poisonous in such water. You will therefore need to incorporate trace minerals and salts into the diet of koi living in softer water areas. The waters in Japan are naturally soft and are buffered by the koi-breeders using oyster shell and coral. The minerals and salts dissolved in hard water reduce the osmotic pressure on koi (see page 75) and tend to bind to, or chelate, toxic metals and pollutants, pulling them out of solution and thereby making them less harmful.

Alkalinity

As the name would suggest, the alkalinity of water is a measure of alkaline substances dissolved in it. The alkalinity of the water is due largely to naturally occurring hydrogen carbonates (bicarbonates, HCO_3^-), carbonates (CO_3^-), plus mineral hydroxides (OH^-) in the mains water. In areas where the water is soft, it is acidic and therefore devoid of any alkalinity. The alkalinity of the water is very important because it acts as a natural buffer, preventing wide fluctuations in pH, which can occur naturally as a consequence of respiration from the koi and microbes in the filtration system. Excessive plant or algal growth, such as blanketweed, can also affect the pH of the water, which is buffered by the alkalinity. Through its buffering action, the alkalinity of the water is used up, and in the absence of water changes in hard water areas, the pond water can become increasingly acidic and subject to wide variation in pH. Where the water is soft and acidic, the pH and alkalinity can be increased by adding marble chippings, oyster shell or the ceramic rock used as a filter medium (rich in calcium carbonate). The mildly acidic water dissolves these alkaline minerals, releasing carbonate and hydrogen carbonate into the water, which improves the alkalinity. Sodium hydrogen carbonate (sodium bicarbonate)

CARBONATE HARDNESS (KH) TEST

1 Add the KH reagent a drop at a time to a 5 ml sample of pond water and gently swirl the tube to mix. Count each drop of reagent.
2 Initially, the sample turns blue.
3 As more reagent is added, the water sample turns yellow. Continue counting the drops added until the yellow color is stable. Each drop added from the beginning of the test represents 1°dH, which is equivalent to 17.5 mg/l of carbonate.

PHOSPHATE TEST

1 Add five drops of the phosphate reagent to a 5 ml sample of pond water and shake gently to mix.

2 Allow the sample to stand until the yellow color has fully developed and then compare it with the chart. Place the tube on the printed chart and look down the length of the tube to compare the color of the solution.

0 mg/l *No phosphate, ideal. However, this reading is still possible if a prolific growth of algae is consuming the nutrient.*

0.25 mg/l *Even such low levels boost algae growth.*

0.5 mg/l *Low but enough to encourage blanketweed. Make partial water changes and test incoming tap water.*

1.0 mg/l *This level and above cause algae blooms such as green water and blanketweed.*

2.0 mg/l *At this level, blanketweed will thrive.*

4.0 mg/l *Very high level of phosphate. Control it with partial water changes and/or by installing a vegetable filter.*

8.0 mg/l *At this level, there will be an algae bloom in the pond to consume the nutrient. Take action as described above.*

has been used in extreme instances to improve the alkalinity, but treat it with caution as it has anesthetic properties when used with carp and therefore koi. Ideally, the alkalinity should be between 100 and 150 mg/l for adequate buffering of the pond.

Phosphate

Phosphate is released by koi into the pond water as a waste product. It is the limiting factor for growth of plants and in most situations is in rather limited supply. However, if there are many koi in the pond they will release considerable quantities of phosphate and this provides the essential nutrient for nuisance algae such as blanketweed to thrive. Using a vegetable filter (such as a bed of watercress through which water from the filter trickles before it returns to the pond) helps to remove the available phosphate and reduce the growth of blanketweed. You can establish phosphate levels using a simple test kit as shown on this page.

Blanketweed

One of the biggest headaches for many koi-keepers is the proliferation of blanketweed, which thrives in warm water with plentiful nutrients and can choke bottom drains, pumps, filters and pipework. Like many other algae species, blanketweed periodically undergoes a form of sexual reproduction that results in the release of spores, which are the likely source of initial contamination in the koi pond. Although ultraviolet (UV) filtration systems can control single-celled algae (green water), they have no effect on the growth of blanketweed. Various chemical treatments are available in the form of liquids, granules or crystals, but they are all only temporary solutions, as the blanketweed inevitably flourishes again once the chemical becomes diluted beyond a specific concentration.

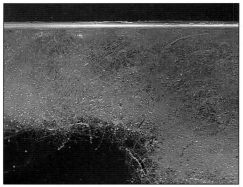

Above: Oxygen — a daytime by-product of photosynthesis — in blanketweed strands. The trapped bubbles cause the mass to rise.

Right: The weed develops rapidly in summer, choking bottom drains, pumps and filters, and causing low oxygen and high ammonia levels.

BLANKETWEED REMEDIES

Pads placed in one of the filter chambers provide a slow-release of a chemical to control algal growth.

Natural control methods include barley straw, here in netting packs, dropped into the pond. The dose rate of barley straw is 50 g/1,000 l of water (2 oz/220 gal).

Blanketweed remedies

In the past there was a range of herbicides that could be used to control blanketweed growth, but most of these have been withdrawn because they are harmful to the environment and wildlife. Many hobbyists resort to removing blanketweed manually, twisting the fibers onto a stick and then pulling them off. Unfortunately, breaking the fibers acts as a growth promoter and can make this nuisance algae grow even more prolifically. Dyes, usually blue or black, have been marketed to control nuisance algae growth in ponds. These filter out the sunlight, causing the blanketweed to die. However, the depth of color in these dyes is intense and therefore unacceptable to most koi-keepers because it becomes impossible to see the koi unless they are at the water surface. Barley straw is another natural means of control, but it must be placed in well-aerated water, as the bacteria and fungi which decompose it need oxygen to produce the hydrogen peroxide that kills the blanketweed.

Products based on enzymes and bacteria can successfully control blanketweed in the summer, with optimum water temperatures. The enzymes promote the blanketweed growth, whereas the bacteria remove the necessary nutrients from the pond water. Thus the blanketweed dies in the absence of essential nutrients.

Ultrasonic algae control

A more recent product controls blanketweed using ultrasound. The device is placed in the water and emits ultrasonic vibrations that are harmless to fish and aquatic plants, but that kill the algal cells in blanketweed. Every plant cell contains a fluid-filled cavity known as a vacuole. The ultrasound ruptures the vacuole in the blanketweed, killing the cells. Chains of single cells comprise blanketweed, which are more susceptible to the effects of ultrasound than are the multicellular aquatic plants.

Blanketweed does not thrive so well in brackish water. Where it is out of control, you can introduce salt or aquarium salt at 1.6 g/l (0.25 oz/gal).

AN ELECTRONIC BLANKETWEED CONTROLLER

Electronic circuitry in this sealed weatherproof unit generates pulses of random electrical pulses.

Power lead

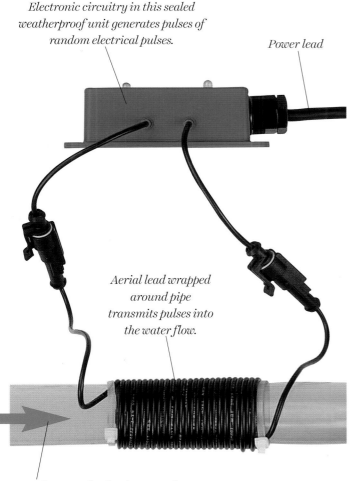

Aerial lead wrapped around pipe transmits pulses into the water flow.

Pond water after having passed through the main filter system.

Particulate organic substances

All the microscopic organisms in the pond system, plus koi debris, such as discarded skin cells, mucus and feces, and decaying plant material such as leaves or treated algae, are described as particulate organic substances. These often form a matrix that causes the filtration system to block and allow the water to track through the system. They also provide a food reservoir for the fish parasite Trichodina (see page 112), which feed on organic material trapped in the mucus layer of the fish. The Trichodina irritate the koi, which respond by producing more mucus, which in turn traps more organic material and so begins the route to a clinical infection of this parasite. The presence of Trichodina in samples of koi mucus indicate the presence of organic material in the pond, filtration and associated pipework. Clearing the filters and removing the organic material is therefore important in controlling outbreaks of Trichodina parasites.

In the laboratory, particulate organic substances are usually measured as "particulate organic carbon," or POC. A sample of pond water is filtered, the material dried and then burnt using special equipment to convert all the carbon within the material to carbon dioxide gas, which is then measured.

Dissolved organic substances

As organic material from the koi, microbes and plant cells decays, it gives rise to an assortment of organic chemicals. Many of these substances are not especially soluble in water, but can be removed using a technique known as foam fractionation or protein skimming (see page 45). Air blowers and airstones, or even venturis, can mimic the action of a foam fractionator, causing a persistent foam on the water surface.

Below: *Be sure not to overfeed the koi, as uneaten food will decay and the protein content will lead to ammonia pollution.*

Filtration

All aquatic animals produce nitrogenous waste, in the form of ammonia, urine and feces, all of which are extremely poisonous to freshwater life. In a natural environment such as lakes, rivers, streams and even ditches, the marginal aquatic plants, pond weeds and algae use this nitrogenous waste, and many of the aquatic invertebrates and microscopic animals consume the feces as a rich source of nutrients. This cycling of nutrients in the freshwater environment creates a balanced, healthy habitat, free of these natural toxic waste products.

Aquatic plants are rarely found in the koi pond as the koi are the focal point. A biological filter is therefore required in order to remove the nitrogenous waste. It usually incorporates some form of mechanical filtration to remove the feces. It is fair to say that some koi-keepers use an additional plant or vegetable filter, but this is primarily to remove nitrate and phosphate, and reduce nuisance algae growth. The biological filter exploits nitrifying bacteria and other micro-organisms, which oxidize the ammonia produced by the koi, first to nitrite and then nitrate. Not only do the bacteria and micro-organisms use oxygen to convert the ammonia ultimately to nitrate, but they also need oxygen to produce energy; in effect the biological filter can be thought of as a living entity. In this section, we look at how filter systems work and consider the practical options available for koi-keepers to maintain the water quality in their ponds.

External filters

When early experiments with undergravel filtration proved unsatisfactory in the long term, it became clear that the filter system of a koi pond had to be sited externally for ease of maintenance, if nothing else. This meant devising a receptacle that could contain filter media with a large surface area to support beneficial bacteria and through which water could flow freely.

Above: *The pond and filter are like an ecosystem, where the bacteria in the filter are totally reliant on the koi in the pond for their source of food, and the fish are dependent on the bacteria to break down their waste products. If the koi were taken out of the pond the bacteria would die, and vice versa.*

EXTERNAL FILTER — ABOVE GROUND OR INGROUND?

Water pumped to filter system

Filtered water returns under gravity

Above: *An above-ground filter system. Water pumped from the pond passes through the biofilter under gravity and returns via a waterfall.*

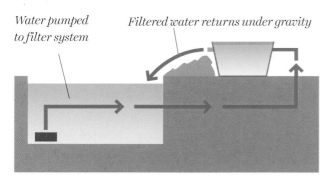

Right: *A gravity-fed inground filter linked to the pond by a bottom drain and pipework. Water is returned by a pump in the last filter chamber.*

Bottom drain gravity feed to the filter

Water is pumped from the filter back to the pond via a venturi

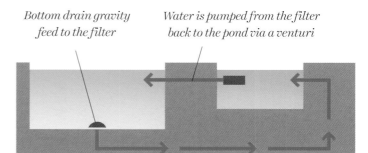

External filters can be either pump-fed or gravity-fed from the pond. They are available in various shapes and sizes, and the number of compartments required is relative to the size of the pond and the intended stocking levels. Of all the filtration methods available, the external filter is by far the best, as the chambers are easy to maintain for cleaning purposes, but they must be fitted with a drainage facility to remove waste products that settle beneath the media. Should the need arise, the system can be completely isolated from the pond simply by switching off the pump, if it is pump-fed, or closing a slide valve, if it is gravity-fed.

If a system like this is installed below ground, it can be covered by decorative wooden decking strong enough to walk over. Alternatively, you could place a bench on top to act as an additional viewing area. Filters installed above ground can be difficult to disguise, but remember that they do not have to be situated close to the pond. Providing the outlet is higher than the water level in the pond, water will run back to the pond under gravity even if it is 15 m (50 ft) away. Another important consideration is that the chambers should have a void beneath the media that is dished toward the base with an independent outlet (at least 4 cm [1.5 in] in size) at the bottom, so that all the debris can be completely removed without having to disturb the media.

Choosing the right filter

You can choose from a number of filtration systems in a wide range of shapes and sizes, each with their own individual features. Choosing the correct system can be a difficult decision, especially if you are on a limited budget. Remember that this will be the single most important purchase that you are likely to make when constructing your dream pond and any mistake could be extremely costly in the long run. As with the design of your pond, research this aspect thoroughly before you decide which system is best for you. Make sure you understand the principles of biological filtration and that your chosen filter is sufficient in size to cope with the intended stocking rate and volume of water to be treated.

Hobbyists on a limited budget may be tempted to construct their own filter from concrete or use a converted coldwater storage tank. However, experience has shown that neither of these methods is particularly successful, as both materials have their limitations. Coldwater tanks have a tendency to distort, bulge and become brittle on exposure to sunlight. By

Above: *If you get the filtration system and water quality right, the fish will look after themselves. Remember to test the water on a regular basis to pre-empt any problems. Keep a record for reference.*

design, they have a flat base, making it impossible to remove the detritus that forms beneath the filter media. Without prior building experience, concrete filters can be extremely difficult to build and render completely watertight, especially around the areas where pipes enter and exit the chamber. Furthermore, it is almost impossible to mimic the cylindrical vortex or octagonal filter shapes that are the most effective in producing the maximum flow rates possible without "dead" spots occurring in the media.

Mechanical filtration

Mechanical filters are an extremely important part of any biological filtration system. Every koi pond system produces particulate waste, such as koi feces, sloughed mucus, dead organisms (including bacteria), algae and bits of cellular material. If this organic material enters the biological filtration system, it causes sediment to accumulate and block the water flow. This leads to tracking, where the water passes rapidly through the filter before the beneficial nitrifying bacteria can oxidize the ammonia waste, resulting in water quality issues.

Mechanical filtration acts as a strainer, removing particulate organic waste from the koi pond, and should therefore be placed before the biological filter to prevent waste from washing in to this vital part of the filtration system. Any mechanical filtration system readily becomes coated in organic detritus and therefore requires frequent maintenance and cleaning. Although cleaning filters is anathema to many koi-keepers, the purpose of mechanical filtration is to allow the organic detritus to be removed easily. It is not designed to house the beneficial nitrifying bacteria, which is the function of the biological filter. If the organic waste is allowed to accumulate in the filters and pond water, it increases the overall bacterial load. This encourages outbreaks of disease, including Trichodina, which thrives in these conditions, moving onto the koi, where the sticky mucus traps their food.

The pump should also be capable of turning over enough water under pressure without affecting its flow rate, otherwise the biological filter's effectiveness will be impaired, especially if the volume of water passing through it is constantly fluctuating.

Some biological filter media, such as brushes sited in the first stage of a multichamber biological system, have natural mechanical properties. However, they must be tightly packed, with each brush overlapping the next, so that the debris is trapped. It is no good having just a few brushes, as the water will take the easiest route, bypassing them altogether and taking the dirt into the next stage. Japanese matting and plastic media have very few mechanical properties, as water passes freely though the channels without restriction. Porous ceramic rock (Alfagrog) is very effective, because it is a fairly dense material, but, even so, small particles still manage to pass through. You can see this happening over a period of time; the ceramic material becomes coated with a very fine dust, which is basically dirt that has managed to pass through the previous chambers and, as it is strained by the ceramic rock, settles on top of the stones.

Some filter systems incorporate layers of foam placed on top of the ceramic rock to prevent this occurring, which is quite effective. Unfortunately, the foam has to be washed regularly, otherwise the water cannot pass through freely and the restriction causes the system to back up and overflow.

So what is the answer to this problem? There are only a few proprietary systems suitable for a koi pond and choosing the right one will depend on the volume of water to be treated and stocking levels.

Below: The water enters a smaller chamber in the drum filter at the far end of the picture via three 110 mm (4½ inch) inlets. It passes into the main chamber by going into the middle of the drum and through the mesh. This means that all the debris is caught on the inside of the drum and there is only clean water on the outside. The clean water is pulled from a 110 mm (4½ inch) outlet in the main chamber (at the closest end of the picture) by an external pump.

Left: There are various models of drum filter on the market, designed for ponds of different volumes. This smaller unit will apppeal to koi hobbyists with compact ponds.

Filter system dos and don'ts

DO

Buy a filter large enough to cope with the volume of water and stocking rate.

Choose a very strong model, preferably made from fiberglass.

Ensure that the method of transferring water between chambers can cope with the flow rate for the pump.

Ensure that all waste products can be completely discharged individually from the base of each filter chamber.

Make sure that aeration can be introduced without disturbing the media.

DON'T

Skimp on size or price, as filtration is the most important consideration when setting up a pond.

Use cold water storage tanks or attempt to build a filter from concrete.

Attempt to "do-it-yourself" until you have sought advice and professional help.

Use inferior filter products not designed for filter media, such as hair rollers.

Put too much filter media in each chamber; a depth of 23 cm (9 in) is sufficient.

Drum filters

In the past, solid waste collecting in the biological filtration system was a common problem in many koi ponds. The result was that the water tracked through the filter too fast for the nitrifying bacteria to break down the ammonia to nitrate. Although drum filters remain in extensive use in industrial recirculating systems used for aquaculture, more recently they have been installed as part of koi pond filtration.

Drum filters, or rotating drum filters, are an effective form of mechanical filtration, which separates the solid waste from the water by using a rotating screen. Water passes into the drum and exits through the screen, where any solid matter is deposited. As the solid matter accumulates on the screen, the drum rotates and spray bars wash the solid waste into the waste pipe. As well as leaving the pond water free of solid detritus, the process also reduces the potential for opportunist fish disease-causing bacteria, such as Aeromonas hydrophila, to establish. These thrive on the organic content of the sludge. Similarly, this mechanical filtration reduces incidents of infection with parasites such as Trichodina, which normally feed on the detritus removed by the drum filters.

Below: *The drive belt and mechanism for the filter drum can be seen on the left side of this picture. The spray nozzles are positioned over the drum.*

Below: *When the cleaning cycle operates, the rinse water and debris are washed down the drain through an outlet at the far end of the unit.*

Sieve filter

Another variation on the mechanical filter theme is a simple box housing a fine sieve that physically strains out solids. The sieve consists of hundreds of laser-cut stainless steel blades arranged in rows at 90 degrees to the water flow, and with aperture options of 50, 100, 150 or 200 microns (millionths of a meter). Water flows through, but fine particles — including weed cells and some immature stages of fish parasites — are trapped.

Pond water is pumped or drawn by gravity over a weir in the body of the device. As it strikes the sharp edges of the blades, surface tension is broken. Dirt particles, or strands of blanketweed, are pushed away from the sieve by the hydrostatic load created. Because the sieve fits into the body of the unit in a curved profile, the particles end up trapped at the lowest point. They can then be removed by hand, flushing to waste or by turning off the pump, sliding out the sieve and rinsing it off.

When water passes through the screen, a pressure drop sucks in air, so the blades act like mini-venturis, oxygenating the water. This device can be used in pump-fed or gravity mode with pumps of flow rates of up to 15,000 l/hr (3,300 gal/hr).

SIEVE FILTER

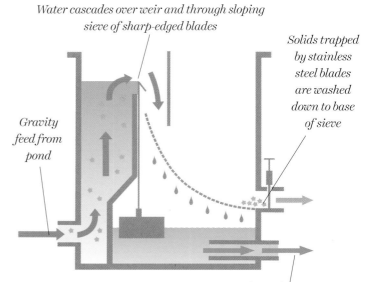

Water cascades over weir and through sloping sieve of sharp-edged blades

Solids trapped by stainless steel blades are washed down to base of sieve

Gravity feed from pond

Pump carries away cleaned water

Above: *The sieve filter is sited so that the internal weir is slightly higher than the pond water. In this way, water is gravity fed from the bottom of the filter, over the weir and passes over the sieve. The sieve creates friction, which breaks the water tension, causing organic particles and sediment to drop out of solution.*

Above: *The sieve filter with the weir in place. Water flows through the weir and exits from the smaller pipe at the base of the filter. The larger pipe discharges the solid matter to waste.*

Above: *The weir mechanism has been removed to show the sieve mechanism and illustrate the bend in the sieve. This traps the solid waste and particulate organic matter. As the water passes through the sieve blades, the surface area of the water is increased, aerating the water and adding oxygen, which improves the efficiency of the next stage of biofiltration.*

Above: *Although the sieve filter appears to be very simple, it is extremely efficient in trapping solid waste, organic material and suspended solids. These are present in the water column of all koi ponds.*

Multichamber filters

The bays, or chambers, in a multichamber filter are used for a number of reasons, but mainly as a means of separating different filtration media. The first chamber will take the brunt of the debris from the pond, so use a mechanical medium to trap this. At the same time, you must make sure that it will not clog quickly, otherwise water will not be able to pass through to the next stage. The bays that follow will contain the main biological media, which are usually preinstalled in these filters. Dense materials were traditionally used to polish the water, but mechanical prefiltration is so efficient now that it removes particulates before they reach the filter. Use a dense material in the final stage to remove any fine particles before the water is returned to the pond.

Look closely at the method of transferring water from one chamber to the next and ask yourself if it is capable of passing the total volume of the pond through the filter every 2 hours. If the size of the connecting pipe or ports between chambers is too small, the water will not pass through quickly enough to supply the pump in the final chamber, which could cause it to burn out. The transfer ports are also an ideal location to house airstones to re-oxygenate the water as it travels between the bays without disturbing the beneficial bacteria contained within the media.

Pumps for koi filters and ponds

A good-quality, reliable pump is an essential and integral part of a pond and filter system, and must be capable of running continuously, 24 hours a day, 365 days a year. All pumps are driven by an electric motor that rotates an impeller inside a casing. As it turns, the impeller draws water into the casing and expels it through the outlet. Generally speaking, the

GRAVITY-FED MULTICHAMBER FILTER

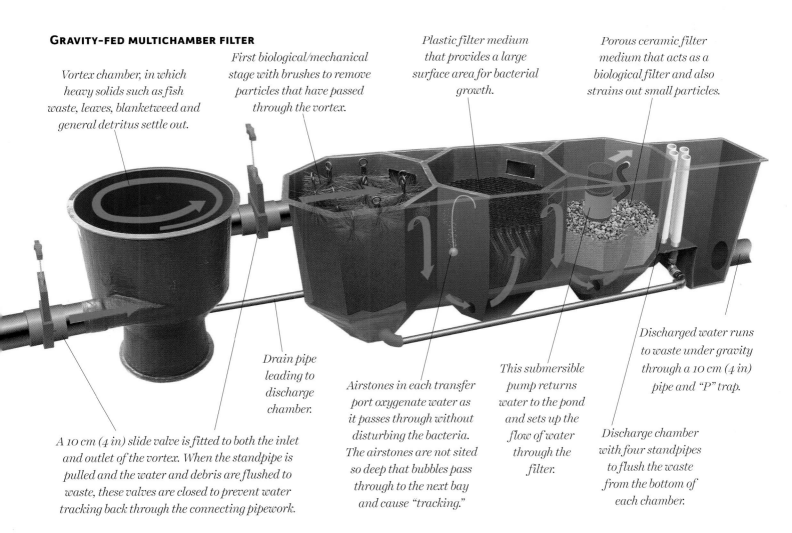

Vortex chamber, in which heavy solids such as fish waste, leaves, blanketweed and general detritus settle out.

First biological/mechanical stage with brushes to remove particles that have passed through the vortex.

Plastic filter medium that provides a large surface area for bacterial growth.

Porous ceramic filter medium that acts as a biological filter and also strains out small particles.

Drain pipe leading to discharge chamber.

Discharged water runs to waste under gravity through a 10 cm (4 in) pipe and "P" trap.

A 10 cm (4 in) slide valve is fitted to both the inlet and outlet of the vortex. When the standpipe is pulled and the water and debris are flushed to waste, these valves are closed to prevent water tracking back through the connecting pipework.

Airstones in each transfer port oxygenate water as it passes through without disturbing the bacteria. The airstones are not sited so deep that bubbles pass through to the next bay and cause "tracking."

This submersible pump returns water to the pond and sets up the flow of water through the filter.

Discharge chamber with four standpipes to flush the waste from the bottom of each chamber.

CALCULATING THE SIZE OF YOUR FILTER

STEP 1

In a pond of 16,000 liters capacity a typical fish population might be as follows. (Use the graph on page 154 to estimate the weight of each fish based on their length.)

Six 50 cm koi at 2.4 kg each.

Six 40 cm koi at 1.8 kg each.

Six 30 cm koi at 0.5 kg each.

Six 20 cm koi at 0.1 kg each.

Total weight of fish in the pond is 28.8 kg.

Double this figure to allow for growth and increased stocking rate and the total fish weight is 57.6 kg.

STEP 3

In a four-chamber filter in which each chamber measures 60 x 60 x 30 cm, the volume of filter media in each chamber is 0.113 m³. The table below shows the surface area provided by different media and how the target of 177 m² is reached.

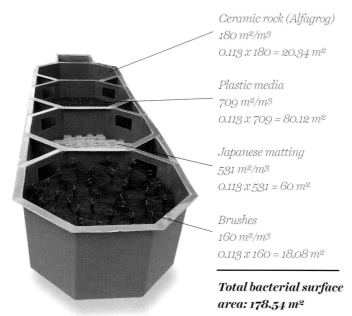

Ceramic rock (Alfagrog)
180 m²/m³
0.113 x 180 = 20.34 m²

Plastic media
709 m²/m³
0.113 x 709 = 80.12 m²

Japanese matting
531 m²/m³
0.113 x 531 = 60 m²

Brushes
160 m²/m³
0.113 x 160 = 18.08 m²

Total bacterial surface area: 178.54 m²

Above: *This filter setup would be ideal for the proposed stocking rate. Add a fluidized bed for extra biological filtration.*

STEP 2

Use this graph to find the bacterial surface area required in the filter system to support the total weight of fish in the pond. In this example, the total fish weight of 57.6 kg needs approximately 177 m² of bacterial filter surface area.

Bacterial surface area in square meters (m²)

800
750
700
650
600
550
500
450
400
350
300
250
200
150
100
50

0 20 40 60 80 100 120 140 160 180 200 220 240 260
Total weight of fish — kg

Conversion factors

Liters to gallons, divide by 4.54; kg to lbs, multiply by 2.205

m² to ft², multiply by 10.76; m³ to ft³, multiply by 35.3

---

speed or flow generated by the pump depends on the size of the impeller and the amount of electricity the motor consumes, although in recent years, manufacturers have successfully produced high-output pumps that use a lot less power. Selecting the right pump for your system can be difficult, as there are several to choose from.

There are two basic types of pump: external and submersible. External pumps are used to draw water through a surface skimmer (see page 68). Because skimmers are sited remotely with an external fitting, i.e., they are not submerged in the pond but sit outside, it is necessary to connect solid pipework to an external pump with a suitable threaded inlet, so it pulls in water directly from the source. If the external pump is sited below the water level, the pipework will be naturally "charged" with water by gravity and the pump will begin to operate immediately. However, if the pump is located above water level, it will be necessary to fit a nonreturn valve to stop water tracking back to the pond when the pump is switched off and having to prime the pump

Top tips for a healthy pump

1 Fit the pump at the final stage of filtration so that all the detritus in the pond is filtered before it reaches the pump.

2 Clean the strainer housing and foam inserts on a regular basis and more often in the summer.

3 If the pump is sited in the pond you can prolong the intervals between regular maintenance by replacing the standard strainer housing with a larger prefilter.

4 Never pull the pump from the pond using its electricity supply cable. Instead, tie a string around the handle on the pump.

5 Site the pump at least 15 cm (6 in) from the base of the pond, as this will prevent it becoming clogged by large objects.

6 If there are no bottom drains in the pond, vacuum it

on a regular basis to prevent the buildup of general debris that may impair the pump's performance.

7 From time to time, it may be necessary to descale the impeller/rotor assembly and soak it overnight in a domestic kitchen descaler.

8 Always fit a ground fault interrupter (GFI) for added protection against possible electrical accidents.

9 Buy a cheap spare pump in case of emergencies. It makes sense to have one, rather than risk losing all your fish.

10 Do not restrict the flow of water through the pump, as this will cause the motor to burn out and may invalidate the warranty. If you need to regulate the flow to a filter, fit a "T" piece before the valve and divert the balance of the water to a further venturi or waterfall.

Above: *Pump technology has advanced considerably, producing compact, external, energy-efficient pumps with good, continuous flow rates. They can cope with quite large items of debris, such as leaves, removing the need for strainer baskets.*

again. Although most external pumps are "self-priming," they cannot pull out the air in the pipework from the pond and will run dry unless the pipework has been filled manually through an access port or similar.

Submersible pumps are designed to operate under water, either in the pond or in the filter system. If a submersible pump is located in the last chamber of a multichamber filter, all the dirt, algae and general detritus will have been filtered out (or at least substantially reduced) before reaching the pump, which will make it perform more efficiently and extend its life expectancy and will involve less maintenance in terms of cleaning the strainer and impeller.

Pump flow rate

It is important to understand that a pump should be capable of turning over the total capacity of the pond through the filtration system every 2 hours to ensure good retention time within the chambers and a healthy biomass. If the flow rate is reduced due to a blockage in the pump, the ammonia and nitrite levels in the water would rise and the oxygen level could fall below the minimum requirements of 6 mg/l, causing stress in the fish and potential losses. The ultraviolet clarifier (UVC) discussed later also needs to have a constant minimum flow rate and if this falls below the recommended level, the water may turn green due to an algae bloom.

All manufacturers state the maximum flow rate the pump is capable of producing at zero head (meaning at the surface of the pond without any pipework or fittings attached). However, it is important to take into account that flow rates can be significantly reduced by the height of the pipework above water level, otherwise known as "head." The head of pipework is calculated from the point where the pipework breaks the surface and NOT the depth of the pump. The flow

A SURVEY OF FILTER MEDIA

Porous ceramic material (Alfagrog)

Manufactured by sintering selected fire clays at very high temperatures, resulting in a porous, foamed ceramic material. The rough surface with many open pores has a high surface area, making it ideal as a filter medium for aerobic bacteria. Its ceramic bonding provides strength and integrity when the water flow is reversed when flushing the bottom drains. Maximum depth of media is 30 cm (12 in).

Advantages
- Lightweight material.
- Good mechanical filtration.
- Easy to clean.
- Does not deteriorate.

Disadvantages
- Needs to be suspended in the filter.
- Clogs over a period of time.

Plastic media

A wide range of different types and shapes of plastic filter media are available, specifically manufactured for biofiltration. Perforations or hollow centers mean this type of filter media allows a good water flow rate through the system, while the fins and other projections provide plenty of surface area for bacterial colonization. The surface area of the filter media is the most important factor in koi pond filtration systems. These plastic filter media can provide a surface area in the region of 1,000 m2, for each cubic meter of filter material. As a rule of thumb, each cubic meter can treat 1 kg (2.2 lb) of food consumed by koi, when they are feeding most actively in the summer.

Advantages
- Lightweight.
- Large surface area.
- Self-cleaning.
- Does not deteriorate.

Disadvantages
- Plastic shapes occupy a large amount of space.
- Not suitable for all filters.

Canterbury spar

This medium has a good, irregular surface area on which bacteria can grow, plus an excellent mechanical "polishing" effect to help keep water clear. Do not completely fill the chamber with spar, as this causes clogging. If this happens, water cannot find its way through the gravel and tracks up the sides of the chamber, bypassing the media entirely. Spar should be 15–20 cm (6–8 in) deep and supported from the base on a unplasticized polyvinyl chloride (uPVC) perforated plate with a void underneath to encourage the heavy solids to settle on the base, where they can be discharged to waste.

Advantages
- Inexpensive.

Disadvantages
- Difficult to clean.
- Water can bypass media over time.
- Dense material that clogs quickly.
- Disintegrates over a period of years to form a solid sediment.

Filter brushes

Made from nontoxic polypropylene, with a stainless steel wire core.
Normally used as a mechanical prefilter to the main biological stage to stop heavier solids, such as leaves, blanketweed, fish waste, etc., entering the main filtration system. When brushes are left uncleaned they become biological. Rinse in pond water periodically (to retain bacteria) to remove solids, otherwise they become completely blocked. Arrange brushes so they just overlap in rows suspended from the top of the chamber. Leave a void under the brushes to aid further settling of heavier solids.

Advantages
- Lightweight material.
- Good mechanical filtration.
- Very little maintenance required.
- Easy to clean.
- Available in a wide range of sizes to suit your filter chamber.

Disadvantages
- Needs to be suspended in filter.
- Can only be used in multichamber filters.
- Relatively expensive.
- The chamber needs to be mass-filled.

These brushes are 40 cm (16 in) long and 15 cm (6 in) across.

Crystal Bio media

Crystal Bio media is formed from glass heated to over 900°C (1,652°F). This produces a highly porous media, with a very high surface area that is ideal for the nitrifying bacteria to colonize.

Lytag

Baked clay spherical granules used in the final stage of filtration. This medium was widely used in the past, but has largely been replaced by porous ceramic rock.

Disadvantages
• Clogs very quickly.

Foam

Open-cell foam, usually placed in three layers on top of ceramic rock in the filter. A dense material that tends to clog quickly and needs regular washing. Unfortunately, when the sponge is cleaned, any bacteria present will be lost, so its use is purely mechanical.

Advantages
• Lightweight material.

Disadvantages
• Little biological benefit.
• Regular maintenance required.

Coarse, medium and fine grades of foam used in filter systems.

Japanese filter matting

A polyester-based material supplied in 2 x 1 m (78 x 39 in) sheets. Cut into 23 cm (9 in) wide strips, with 5 cm (2 in) spacers in between to fit the filter chamber exactly, otherwise it will not function correctly. Install on a support tray so that water passes evenly through the holes. Bacteria will then develop on all the internal surfaces and will increase the surface area threefold. Because of the vast surfaces, the matting takes longer to establish the necessary nitrifying bacteria and other microorganisms that will remove the fish wastes. To speed up this process, introduce a live bacterial additive, which has the required bacteria held in liquid suspension. Introduce this to the filter system on a regular basis until the water is mature.

Advantages
• Lightweight material.
• Large surface area for bacterial growth.
• Very little maintenance required.

Disadvantages
• Solids pass through unrestricted.
• Can only be used in multichamber filters.
• Relatively expensive.

Matala

Similar to Japanese matting, but supplied in 1.2 x 1 m (48 x 39 in) rigid sheets that can be installed vertically or horizontally. Water flows freely through its matrix of stiff fibers. The material is self-supporting in the chamber and there is no need to use a perforated plate. It is available in four densities: low (0.18 mm), medium (0.09 mm), high (0.06 mm) and super-high fiber diameter (0.045 mm), fitted in the first to last chambers respectively.

Advantages
• Even adhesion of nitrifying bacteria to the filter mat fibers.
• Lightweight.
• Easy to clean.
• Nontoxic.
• Self-supporting.

Disadvantages
• Takes a long time to mature biologically.

Three grades of Matala, the finest on top.

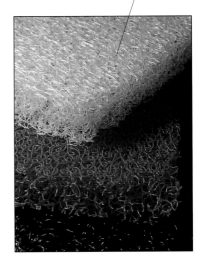

rate would be the same at the surface whether the pump was 6 m (20 ft) or 1.5 m (5 ft) deep, because the pressure of water in the pipe is equal to the outside volume. In addition to the flow restrictions caused by the pumping head, the length of run from the pump to the filter or the return to the pond, the number of inline elbows, the bore of the pipe used, UVCs, heaters, venturis and other equipment can all adversely affect the flow rate. It is no good buying a pump for a 22,700 liter (5,000 gallon) pond that produces a maximum flow of 11,350 liters/hr (2,500 gal/hr) if there is, say, a 2 m (78 in) head, several elbows and a long pipe run, plus several items of equipment, as the flow will fall below the minimum requirement.

Coping with clogged pumps

The most common reason why pumps become clogged is the scourge of every koi-keeper — blanketweed. The long strands of algae pass through the pump's strainer housing and entangle themselves around the impeller, causing it to slow down or come to a complete standstill. During the height of summer, when the weed problem is at its greatest, you may have to clear the pump twice a day to maintain the full flow rate. In the autumn, leaves that are not removed from the surface will fall to the bottom of the pond, be drawn toward the pump and sucked against the strainer. Fish feces, leaves and organic detritus can all cause problems, especially if the pump is sited in the pond. The best solution is to have a gravity-fed filter system and install the pump in the final stage. This way, all foreign objects will be removed before they can affect the pump.

The pumps that suffer most from clogging are the ones with relatively small strainer housings and foam inside. Because of the dense nature of the foam, it is not long before it becomes obstructed. Choose a pump with an impeller that will allow solids up to 8 mm (0.3 in) to pass through, which can then be dealt with by the filter system.

There is a misconception that external pumps do not become clogged as quickly as their submersible counterparts; however, this is not true, as both take their feed directly from the pond and suffer the same consequences. External pumps are more difficult to install as they generally need to be sited in a dry chamber away from the elements and must be fitted with a nonreturn valve to prevent them running dry, especially if they are above water level.

Above:
Submersible pump with a large strainer assembly that allows solids up to 8 mm (0.3 in) to pass through without clogging the impeller. The universal hosetail is attached to a swivel balljoint.

It is good practice to clean the pump regularly to ensure that the impeller within the motor does not become clogged, thus causing the flow rate to slow down or stop completely. This will help to maintain its full life expectancy and avoids the unnecessary expense of having to replace it.

If, after you have cleaned the strainer and impeller, a pump fails to operate, return it to your dealer for a replacement if it is still under warranty. If it is outside the warranty period, it may be possible to service the better-quality pumps.

If the pump should fail when the water temperature is above 10°C (50°F), you must replace it immediately. With the pump out of commission, the aerobic bacteria in the filter will begin to die and the oxygen content will fall to critical levels. If you cannot replace the pump straightaway, do not feed your fish until you have installed a new one and flushed the stagnant water out of the filter.

Bubble bead filter

These filters use a medium consisting of small (3 x 5 mm), floating plastic beads. In normal running, the beads float in the upper part of the device, forming a filter bed that carries out biological filtration as well as straining out solid particles down to 15 microns (millionths of a meter) in size — a fine sand particle is 50 microns.

Several models are available, depending on the size of the pond being treated. All have the capability of being fitted with an integral UVC unit to control green water. Cleaning the filter is made easy by a valve system that enables automatic backwashing, with collected wastes being flushed out on a regular basis.

Bead filters can maintain acceptable water quality with a loading of up to 8 kg of food/day/m^3 of filter media (0.5 lb/ft^3). This is equivalent to 23 kg (50 lb)of koi feeding at a 1 percent rate. For maximum water quality, this figure is halved to an upper limit of 4 kg of food per day per m^3 of bead media (0.25 lb/ft^3). These figures are based on standard bead media and typical pelleted foods with a protein content of around 35 percent.

Providing sufficient aeration

Biological filters should be considered as a self-contained ecosystem, and the oxygen consumption by nitrifying bacteria and other microorganisms is very high. If there is insufficient dissolved oxygen in the water, the filtration system can be affected, leading to an accumulation of ammonia or nitrite. To prevent this occurring, multichamber filters should be fitted with airstone diffusers to provide extra aeration as the water travels through. This is essential, because as the water proceeds through each filtration stage, a certain amount of oxygen is removed by bacteria as they convert ammonia to nitrite and nitrite to nitrates (see page 26). Aerating the water in the transfer ports will create the optimum environment for bacteria to thrive on the surface of the filter media.

Other factors that influence the oxygen content of the water are the numbers and size of koi stocked in the pond. Large koi have a higher demand for oxygen than small ones, but a pond heavily stocked with small koi also places a high oxygen requirement on the water. It is easy to monitor the koi pond routinely for oxygen levels using a dissolved oxygen test kit (see page 24).

BUBBLE BEAD FILTER

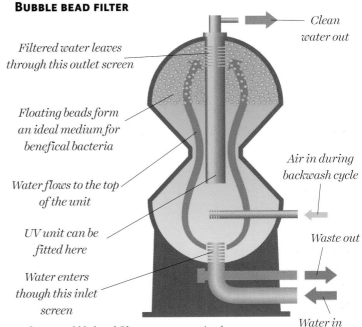

Clean water out

Filtered water leaves through this outlet screen

Floating beads form an ideal medium for benefical bacteria

Water flows to the top of the unit

UV unit can be fitted here

Water enters though this inlet screen

Air in during backwash cycle

Waste out

Water in

Above: *Bubble bead filters are pressurized systems that contain thousands of floating plastic beads. These are in constant motion as the water flows through the system. The movement of the beads acts as mechanical filtration and the beads provide the surface area for biological filtration bacteria to colonize.*

Left: *An ozonizer coupled onto a bubble bead filter provides disinfection and increases the oxygen content of the water, allowing the bacteria to work more efficiently and breaking down dissolved organic debris.*

An aerated dome or adding a conversion kit in an existing pond will promote more efficient water circulation into the bottom drain, thereby improving the removal of solids from the pond bottom. It will also provide additional aeration when oxygen levels are low during the summer months or if treatments are introduced into the pond (see page 66).

Below: *The fine bubbles created by an air diffuser are extremely efficient at delivering oxygen into the water. The small bubbles contain atmospheric air and for their size have a large surface area, which allows oxygen to readily dissolve into the water.*

Above: *The sieve filter shown at the back removes particulate matter from the water and provides the bubble bead filter (blue) with well-aerated water that enhances the bacterial activity in this biological filtration system. A UVC is also included.*

Below: *An air pump suitable for a koi pond. It needs to deliver a minimum of 40 liters/hour to supply six airstones or an aerated bottom drain.*

Airstones and air pump

Airstones, or similar bubble-forming devices driven by an air pump, should be standard pieces of equipment in the filtration system of a koi pond to provide supplementary air. As we have seen, they should be fitted in the transfer ports of the filtration system to ensure maximum saturation as the water passes through the chambers to feed the nitrifying bacteria contained within the filter media. If you do not have an aerating bottom drain, it is also a good idea to have a couple of airlines in the pond, so that if the main biological filter pump were to fail, the air pump would maintain oxygen levels and act as a backup. Do not place the airstones on top or below the media, as this can cause unwanted tracking of water through the filter and disturbs the bacteria. In addition, too much disturbance within the filter chamber does not allow solids to settle freely on the base.

HOW A PROTEIN SKIMMER WORKS

The dissolved organic carbon sticks to the surface of the bubbles and is carried up and out of the top of the tube as foam.

As the bubbles collapse, a yellow liquid builds up in the collecting cup and can be discarded.

Water from pond flows downward into a rising stream of air bubbles.

Airstone connected to a powerful air pump.

Cleaned water returns to the pond.

Top aeration tips

Always site the air pump above water level, because if there were to be a power outage, water would run back into the pump by capillary action. This would result in a loss of water from the system to the depth of the airstones, possibly causing the pump to burn out. If this is not an option, fit an inline nonreturn valve.

Air pumps are not suitable for outdoor use and should always be located in a dry housing.

Small air pumps are ideal for aerating filter systems and when dipping koi in medicated baths.

In larger koi ponds, have at least two airstones running as a backup in case the main biofilter pump fails.

A venturi can be quite noisy as it draws air into the breather pipe. You can silence the venturi simply by placing a small piece of sponge in the air intake.

Do not solvent-weld the venturi to the pipe in the pond wall as it could get blocked up with blanketweed at a later date and would have to be cut out and replaced. Instead, drill a small hole through the venturi and pipe, and secure them together with a stainless steel self-tapping screw.

The venturi

A venturi (devised by the Italian G.B. Venturi) is a piece of equipment that injects air into the water. It is made from 2 to 4 cm (0.75–1.5 in) pipework, with a restrictor inside and an air tube that extends above water level. When water is pumped through the venturi, the restrictor forces air to be sucked in from the tube above water level and mixed with water inside the venturi to cause thousands of tiny bubbles that both aerate the water and improve circulation.

Protein skimmers

If the surface of your pond takes on an oily appearance and bubbles from a venturi or waterfall take a long time to burst, then the problem is protein waste, or dissolved organic carbon (DOC). This can also give the water a yellowish tinge. The cause is decaying organic matter, including food, algae, blanketweed and fish waste. The reason for the surface of the pond appearing oily is that the dissolved organic carbon is attracted to the water/air interface. The answer to this problem is a device called a foam fractionator or protein skimmer. In its simplest form, water from the pond is passed down a vertical tube against rising air bubbles from an airstone. The DOC sticks to the surface of the bubbles and is carried up and out of the top of the tube as foam. In more advanced units, water enters a vessel through a downward-

Above: *Typical signs of a buildup of dissolved organic carbon, or protein waste, in the pond. Look for an oily appearance and long-persisting bubbles. Fitting a foam fractionator, or protein skimmer, will solve the problem.*

ULTRAVIOLET CLARIFIER

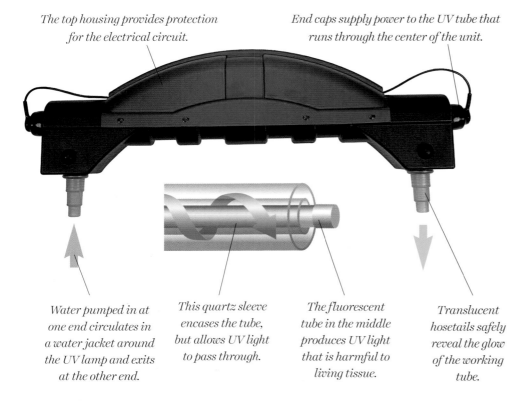

The top housing provides protection for the electrical circuit.

End caps supply power to the UV tube that runs through the center of the unit.

Water pumped in at one end circulates in a water jacket around the UV lamp and exits at the other end.

This quartz sleeve encases the tube, but allows UV light to pass through.

The fluorescent tube in the middle produces UV light that is harmful to living tissue.

Translucent hosetails safely reveal the glow of the working tube.

At the heart of each UV unit is an ultraviolet lamp sealed inside a quartz glass sleeve. Although more expensive than normal glass, quartz glass is used because it is purer, will not filter out the UV light given off from the bulb and maximizes the unit's efficiency.

UVCs have no adverse effect on sensitive plant and pond life, and as no chemicals or other environmentally harmful processes are involved, there is no danger of pollution or overtreating the water. Providing the unit is installed in accordance with the manufacturer's instructions, and the unit is the correct wattage for pond capacity, stock level and situation, all that is left is clear water. If you dose the pond with any treatment containing malachite green, turn off the UVC for 24 hours, otherwise the UV light will weaken the dosage.

Be sure to fit the UV before the biofilter to ensure that the pipework is fully charged with water. If you put it in after the filter in the gravity return, only half the pipework will be full of water and you risk burning out the electrics. UV light is used to control algae blooms because the contact time the water is exposed to the UV light is too short to have any significant effect in eliminating bacteria. Most parasites are on the body of the koi, so UV light has no effect on these. However, white spot has a free-living stage and there is good evidence that the infective stage is affected by UV. All the water should pass through the UVC before teeing off to ornaments, waterfalls and venturis, etc., to make sure it is treated.

Although most manufacturers state that a UV bulb will last between 8,000 and 10,000 hours, its efficiency will be reduced by anything up to 15 percent after 5,000 hours of continuous use (about 6 months), and water clarity will begin to deteriorate. To ensure that the pond remains crystal clear all year-round, it is a good idea to replace the bulb before it

pointing venturi, which ensures that the bubbles remain in contact with the water for a much longer time. With both of these types the critical factor is to keep the water level at just the right height so that only foam emerges from the top. As the foam collapses, the resultant yellow-brown liquid produced can be removed and discarded.

UVCs

UVCs tend to be fitted onto koi ponds as a standard piece of equipment to control phytoplankton, or algae, that cause green water. These microscopic algae thrive where there is an abundance of nitrate and phosphate, which are typically found in koi pond water. The UV light damages the green pigment, or chloroplasts, in the algae, which prevents them using the energy from sunlight and dissolved carbon dioxide to produce sugars in a process known as photosynthesis. Photosynthesis is essential to all plant life; once disrupted, the algae die.

loses its algal qualities. Do not be fooled if the bulb can be seen glowing through the hosetails — it still needs replacing. Never look into an unprotected UV bulb, as this could seriously damage your eyes.

Over a period of time, the quartz sleeve may get dirty or a buildup of limescale could prevent the UV light shining through the water as it passes through the unit. To remove the bulb, pull off the end caps and carefully slide it out of the quartz sleeve. Carefully remove and wash the quartz sleeve in warm soapy water, which should be enough to clean it. To remove stubborn limescale, use a long-handled bottle brush.

Ozone

Ozone (O^3) is very unstable, producing potent free radicals as it breaks down to oxygen gas. Free radicals are very effective at killing bacteria and viruses, which make them a powerful disinfectant, but they should never come into contact with koi or filter bacteria.

Modern ozonizers consist of two main elements: a generator (in which the gas is produced by a high-energy electrical discharge that literally bonds an extra oxygen atom onto each oxygen molecule) and a reactor vessel or skimmer (where it is mixed by venturi action with pond water, and protein froth and residual gas are removed before the water returns to the pond). A probe in the water flow constantly monitors the level of ozone, so there is no possibility of overdosing.

OZONIZER AND PROTEIN SKIMMER

Ozone generator

Ozone passes into the water flow through venturi

Protein waste

Water in from pond

Ozone reacts with water as it flows through the protein skimmer

Water return to pond

Redox probe in pond ensures correct ozone dosage

MULTICYCLONE PREFILTER

The Multicyclone is a prefilter designed to remove up to 80 percent of the particulate sediment from the water before passing through the koi pond filtration system. It can be fitted directly to the outlet of an external, dry pump. There are no moving parts. Water enters from the base of the bottom unit and passes up the gray tube into the top chamber, where it flows down through conical hydro cyclones that force it to spin into the transparent sediment chamber. The water continues spinning in this chamber, forcing the clean water into the center, from where it passes upward and through the outlet at the top. Centrifugal action spins the debris out to the walls of the sediment chamber, from where it spirals down to the base of the chamber and can be purged from the unit via the waste pipe shown on the left.

Below: Water enters the top of the shower filter (shown at right) through spray bars, which break up the flow, creating trickles of water that run over the filter media as a fine film. This produces the moist, well-aerated conditions favored by bacteria.

SHOWER FILTER

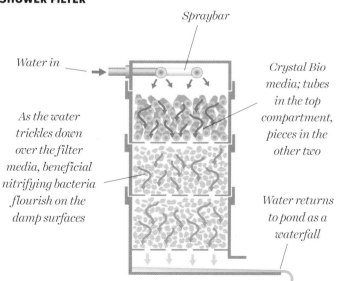

Spraybar

Water in

Crystal Bio media; tubes in the top compartment, pieces in the other two

As the water trickles down over the filter media, beneficial nitrifying bacteria flourish on the damp surfaces

Water returns to pond as a waterfall

Above: Water passes through a shower filter by gravity to pool at the bottom, where it exits. The shower filter shown here produces a waterfall as it flows back into the koi pond, which ensures the water returning to the pond is well-aerated.

Ozone units supersaturate the pond with oxygen, kill blanketweed and single-celled algae and allow filter bacteria to work more efficiently. The water achieves an unparalleled clarity, and koi are far less prone to niggling infections. Damaged tissue heals rapidly.

It is a myth that koi immune systems suffer when ozone is used. Rather, because the fish are not constantly under low-level stress from resisting pathogenic attack, they become stronger and fitter than ever. Ozone units are not cheap, but are a worthwhile investment for people serious about keeping koi.

Shower filters

In the summer months, oxygen becomes less soluble in the warm water, but this season is when the koi are at their most active, feeding several times a day, and their oxygen requirement is greatest. Not only do the koi have an increased oxygen demand, but they are also producing high volumes of ammonia, which must be oxidized by the bacteria in the filter system. The biological filter is the biggest oxygen sink in the koi pond system, consuming oxygen more easily and readily than the koi in the pond. It is at this time of year that shower filters become advantageous. The shower filter works on the basis that beneficial bacteria thrive in moist conditions, rather than being totally submerged, as occurs in conventional pond biofiltration. Water is pumped to the top of the shower filter and flows through the filter media by gravity and back into the pond. The advantage of the shower filter is that the film of water passing over the filter media becomes very warm, thereby creating the perfect conditions of warmth and moisture for the nitrifying bacteria to thrive.

As the water trickles over the media as a fine film, it readily absorbs atmospheric oxygen, supplying the nitrifying bacteria with oxygen to convert ammonia to nitrite and then harmless nitrate. The ability of shower filters to utilize atmospheric oxygen for the nitrifying bacteria reduces the burden on any aeration system installed in the pond system for the benefit of the koi.

Qube filters

Qube filters incorporate both mechanical and biological filtration. They consist of a dual chamber filter, containing "oxygen reactive biological spheres" (ORBS). The pond water flows through the Qube from the first chamber and through a UV light system before entering the second chamber. The ORB media provide a large surface area for bacterial

colonization and are designed to create minimum friction so that water flows evenly over them. As the water passes through the Qube system, debris collides with the ORB media and drops out of suspension to the base of the filter. The system is self-cleaning and solids are removed from the base via a slide valve. Because the water flow through the Qube is linear, these filters can operate on low-wattage pumps.

Plant filters

There has been increasing interest in plant filtration, not just for treating koi ponds, but also to deal with human waste and gray water. From an ecological standpoint, plant filters can work with minimum water use and have a low environmental impact. All animal waste contains high concentrations of phosphate, and the biological filter on a koi pond gives rise to copious amounts of nitrate. Of these by-products, phosphate is the most potent plant fertilizer and promotes the growth of nuisance algae if allowed to accumulate in the pond. Plants are very efficient at utilizing nitrate and phosphate, hence their increasing use as a supplement to the biological filter. Ideal plants include iris, reeds or watercress. As a general rule, a plant filter needs to be roughly equivalent to 25 percent of the pond surface area.

Above: A simple plant filter consisting of a "runway" with aquatic plants that absorb nitrates (NO_3) given off by the biofilter.

A PLANT FILTER

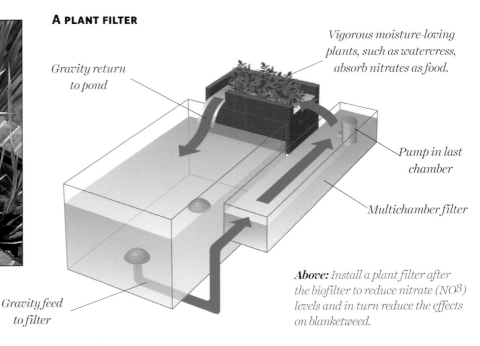

Vigorous moisture-loving plants, such as watercress, absorb nitrates as food.

Gravity return to pond

Pump in last chamber

Multichamber filter

Gravity feed to filter

Above: Install a plant filter after the biofilter to reduce nitrate (NO_3) levels and in turn reduce the effects on blanketweed.

Designing and building a koi pond

Building your own pond following your design and carrying out or overseeing the work yourself is one of the most rewarding aspects of becoming a koi-keeper. It is one of the few areas in which complete novices can express themselves, choosing designs that are imaginative, outrageous, conventional, traditional or even Japanese — there is no limit to the possibilities. However, to succeed, it is vital to plan every aspect of the proposed pond before starting any work, because once the project is finished it will be very expensive to alter. Before putting a spade into the ground, read plenty of books and specialist magazines and talk to people who have an up-to-date working knowledge of pond design and construction. There are plenty of koi clubs you can join, whose members will be only too willing to show you their efforts and share experiences, both good and bad, so that you can avoid making basic mistakes.

Equipment can be purchased from koi retailers, but many hobbyists prefer to research the many different types and specifications of filters, pumps and other koi pond essentials on the web and either buy them directly from the manufacturers or via the Internet.

Choosing the location for your pond

The most suitable place for the pond has to be as close as possible to the house, so that you can view the fish all year-round and in all weathers. However, the excavation must be at least 1 m (39 in) away from the house, otherwise you risk undermining the foundations. If this were to happen, the property would have to be underpinned — a very expensive procedure that would not be covered by your household insurance.

The pond will become a major feature of the garden, so consider all the options before you start digging. Bear in mind the practical day-to-day chores, such as cutting the grass; will the cuttings fall into the water when you trim around the pond perimeter? Could any pesticides such as slug pellets pollute the water? Overhanging trees may become difficult to prune, especially if you intend to build a pond with a large surface area, and falling leaves can be a big problem in the autumn, clogging bottom drain inlets and skimmer baskets. Roots from nearby trees and large shrubs can also become a problem, especially if you intend to build the pond using a liner, which could easily be punctured at a later date.

Locate the pond in an area that enjoys the most natural light without too much shade from trees or buildings. The only disadvantage of this position is sunlight, which encourages the growth of blanketweed; you will have to use a treatment regularly to keep this unsightly filamentous algae under control.

Designing your new pond

Planning a koi pond is essential. It allows you to visualize where and how it will fit into the garden, taking into account any utility supply. A scale version of your garden and proposed pond is easy to create using one of the many garden design apps or software available on the Internet, many of which are free. Measure any outbuildings and enter them on the plan. Then add permanent features, such as large trees and shrubs,

Below: Before you start building, make a simple plan either on paper or using a computer design program. Changes are easy at this stage and you can check that the pond design and position are right for your garden.

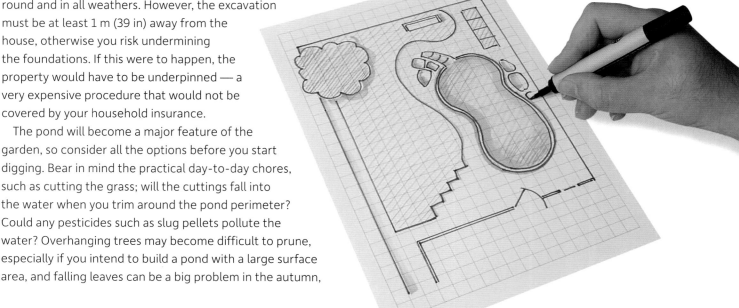

Above: *This is a good example of a formal pond raised out of the ground, with an attractive pergola built over the top to provide shade. Bonsai trees and ornaments have been placed around the perimeter of the pond to provide a Japanese atmosphere.*

Right: *A more natural pond, with plenty of mature shrubs and other planting to disguise the pond structure and filtration system. It is a good idea to leave one area open and accessible so that you can get close to the fish, especially when feeding.*

as well as hard landscaping, including patios, pathways, raised borders, etc. Before sketching in the pond, make a few photocopies of what you have done so far, so that if you decide to alter the shape or position of the pond you will not have to draw in the existing features again. Alternatively, cover the paper plan with adhesive-backed plastic and use water-based felt pens to draw the shape of the pond. If you want to make any alterations, simply rub out unwanted lines with a cloth. If you have a computer, there are some very good and relatively inexpensive garden design packages available that can help you create a visual of the finished pond and how it will look in your garden surroundings.

Spend plenty of time on the design and location of the pond. Show your ideas to fellow hobbyists and to your local dealer, who will be only too glad to offer you help and advice.

Pond designs

Anyone can have a pond, even in a modest-sized garden. In Japan, most hobbyists' gardens are quite small, but what they lack in surface area they make up for in depth to ensure a good volume of water.

The shape of the pond will be determined by a number of factors, such as the area it is intended to occupy, the existing hard landscaping and the overall concept. For example, if it is to be built within or adjacent to a patio, the design is likely to be very formal — rectangular, L-shaped, above ground with brick walling, etc. When designing a pond of this nature, you need to consider "dead spots," which are areas where the water is almost stationary and does not circulate properly

around the pond and into the filter system. These areas can be agitated by aerated drains and additional venturis to regulate the flow of water.

Informal circular and kidney shapes are usually associated with a natural design and it is easier to control the water flow in such ponds because of the soft curves that allow a good flow of water around the surface. In addition, there are fewer areas where fish can damage themselves by "flicking" off sharp walls.

Sometimes it can be an advantage to have a natural fall in the garden, as it can open up all sorts of landscaping possibilities, such as streams, waterfalls, rockeries, bog gardens and raised patios. If the ground slopes toward the house, you could construct a very natural-looking waterfall or stream at the far end of the pond, with an impressive drop onto the water surface. The front of the pond could be raised out of the ground with paving stones. You could install a window as an added feature. Never build a pond more than 60 cm (24 in) out of the ground, as it very rarely looks right.

An interesting concept is building a pond partly in the garden and partly in a conservatory, so that you can enjoy the hobby all year-round. However, there are a number of

Right: A formal design in which brickwork has been used to achieve a circular shape with a Japanese-style backdrop and pergola. Granite ornaments, cobbles and shingle are also used to create the desired oriental effect.

Left: *A large formal pond covered by a pergola. Make sure that the wood is treated with a nontoxic preservative; otherwise, the stain could leach out and pollute the water.*

Above: *A raised pond with a bridge over the center onto a decked area that hides the filter system. The water clarity in this pond is so good that the fish seem to be held in suspension.*

Right: *A natural-looking pond incorporating a window that provides an interesting viewing perspective. It is quite useful for checking the fish for damage and disease. Seek professional help if you contemplate fitting a window in your koi pond.*

house could fall into the pond! Subject to the surveyor's advice, and if the proposal is feasible, the pond would have to be built using reinforced concrete and sealed with fiberglass. In such an elaborate design, the filtration system should be located in the garden, because you would not want to put up with the smells from the discharge chamber when purging the bottom drains. Also, pond filter systems tend to attract flies, which is the last thing you want in a conservatory.

Condensation could be a problem within the conservatory, but a space heater or dehumidifier will prevent a buildup of moisture. Consult the conservatory manufacturer regarding the strength of the joists that span the expanse of water, and fit the glazing below water level to prevent cold air entering the room.

Coping with the ground conditions

The type of soil found in your garden is mostly irrelevant, especially if you are constructing a block-built pond, which could freestand without relying on the surrounding backfill. This is the case even if the pond is constructed using a liner, because a liner pond has a ring beam (footing) to act as a stabilizer and does not require additional external support above ground. However, the construction of a liner pond will rely on the state of the ground below the ring beam.

Above and right: *A raised koi pond that extends into a conservatory. Two windows in the pond wall mean that the your favorite koi are up close and personal the whole year.*

potential problems associated with constructing such a pond and you should seek the advice of a building surveyor before undertaking the project. You will need to take into account considerations such as the depth of the foundations. If these are undermined, the side of the

COPING WITH A HIGH WATER TABLE

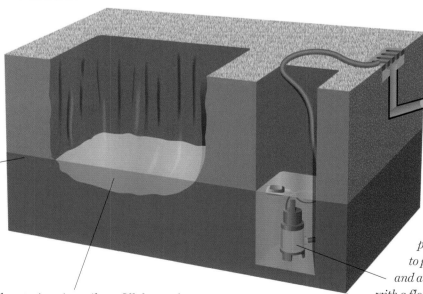

If you encounter a high water table, dig a dewatering pit to divert ground water away from the excavation.

Ideally, pump ground water direct to a main drain. If there is no drain nearby, make sure that you discharge the water well away from the excavation, otherwise water will percolate through the soil and back to the excavation.

Use a dirty water type of pump that will allow solids to pass through the impeller and away to waste. Choose one with a float switch so it will turn on automatically as the water rises, and off again when the level drops.

Do not backfill the dewatering pit until you fill the pond, otherwise water could build up underneath a liner, causing it to bulge and potentially tear the bottom drain connection.

Left: *This koi pond has been built on a sloping site where one end is at ground level and the opposite side is raised, with steps to a deck hiding the filter. The perimeter wall provides an ideal sitting area for viewing and feeding the fish.*

It is not really possible to predict where the water table is unless you dig pilot holes in strategic places in the garden. Although a high water table can cause certain problems, do not let it affect your chosen pond location because the difficulties can be overcome, although it may involve extra work.

If you are unlucky and hit the water table, the only way to ensure that the excavation remains dry is to dig a dewatering pit, or sump, close by. Make this about 60 cm (2 ft) across and 60 cm (2 ft) deeper than the pond. (A post hole borer is useful for digging this relatively narrow shaft.) Put a paving slab at the base of the pit and lower an automatic submersible pump on top — the slab will prevent dirt clogging the strainer. Then run a flexible hose to a main drain or a lower part of the garden. As the pit is lower than the base of the pond, water will begin to fill the pit, causing the float switch on the pump to rise. This will activate the pump and the water will be drawn away to waste. When the pit is empty, the float switch will fall and turn off the pump automatically. Leave the pump in place until the pond is built and full of water and then backfill the sump.

Most of the obstructions that you find during excavation can be overcome, but you may come across something totally unexpected, such as an abandoned septic tank or the foundations of a building not shown on the deeds of your

Pond building dos and don'ts

DO

Thoroughly research and plan your proposed pond. Read books, articles, watch videos and talk to the experts before you start digging in your garden.

Make drawings of the layout with cross-sections and plan views showing all pipe runs and dimensions, and keep this for future reference.

Work out the cost of the building materials and equipment, and make sure you stay within your budget.

Choose the right biological filter. Ask yourself the following questions: Is it manufactured from good-quality fiberglass? Can all detritus be removed without disturbing the media? Is it big enough to cope with your pond volume and intended stocking levels? Dealers should be able to demonstrate the filters on sale on their own systems.

Invest in a good pump. Most of the top manufacturers offer a 3-year warranty.

Show your proposals to your local koi specialist, who will check for any mistakes and give you practical advice and guidance.

DON'T

Dig a big hole and wonder what to do next.

Take advice from amateurs who think they know everything there is to know about ponds. Talk to people who do it for a living — they don't want you to make mistakes because you are their future customers.

Cut corners or compromise on quality if you stray over your budget limit. Remember, you only want to do this once — get it right first time and if necessary reduce the pond size and the material costs will reduce pro rata.

Penny pinch on the filter system — this is the most important aspect of koi-keeping. Savings on a cheap filter now could cost you more in the long run. Do not try to build a filter yourself. Manufacturers have invested a great deal of money developing efficient systems that you cannot emulate using domestic cold water tanks.

Buy a pump with a high power consumption. This pump will be running 365 days a year so you want maximum output with a low wattage.

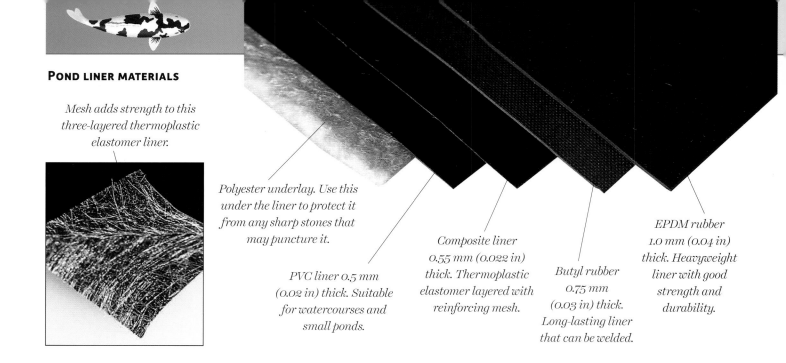

POND LINER MATERIALS

Mesh adds strength to this three-layered thermoplastic elastomer liner.

Polyester underlay. Use this under the liner to protect it from any sharp stones that may puncture it.

PVC liner 0.5 mm (0.02 in) thick. Suitable for watercourses and small ponds.

Composite liner 0.55 mm (0.022 in) thick. Thermoplastic elastomer layered with reinforcing mesh.

Butyl rubber 0.75 mm (0.03 in) thick. Long-lasting liner that can be welded.

EPDM rubber 1.0 mm (0.04 in) thick. Heavyweight liner with good strength and durability.

property, and conclude that the additional cost of eliminating the problem is prohibitive. However, the usual obstacles are services leading to and from the house, such as electricity cables, sewage and water main pipes, which can usually be rerouted without too much trouble. There may be plans available that illustrate any utility supplies to your property, but these can be misleading or wrong. It is better to use a cable and pipe locator, which accurately tracks buried pipes and cables.

Access and waste disposal

Access is an important consideration, especially if you want a large pond and need a backhoe to carry out the excavation. Most are over 1 m (39 in) wide and will not fit through a standard garden gate, although it is possible to hire smaller machines. Construction will be a bit trickier if you live in a property with no access to the backyard, as all the excavated soil and building materials will have to be transported through the house.

If you are unable to dispose of the waste soil around your garden, you will need a dumpster. Contact several dumpster rental companies to obtain the best price and find one that offers a convenient pickup service. Site the dumpster as close as conveniently possible to the excavation site.

The cost involved

Remember, you only want to carry out building work once,

so make sure it is done properly the first time, and stay within your budget. If you discover that you cannot afford to buy the best materials or filtration system, do not cut corners; wait until you have the funds. When you have decided on the size of the pond, it is reasonably straightforward to calculate the cost. Throughout this section we will use the example of a pond measuring 3.6 x 3 x 1.2 m deep (about 12 x 10 x 4 ft), with a capacity of 13,000 liters (about 3,000 gallons) to help you calculate quantities, materials and costings, etc.

Children and animals

If you have young children or pets, it is important to locate your pond carefully to avoid any accidents. Remember that a pond will contain deep water and is a potential deathtrap. If you are lucky enough to be able to construct a pond in a conservatory, it should be fairly easy to keep children out of this area by fitting a self-closing mechanism on the internal door and positioning the catch high up. For outside ponds, it is better to build a raised pond and fit a decorative panel onto the wall around the perimeter. When the children are old enough to understand the danger, you can remove the paneling. Be sure to check your municipal bylaws with regards to fencing requirements around ponds and pools.

Construction methods

When building a new koi pond, the first consideration must be what material to use. Your eventual decision may be influenced by a number of factors, such as the ground conditions in the intended location, financial constraints and the shape. Here we look at the advantages and disadvantages of the three most popular pond construction methods, so that you can choose the one that suits you best. These are: precast fiberglass ponds, liner ponds and block-built rendered ponds.

Precast fiberglass ponds

The advantages of fiberglass ponds are that they are tough, made of a long-lasting material and quick to fit. Little building knowledge is needed to install them and they are available in interesting shapes and designs from several manufacturers. There are no unsightly creases to deal with and no restriction on suitable sites. On the other hand, they are relatively expensive and most are too shallow to be suitable for koi. In shallow water, temperatures fluctuate very quickly. The only way to overcome this problem is to find a pond that can hold in excess of 4,500 liters (about 1,000 gallons), as this volume reacts more slowly to changes in ambient temperatures.

If you do decide to install a fiberglass pond, it is a good idea to add an inline heater to stabilize the water temperature. These heaters are available from most koi outlets and are very easy to fit. They are typically made of stainless steel with a 3.75 cm (1.5 in) threaded inlet and outlet and a digital thermostatic control (see page 21).

Liner ponds

Probably the quickest and cheapest method of building a koi pond is to fit a liner. You can buy these off the roll or in prepack form. The three main options are PVC, butyl rubber and EPDM rubber.

Plasticized polyvinyl chloride (PVC) liners are relatively inexpensive and available with or without nylon reinforcing. The material is generally manufactured in rolls 2 m (6.5 ft) wide and is sold off the roll or seam-welded by the distributor to be sold in prepack form. It is typically 0.50 or 0.80 mm (0.02 or 0.03 in) thick and has a limited life expectancy. This material should only be used for smaller ponds or watercourses.

Isobutylene isoprene rubber (BUTYL) is 0.75 or 1.0 mm (0.03 and 0.04 in) thick and is produced by polymerization of specific fractions from the oil refining process. The manufacturers of butyl rubber sheeting will not disclose their formulations except to say that 40 to 45 percent by volume

of the finished sheet is butyl polymer combined with a small proportion of EPDM polymer to improve the end product's weathering properties.

The distributor uses a hot bond tape to vulcanize the butyl sheets together to form a perfect weld. This should not be seen as a weak point; in fact, it constitutes the strongest part of the liner. These liners are available in almost every conceivable size in prepack form or off the roll and can be tailor-made with on-site vulcanizing for larger installations, such as lakes and reservoirs. For the discerning koi-keeper who does not want to see any pleats or folds, the liner can be

What you need for a liner pond

To help you plan and budget for your own system, here is a typical "shopping list" of the materials and equipment you will need to build a pond measuring 3.6 m long, 3 m wide and 1.2 m deep (approximately 12 x 10 x 4 ft) containing 13,000 liters (about 3,000 gallons) of water. The list can be adapted to suit a pond of any size.

Quantity	Description
3 days	Rental of backhoe
1	Insurance policy on above
36 m³ (48 yd³)	Spoil/waste removal capacity
1 m³ (1.3 yd³)	Ballast for ring beam and to encase bottom drain and pipework
7 x 25 kg (55 lb)	Bags cement powder
1	Liner 6.6 x 6 m (about 22 x 20 ft)
20 m (66 ft)	Polyester underlay off a roll, 2 m (6.5 ft) wide
2	25 cm (10 in) bottom drains with flange seals
4 m (13 ft)	10 cm (4 in) PVC pipework from drains to filter
4	10 cm (4 in) PVC elbows
2	venturi returns
2	3.75 cm (1.5 in) tank connectors for venturi
1	Fiberglass biological filter complete with media and pipework
1	Submersible pump to run system
1	30 w UVC

Optional extras	
1	Surface skimmer with liner adapter
1	Pump for skimmer
1	Electronic blanketweed controller
1	Underwater light
1	Mechanical filter

box-welded (a method used to fit the excavation exactly) to your specifications, but this is typically twice as expensive as buying a flat sheet. A template would be required if the liner is intended to fit a more complex shape.

Ethylene propylene diene monomer (EPDM) rubber is sold under various trade names. It is not supplied in prepack form but can be cut from rolls available in a range of widths, all 1.0 mm (0.04 in) thick. Although it does not contain any butyl, it has the same specification and is ideal for any pond size. The only drawbacks are that it cannot be box-welded and butyl tape will not adhere to it unless the surface is first prepared with solvent and sanded. It is an ideal alternative to butyl.

Warranties for liners

When setting out to buy a liner, the temptation is to get the best price possible; after all, it's only a hole in the ground, isn't it? However, choosing a cheap liner could be a disastrous mistake.

Read any warranty carefully, as it does not cover all potential contingencies. Most only offer to repair or replace the product in the event of failure due to faulty seams, materials or manufacture. There is no cover for consequential loss, excessive stretching, misuse, puncturing or mechanical damage. Imagine this scenario:

a company installs a liner pond in accordance with the manufacturer's guidelines, but it develops a fault 6 months later. Who will bear the cost of removing the fish, providing temporary accommodation, draining the pond, taking out the faulty liner, returning it to the supplier, taking delivery of a new one, refitting it and returning the fish? Meanwhile, one unfortunate but valuable koi suddenly dies.

The moral of this is that you should only buy a liner from a long-standing, reputable company that is more likely to honor the sale. Be wary of cheap liners; some are intended for roofing and may contain harmful fungicides that could be lethal to your fish.

Installing a liner pond

Try to keep the shape of a liner pond fairly simple; an informal kidney design or formal shapes such as a square or rectangle work well. The more complex the shape, the more you will be able to see unattractive pleats and folds that act as collection points for blanketweed and dirt once the pond is up and running.

When you have decided on the size and shape of a liner pond, do not dig it out right away. Remember that you need a firm edge around the pond on which to lay the liner, so that it can be disguised by the lawn, paving, brickwork or decorative stone cappings. To make this, you should construct

How big a liner do I need?

To work out the size of the liner, simply double the depth measurement of the pond and add this figure to both the length and the width. For example, if the excavation measures 3.6 m long, 3 m wide and 1.2 m deep (approximately 12 x 10 x 4 ft), you need a liner measuring 1.2 x 2 = 2.4 + 3.6 = 6 m (20 ft) long and 1.2 x 2 = 2.4 + 3 = 5.4 m (18 ft) wide. However, this does not allow for any overlap, so add 60 cm (2 ft) to each figure to produce a 30 cm (12 in) overlap around

the perimeter. The final sheet size will be 6.6 x 6 m (about 22 x 20 ft).

Polyester underlay is normally sold from a roll measuring 2 m (6.5 ft) wide. To calculate the length needed from the roll for the above pond, divide the area of pond liner by the width of the roll. This works out as follows: 6.6 x 6 m = approximately 40 m^2 divided by 2 = 20 m (66 ft) off the roll. You can also buy underlay in prepack form.

MEASURING YOUR POND FOR A LINER

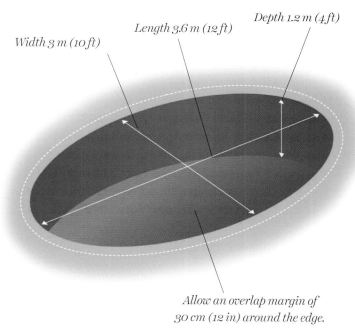

Width 3 m (10 ft)

Length 3.6 m (12 ft)

Depth 1.2 m (4 ft)

Allow an overlap margin of 30 cm (12 in) around the edge.

a ring beam, or concrete collar, as it is sometimes called. This acts as a foundation for the pond perimeter or a footing for brickwork if the pond is to be raised above ground level.

Mark out the ring beam using pegs driven into the ground about 60 cm (24 in) apart. Tie a string around the pegs to give you a better idea of how the eventual shape will look. If you are not totally happy with one particular area, simply lift the pegs and move them around until you achieve the desired effect. When you are satisfied, set out a second series of pegs 23 cm (9 in) away from and outside of the first series to mirror the internal shape. Check around the perimeter using a bubble level. Dig out the area between the two peg shapes to a depth of 23 cm (9 in).

At this point you need to check that the top surface of the ring beam will be level. To do this, take out the wooden pegs that you have used to mark the shape and drive in a series of pegs along the centerline of the trench all the way around. Make sure these are vertical and sticking up about 23 cm (9 in) above the bottom of the trench. Using a long bubble level (or one on top of a long wooden board), check that the tops of

How to construct a liner pond

Building a concrete ring beam or collar around the perimeter provides a firm, level base for the liner and edging stones and prevents cave-ins during excavation.

1 Mark out the internal shape of the pond using string and then place pegs around the perimeter at regular intervals. Then measure out 23 cm (9 in) from each peg, mirroring the internal shape.

2 Dig out the trench to a depth of 23 cm (9 in) inside the pegged area. For uneven ground, drive pegs into the trench and check the levels with a bubble level.

The concrete forms a ring beam in the trench.

Position surface skimmers and pipework for venturis, etc., before filling the trench with concrete.

3 Fill the trench with concrete, completely encasing any return pipework and skimmers, etc. If you have used pegs to establish levels within the trench, lay the concrete up to the top of each peg and leave them in position.

4 When the concrete has set, you can excavate the soil inside the beam without the risk of a collapse or cave-in.

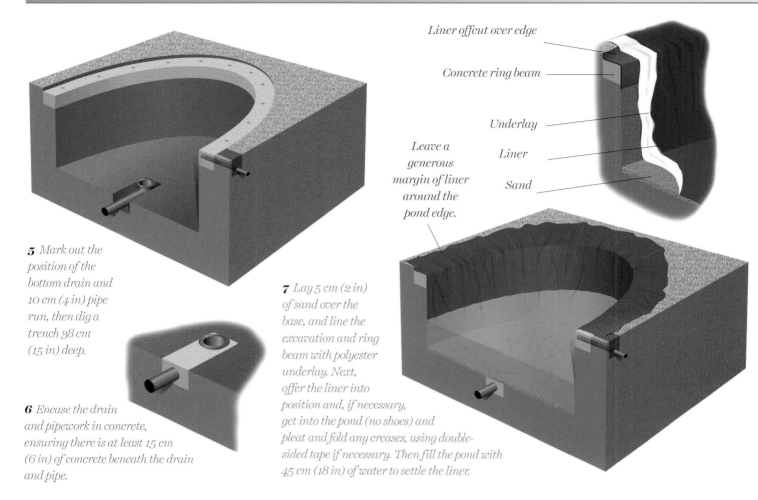

5 Mark out the position of the bottom drain and 10 cm (4 in) pipe run, then dig a trench 38 cm (15 in) deep.

6 Encase the drain and pipework in concrete, ensuring there is at least 15 cm (6 in) of concrete beneath the drain and pipe.

7 Lay 5 cm (2 in) of sand over the base, and line the excavation and ring beam with polyester underlay. Next, offer the liner into position and, if necessary, get into the pond (no shoes) and pleat and fold any creases, using double-sided tape if necessary. Then fill the pond with 45 cm (18 in) of water to settle the liner.

Liner offcut over edge

Concrete ring beam

Underlay

Leave a generous margin of liner around the pond edge.

Liner

Sand

the pegs are level all around the perimeter. Simply raise or drive in those that are not level as you go around.

The next step is to fill the trench with a 3:1 mix of aggregate/cement up to the tops of the pegs, which will create a level surface to the ring beam when the concrete has set. Leave the pegs embedded in the concrete. Remember to lay any return pipework and skimmers (see page 68) in the trench before filling with concrete. When the concrete has set, you can excavate the pond inside the ring beam without the risk of the sides collapsing.

Fitting a bottom drain

When the excavation is complete fit the base of the bottom drain, which is 25 cm (10 in) in diameter, with a 10 cm (4 in) pipe outlet on the side. (A domed cover fits on this to prevent fish swimming into it, but do not attach this now.) The 10 cm (4 in) pipework from the drain runs directly to the first

chamber of the filtration system. The drain and pipe run must be totally encased in concrete and to achieve this you need to dig a trench in the base of the excavation. The depth of this trench depends on the exact dimensions of your bottom drain, but aim to have 15 cm (6 in) of concrete supporting the drain and pipe. For example, if the drain is 23 cm (9 in) deep, excavate the trench to 38 cm (15 in) and fill it with 15 cm (6 in) of concrete. When dry, position the drain and pipe on top of the concrete base and fill the entire trench with concrete.

Fitting the liner

Remove any sharp stones in the excavation, then line the entire floor and wall area with polyester underlay to protect the liner. (Do not use old carpet, as this will eventually rot.) Put the liner into the pond and add about 45 cm (18 in) of water, so that the liner is drawn properly to the base. At this stage you should be prepared to get into the

Calculating pond capacities

Using a flowmeter when you fill your pond is the most accurate way of registering the volume of water in the pond (see page 69). To estimate the capacity of various shapes of pond based on their overall dimensions, the following guidelines will be helpful.

To calculate the capacity of a rectangular pond, multiply the length by the width and the depth. Thus, our example of a pond measuring 3.6 x 3 x 1.2 m deep (12 x 10 x 4 ft) has a volume of 13 m^3 (480 ft^3). Each cubic meter is equivalent to 1,000 liters. (A cubic foot is equivalent to 6.25 gallons.) The capacity of the pond is therefore 13,000 liters (3,000 gallons).

To determine the capacity of a circular pond, use the formula πr^2, which is 3.142 (π) x radius x radius, to calculate the area of the surface. Then multiply this number by the depth. For a circular pond measuring 3.6 m (12 ft) across and 1.2 m (4 ft) deep, the surface area is 3.142 x 1.8 x 1.8 = 10.2 m^2 (113 ft^2). This number multiplied by the depth of 1.2 m (4 ft) produces a volume of 12.24 m^3 (452 ft^3), and therefore a capacity of 12,240 liters (2,825 gallons).

For other shapes, divide up the pond into easy to measure rectangular, square or circular portions, calculate the volume of each and then simply add them all together.

Right: *Slabs form a neat and stable edge for a koi pond. The underlay and liner overlap the ring beam and are covered by paving.*

Left: *If you place boulders around the edge, support them on a liner offcut to protect the pond liner.*

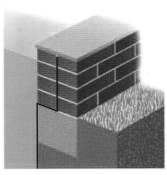

Right: *You can conceal the edge of the liner between vertical courses of bricks, as shown here. The concrete ring beam acts an ideal foundation for the brickwork.*

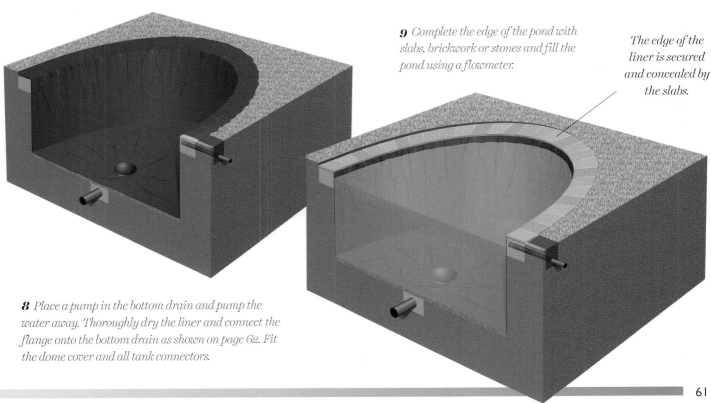

8 Place a pump in the bottom drain and pump the water away. Thoroughly dry the liner and connect the flange onto the bottom drain as shown on page 62. Fit the dome cover and all tank connectors.

9 Complete the edge of the pond with slabs, brickwork or stones and fill the pond using a flowmeter.

The edge of the liner is secured and concealed by the slabs.

pond and fold and pleat the liner to remove as many creases as possible, as these will look unsightly when the pond is finished. You can pleat stubborn creases against the main body of the pond using double-sided butyl tape so that they do not protrude into the pond.

Sealing the liner around the bottom drain

Pump the water from the pond and fit the liner between the flanges around the perimeter of the bottom drain, using plenty of adhesive to ensure a good seal. Most good-quality bottom drains are now supplied with a disc pre-drilled with holes at regular intervals around the perimeter. These line up with countersunk threaded slots built into the flange around the drain. Trim the liner inside the drain using a sharp blade, then apply a generous layer of a nontoxic sealant on top of the liner all around the perimeter of the flange. Put the disc on the flange, aligning the holes, and secure them with stainless steel screws (usually provided), wiping away any

excess sealant. Wait at least 24 hours before filling the pond to ensure that the sealant has cured and a skin has formed. Drill a 6 mm (0.25 in) hole in the domed lid of the bottom drain before you start filling, as air may become trapped under the dome, causing it to become dislodged and float to the surface at a later date. Over a period of time, the weight of water can distort the dome cover. To prevent this from happening, you can place "feet" (offcuts of pipe on their side) to support the edge of the dome.

Installing a venturi

The pipe that you laid across the ring beam now protrudes into the cavity of the pond and is covered by the liner. Cut a hole through the liner and solvent-weld a tank connector to the return pipe so that you can install a venturi, which injects air into the water. Once again, use plenty of sealant when fitting the flange and use self-tapping stainless steel screws to secure it firmly.

FITTING A BOTTOM DRAIN IN A LINER POND

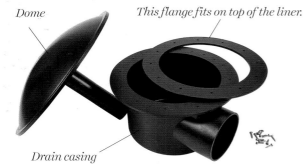

Dome

This flange fits on top of the liner.

Drain casing

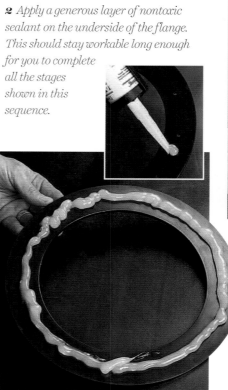

2 Apply a generous layer of nontoxic sealant on the underside of the flange. This should stay workable long enough for you to complete all the stages shown in this sequence.

3 With the flange in position, pierce holes through the liner and secure the flange to the bottom drain casing using the stainless steel screws supplied. The sealant will be squeezed out around the edge — you can clean this up later.

1 Put the flange into position and line up the holes with those in the drain casing. Using a sharp knife, pierce a hole in the center and make four cuts toward the perimeter. This will prevent the liner tearing beyond the flange.

FITTING A VENTURI

4 cm (1.5 in) pumped return pipe

Venturi, with air tube attached.

Do not glue the venturi to this elbow. Fix it with a self-tapping screw for easy removal should it become clogged with weeds.

Fit and seal this flange to the connector in the same way as the bottom drain shown below.

Completing the surround

With the venturi installed, all that remains is to tuck the liner under your chosen surround. It is a good idea to place some "offcuts" of liner beneath any large rocks or boulders to protect the pond liner from piercing or tears. If the pond is raised out of the ground with bricks, lay the liner over the ring beam and construct the wall with the liner sandwiched between the two courses of bricks. Seal the internal pointing with resin to prevent lime from the cement leaching into the water. If you intend to use paving slabs, again use offcuts of liner where the slabs are laid and bed them down on cement.

Filling the pond

When you fill the pond, use a flowmeter at the end of the hosepipe. You can rent one of these from your local aquatic specialist and it simply registers the

4 With the flange firmly fixed, carefully trim off the excess liner around the inside of the opening. Use a sharp blade to create a clean edge.

6 Drill a 6 mm (0.25 in) hole in the dome to release any air trapped beneath it that may cause it to lift off.

7 The ideal gap between the edge of the dome and the pond just allows you to slide your hand underneath like this.

8 A side view of the bottom drain and dome. Note the even gap around the edge.

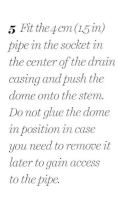

5 Fit the 4 cm (1.5 in) pipe in the socket in the center of the drain casing and push the dome onto the stem. Do not glue the dome in position in case you need to remove it later to gain access to the pipe.

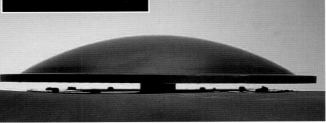

volume of water on a dial as it flows through. It is important to know the exact volume of the pond because in the future you may need to treat the water to remedy, say, a parasite problem and precise dosing rates are recommended.

A rendered block-built pond

A rendered block-built pond gives you the greatest degree of flexibility with regard to location and design. These ponds are strong and there will be no unsightly creases, such as you might find in a liner pond. However, they are relatively expensive and time-consuming to install and not a project for an inexperienced, albeit enthusiastic pond builder, as mistakes can be very costly to rectify. You may decide to use the services of a professional company that will provide you with plans and a detailed estimate. Remember that the pool will be a major building project similar to an extension of your home. If you intend to build it yourself, you must prepare or commission detailed drawings of your proposals and seek professional advice before you even think of getting out your spade or hiring a backhoe.

Building a rendered block-built pond demands a wide range of skills, including bricklaying, plastering (rendering), plumbing, fiberglassing and carpentry, as well as a thorough understanding of electricity supply, loading and wiring.

Above: *For larger excavations, and where access allows, a backhoe can save time. This 113,500 liter (25,000 gallon) pond was dug in just 4 days.*

However, once you appreciate what is required and have a good idea what you want, you could carry out some tasks yourself and call in the professionals when you need them.

The excavation

The excavation work does not require any specific skills, just a lot of hard work — so you can do this part yourself. If you are building a large pond, it is well worth considering renting

What you need to build a rendered block-built pond

To help you plan and budget for your own system, here is a typical "shopping list" of the materials and equipment you will need to build a pond measuring 3.6 m long, 3 m wide and 1.2 m deep (approximately 12 x 10 x 4 ft) containing 13,000 liters (about 3,000 gallons) of water. The list can be adapted to suit a pond of any size.

Quantity	Description
3 days	Rental of backhoe
1	Insurance policy on above
36 m³ (48 yd³)	Spoil/waste removal capacity
2.5 m³ (3.3 yd³)	Ballast for pond base
22 x 25kg (55 lb)	Bags of cement for pond base
140	Hollow concrete blocks, 45 x 23 cm (18 x 9 in)
0.75 m³ (1 yd³)	Ballast to fill blocks and backfill
3 x 25 kg (55 lb)	Bags of cement for above
2 sheets	Steel matting measuring 3.6 m x 2 m x 6 mm (12 x 6.5 ft x 0.25 in)
2	25 cm (10 in) bottom drains
4 m (13 ft)	10 cm (4 in) PVC pipework from drains to filter
4	10 cm (4 in) PVC elbows
2	Venturi returns
0.75 m³ (1 yd³)	Sharp sand to render pond walls
13 x 25 kg (55 lb)	Bags cement for above
3 kg (6.5 lb)	Glass fibers for render
10 kg (22 lb)	Clear resin
10 kg (22 lb)	Pigment resin
1	Fiberglass biological filter complete with media and pipework
1	Submersible pump to run system
1	30 w UVC

Optional extras

Quantity	Description
1	Surface skimmer
1	Pump for above
1	Electronic blanketweed controller
1	Underwater light
1	Mechanical filter

an excavator on tracks from your local rental center. If you have never used one before, it may take you a lot longer to complete the excavation than it would a professional. Furthermore, the DIY pond builder is generally over enthusiastic and tends to excavate more than is required, which will result in extensive backfilling.

Some equipment rentals offer a price for the backhoe and operator, which is well worth considering. Most equipment rentals do not provide any insurance while the backhoe is on hire, so you must arrange this yourself through your broker.

Ask the rental center for details of the make, model and value of the backhoe and insure it for theft and accidental damage, otherwise you could be faced with a huge unexpected bill if it were stolen or damaged.

The bottom drains and pond base

When the excavation is complete, and if you are installing a gravity-fed filter system, this is the time to install the bottom drain or drains. Place them evenly and centrally on the base and run the 10 cm (4 in) pipe to a convenient area where the filter is to be located. Mark out 10 cm (4 in) away from the

CONSTRUCTING A RENDERED BLOCK-BUILT POND

Right: *Begin digging in a methodical way, digging down to the required finished depth at one end of the area and working back. Where needed, use plywood sheets to retain the soil and prevent the sides collapsing as you dig out further areas.*

Below: *Space the bottom drains and pipes equally in the excavation on top of a layer of steel reinforcing mesh.*

Backfill the hollow section of the blockwork with steel rods and concrete, ensuring that they are completely filled.

Above: *Place concrete blocks on top of the bottom drains to prevent them and the connecting pipes floating up while the concrete base of the pond is setting.*

Right: *Begin building the walls using hollow concrete blocks measuring 45 x 23 cm (18 x 9 in) for the straight and slightly curved sections of the pond, and using bricks to create the tight curves.*

drain and pipe and dig a trench 15 cm (6 in) deep along the entire run. Fill it with concrete to act as a base for the drains and pipe. Lay broken bricks, blocks or gravel on the remainder of the pond base, followed by steel matting across the floor area to reinforce the base. The matting consists of 6 mm (0.24 in)-thick steel rods joined together to form a mesh.

Once you are happy that the drain or drains and the pipework are spaced centrally, glue them with solvent cement, which melts the two plastics together. The pipework is standard waste pipe made from PVC. Remember to paint the glue over both surfaces to be joined and twist the pipe in the fitting to ensure that the glue covers the entire surface area.

The next step is to mass-fill the entire base with 23 cm (9 in) of concrete, completely encasing the drains and pipework. This must be carried out in one operation, using a strong 3:1 ballast/cement mix. If you prepare half the base one day and go back at a later date, there will be a weak spot at the join, which could fracture in the future. Remember that our sample pond measuring 3.6 x 3 x 1.2 m (12 x 10 x 4 ft) contains 13,000 liters (about 3,000 gallons) of water, weighing approximately 13 tons, bearing down on the base.

Another option is to employ the services of a cement truck to pump the concrete directly into the excavation. Although relatively expensive, you can be sure of an even mix of concrete that will be laid in a matter of hours.

In the past, pond-builders would slope the base into the drains, and although this appears to be a good idea in theory, in practice, solids are drawn to the drain more effectively if the base is level. As the fish are constantly swimming around, they have a tendency to disturb any particles that settle, causing them to be mobile and naturally drawn into the drain.

Aerated bottom drain

Recently, more and more hobbyists have been fitting a bottom drain with an aerated dome, which promotes more efficient water circulation into the drain, thereby improving removal of solids from the pond bottom. It also provides additional aeration when oxygen levels are low during the summer months or if treatments are introduced. The most noticeable feature of this drain is the extra connection in the wall of the sump. This allows the air supply hose to enter the sump independently of the water outlet pipe, thus eliminating the possibility of restriction to the water flow and somewhere else for blanketweed to attach. A recess in the perimeter of

AERATED BOTTOM DRAIN

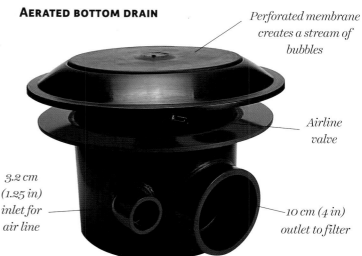

Perforated membrane creates a stream of bubbles

Airline valve

3.2 cm (1.25 in) inlet for air line

10 cm (4 in) outlet to filter

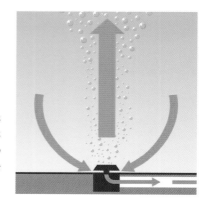

Above: *An aerated bottom drain with a separate inlet for an air line to connect to the valve visible beneath the dome.*

Right: *Air pumped through the membrane rises in a stream of bubbles that help to circulate the water into the bottom drain.*

the dome prevents the membrane from becoming detached when air is injected into it.

Building the walls

When the base is dry, build the wall using either solid or hollow 23 x 45 cm (9 x 18 in) concrete blocks. If you choose hollow blocks, fill the cavities with steel rods and backfill them with poured concrete from the base to the top of the construction.

Fitting venturi returns and a surface skimmer

As you get near to ground level, leave room for at least two 4 cm (1.5 in) pipes to fit through the wall for venturi returns from the filters. If you want to include a surface skimmer, now is the time to fit it into position. Skimmers are useful for removing the leaves and general debris that fall onto the water surface into a collection basket. The pipework from

COMPLETING THE POND STRUCTURE

Left: *The walls are complete and the cavities in the hollow blocks have been filled with concrete. Steel rods embedded in these cavities give the walls additional strength. Wait until everything dries out before applying sealant or fiberglass.*

Left: *The surface skimmer cemented in position. An external pump will draw water to a venturi or waterfall.*

Left: *All the internal surfaces of this pond have been lined with fiberglass and finished with a top coat of black resin sealer creating a durable and attractive finish.*

Right: *A three-bay filter and vortex chamber with isolating valves.*

Above: *The aerated drain is sited so that the bubbles are visible through the window in the side of the pond facing the house.*

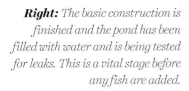

Right: *The basic construction is finished and the pond has been filled with water and is being tested for leaks. This is a vital stage before any fish are added.*

the skimmer is connected to the suck-side of a separate submersible or external pump. As the water flows into the mouth of the skimmer, the floating debris is trapped in a mesh collection basket. The return water from the skimmer can be run to another venturi, a waterfall or an ornamental water feature.

An additional feature of a skimmer is that you can vacuum the pond by placing a cornea over the skimmer basket. This is a see-through, "contact lens"-shaped fitting with a 4 cm (1.5 in) thread in the center. Screw a universal hosetail into the female thread, then simply attach a flexible pipe to the cornea and the other end to the vacuum head, which is fixed to a telescopic pole to enable you to reach the bottom of the pond. Using this device, all the waste gathered by the vacuum head will be collected in the skimmer basket.

At this stage, you can also consider installing an underwater light into the wall of the pond. The best types are those commonly installed in swimming pools and jacuzzis. You can choose between small stainless steel fittings or a larger bowl-shaped unit secured in its own housing and connected to an umbilical cord. This in turn fits into an external deck box and a transformer before being plugged into the main electrical supply. Should the bulb need changing, release the two locking screws on the outer casing, pull the bulb above water level and change the fitting attached to the umbilical cord. Put the cord back into the casing, line up the bulb with the screws and secure.

Completing the construction

Once the shell has been constructed, fill the void between the walls and excavation with a wet concrete mix to ensure that the soil does not subside onto the blockwork. When this stage is complete, you will have to decide how to waterproof the structure. Fiberglass is probably the best option, but it is expensive and should only be installed by a competent person. Two layers of 350 g/m^2 matting are applied to the walls and floor of the pond in sheets and a special gel coat is added to make them adhere to the cement. A tissue mat is then laid over the previous two coats to give the pond a smoother finish. When dry, all the surfaces are painted with the color of your choice. "Glassers" advertise in most aquatic magazines, but if you have difficulty finding one, ask your local dealer for guidance.

Another popular option is to plaster the structure twice, incorporating fiberglass strands in the first sand/cement mix. This means that the cement content can be proportionately

HOW A SURFACE SKIMMER WORKS

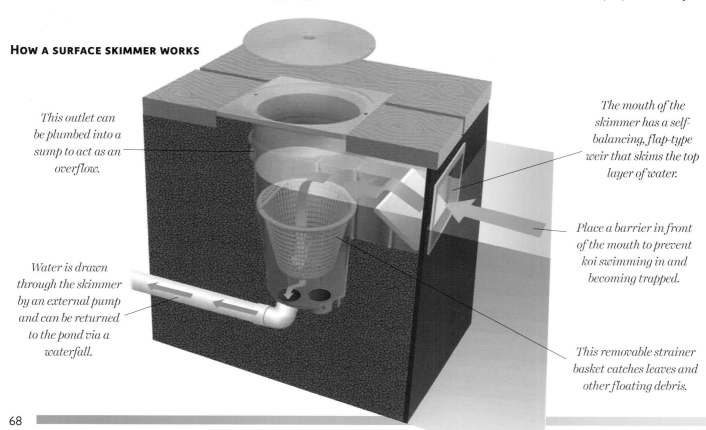

This outlet can be plumbed into a sump to act as an overflow.

Water is drawn through the skimmer by an external pump and can be returned to the pond via a waterfall.

The mouth of the skimmer has a self-balancing, flap-type weir that skims the top layer of water.

Place a barrier in front of the mouth to prevent koi swimming in and becoming trapped.

This removable strainer basket catches leaves and other floating debris.

VALVES USED IN KOI PONDS

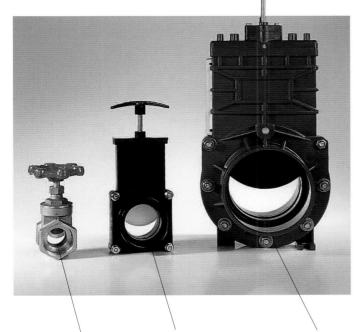

Gate valves, such as this 4 cm (1.5 in) brass one, provide precise control. This one is ideal for regulating the flow on fluidized bed filter systems.

5 cm (2 in) slide valves such as this would be used in pipework that provides a winter bypass and for closing off flow to waterfalls.

10 cm (4 in) slide valves such as would be used in the main pipework runs of gravity-fed filter systems, such as isolating vortex units.

How much resin sealer?

With a rectangular pond measuring 3.6 m long, 3 m wide and 1.2 m deep (approximately 12 x 10 x 4 ft) calculate the total surface area to be covered, namely four walls and the floor, as follows:

Wall 1: 3 x 1.2 m (10 x 4 ft) = 3.6 m² (40 ft²)
Wall 2: 3 x 1.2 m (10 x 4 ft) = 3.6 m² (40 ft²)
Wall 3: 3.6 x 1.2 m (12 x 4 ft) = 4.3 m² (48 ft²)
Wall 4: 3.6 x 1.2 m (12 x 4 ft) = 4.3 m² (48 ft²)
Floor: 3.6 x 3 m (12 x 10 ft) = 10.8 m² (120 ft²)

Total surface area: 26.6 m² (296 sq ft)

1 kg (2.2 lb) of clear resin sealer covers about 1.8 m² (20 ft²) with three coats, so dividing 26.6 by 1.8 (296 by 20) shows that you will need about 15 kg (33 lb) of sealer for three coats, or 5 kg (11 lb)/coat. For a color finish, apply two coats of clear and two coats of pigmented sealer. Thus you will need 10 kg (22 lb) each of clear and pigmented sealer.

---

increased. This, in turn, will reduce the porosity of the mortar and increase its strength. When dry, apply a second sand/cement coat to cover the protruding fibers. When the plastering has cured, paint all the internal surfaces with at least three coats of a resin sealer. This is a moisture-cured, one-component polyurethane that forms a nonporous, tough, durable but flexible seal designed for porous substrates such as cement. If you prefer a color finish, such as black or dark green, apply two coats of clear resin sealer, using rollers on the floor and walls and brushes to cut in around the edges, followed by two coats of pigmented resin sealer. Do not allow the resin to dry between coats, as any subsequent applications will not adhere correctly. Resin sealing can easily be undertaken by the DIY pond builder. The pond will be ready to fill after 48 hours. Remember to use a flowmeter so that you can record the pond capacity.

Left: *Fill the completed pond using a flowmeter attached to a hosepipe. Close the slide valve to the filter, fill the pond and note the volume. Then fill the filter system and record its capacity. Add the two figures for the total volume. It is useful to know the pond volume in case you need to treat the pond with a medication and isolate the filter.*

THE COMPLETED POND

This cutaway reveals how the filtration system and its associated pumps, valves and pipework connect and function in the finished pond.

Two bottom drains connected to 10 cm (4 in) pipework draw water by gravity to the multichamber filter system.

One of two venturi returns that boost oxygen level and create currents. They point away from the skimmer.

The surface skimmer strains out any floating debris.

A window in the side wall of the pond provides a view of the koi from the house.

Autofill unit beneath the bridge introduces mains water through a pipe below the surface.

2.5 cm (1 in) brass gate valve to control water flow from mains supply.

2.5 cm (1 in) pipe takes mains water to an autofill unit located under the bridge.

As the plants grow and mature, they will soften the stark edges of the newly finished hard landscaping.

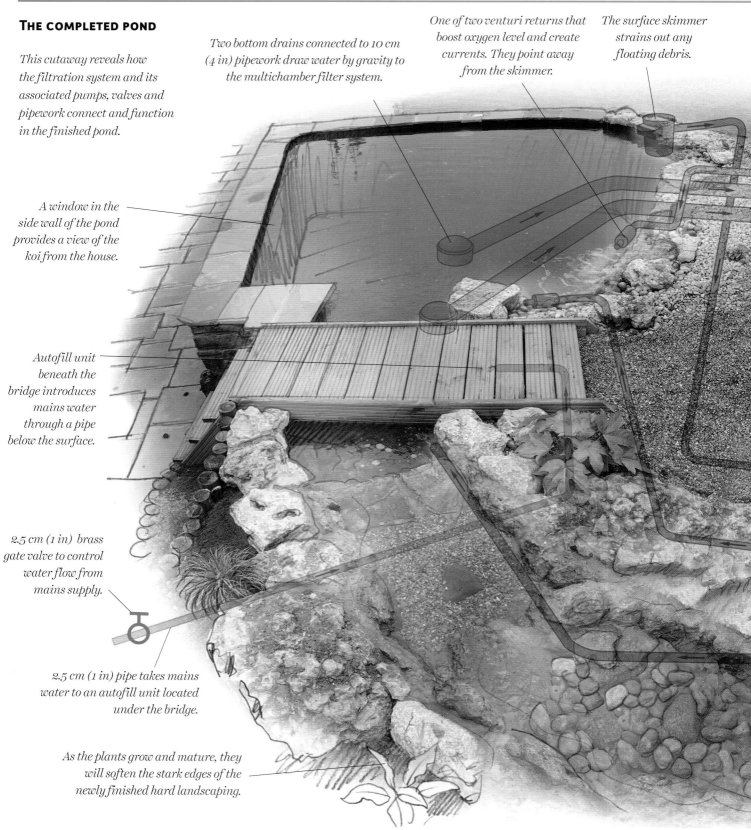

MULTICHAMBER FILTER SYSTEM

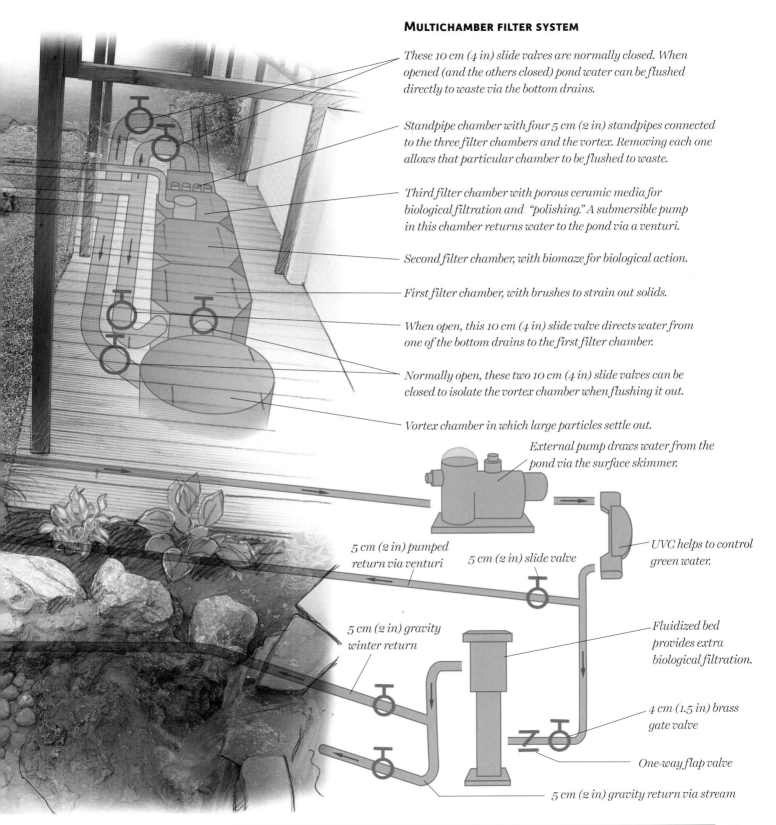

These 10 cm (4 in) slide valves are normally closed. When opened (and the others closed) pond water can be flushed directly to waste via the bottom drains.

Standpipe chamber with four 5 cm (2 in) standpipes connected to the three filter chambers and the vortex. Removing each one allows that particular chamber to be flushed to waste.

Third filter chamber with porous ceramic media for biological filtration and "polishing." A submersible pump in this chamber returns water to the pond via a venturi.

Second filter chamber, with biomaze for biological action.

First filter chamber, with brushes to strain out solids.

When open, this 10 cm (4 in) slide valve directs water from one of the bottom drains to the first filter chamber.

Normally open, these two 10 cm (4 in) slide valves can be closed to isolate the vortex chamber when flushing it out.

Vortex chamber in which large particles settle out.

External pump draws water from the pond via the surface skimmer.

5 cm (2 in) pumped return via venturi

5 cm (2 in) slide valve

UVC helps to control green water.

5 cm (2 in) gravity winter return

Fluidized bed provides extra biological filtration.

4 cm (1.5 in) brass gate valve

One-way flap valve

5 cm (2 in) gravity return via stream

Physiology and health care

In order to understand how best to keep koi, it is necessary to become acquainted with some basic anatomy and physiology. It is only by learning how healthy koi function that we can understand what happens when they become sick, which in turn will help to us to implement an appropriate treatment.

Living in water

Life in the aquatic environment is presented with a completely different set of conditions from those experienced by animals living on land. Water is denser than air and more energy is needed to move through it, so a koi's body is elegantly streamlined to reduce drag. In addition to streamlining, koi conserve energy in the way they swim. The body musculature literally pulls the tail from side to side and it is the tail that provides the propulsive force that moves the fish forward.

Above: As the koi moves forward, the erect dorsal and anal fins prevent it from rolling from side to side with each movement of the tail. The erect pectoral and pelvic fins help to prevent pitching and are used to steer. The pectoral fins also control fine movements.

Because the water is forced in a stream behind, it creates minute vortices that act together to push the fish forward. The fins act as stabilizers, preventing pitching, rolling and yawing. However, the pectoral fins have a further important function in controlling fine movements at slow speed.

For land animals, breathing air to extract oxygen requires very little effort, but the density of water means that koi use up a large amount of energy to perform the same function. It has been estimated that about 10 percent of the oxygen they extract from the water is required just to pump water across the gills. The intimate contact between the gills and water presents yet further problems of osmotic and ion regulation (see page 74).

In addition to the physical demands of the aquatic environment, microbes such as bacteria thrive in water and although most are harmless, a limited number are pathogenic, or disease-causing. In this section we not only examine how koi defend themselves against such pathogens, but also look at their anatomy and physiology. We then consider possible health problems in more detail and how koi-keepers can recognize and treat them.

Skin and scales

One of the most characteristic features of any fish is the presence of mucus over the body surface, which makes it feel slimy to the touch. The mucus is not a living tissue but is secreted by the skin and acts as a lubricant as the fish moves through the water, so it is continually sloughed off and replaced. The second function of the mucus is to act as a primary barrier to microbes, including bacteria, viruses, fungus and parasites. It succeeds in this role, not only because it is continually shed (and with it the microbes), but also because it contains natural antibodies, lysozymes and bacteriolysins (enzymes and chemicals that literally dissolve bacterial cells). Mucus also plays a role in the release of pheromones and odors.

Koi skin consists of two layers. The outermost layer — the epidermis — is a very fine, delicate tissue that lies on the outside of the scales. The fact that you can feel the scales of a koi beneath the epidermis indicates just how fine it is. This layer of living cells forms a barrier between koi and their

SKIN, SCALES AND FINS

The outermost layer of skin produces mucus and acts as a barrier between the koi and the surrounding water. The overlapping scales form a tough but flexible protection. The scales of the lateral line, found on both sides of the body, each have a pore in the center and are part of the sensory system.

Overlapping scales

Dorsal fin

Lateral line

Tail, or caudal fin

Anal fin

Pectoral fin (paired)

Pelvic fin (paired)

environment and is responsible for secreting the mucus. The cells of the epidermis multiply on a continuous basis to replace older cells at the surface and repair any injury.

The second layer of skin is called the dermis and contains blood vessels, nerves, connective tissue, certain sense organs and chromatophores — pigmented cells that give rise to the color patterns. The scales are formed in this layer of skin and if one is lost, a new one is produced by the cells of the dermis. Koi scales are described as cycloid and consist of a fibrous layer, or fibrillary plate, impregnated with calcium phosphate and calcium carbonate. With the exception of doitsu fish, the scales overlap one another rather like roof tiles and provide a flexible, bony protection on the outside of the fish. They are more or less uniform in appearance and shape, apart from those that make up the lateral line.

The lateral line

All fish have a sensory system known as the "lateral line," a series of scales along each flank with an opening, or pore, visible as a row of dots. The pores open into a canal that runs along the flanks just beneath the scales. Positioned along the inside of each canal are a number of hair cells connected to nerve fibers that relay their impulses to the spinal cord and then to the brain. Any movement of water within the lateral line canals disturbs the hair cells and enables the koi to detect vibrations in the water, which may be reflected off other fish, obstacles or even people's footsteps as they approach the pond. In fact, koi can distinguish between the footsteps of their owner and those of a visitor.

Muscles

Three basic types of muscle are found in all vertebrates: one is smooth muscle, found in the walls of arteries and larger veins and in the gut, where it is responsible for the movement of food; another is cardiac, or heart, muscle, and the third is striated, or striped, muscle. Striated muscle is associated with movement and is attached to the skeleton by gristly tendons. In fish it is formed into a series of W-shaped blocks called myotomes that encircle the body and provide the thrust for movement.

The skeleton

Overall, fish have far more bones than other vertebrates. For example, there are 28 bones in the human skull, but over three times as many in a koi skull. The skeleton is a complex structure with two main functions. The first is to provide support, forming a rigid structure for muscles to attach to, either directly to bone or via cartilage. The action of bone and muscle allows movement to take place. Second, it provides protection for delicate and sensitive tissues and organs, which are surrounded by bone. For example, the skull encases the brain and eyes.

The main skeletal elements are the skull, vertebral column (the backbone), pectoral and pelvic girdles, the numerous bones associated with the unpaired fins — dorsal, anal and caudal (tail) fins — and finally the ribs, forming the lateral walls of the abdomen.

INTERNAL ANATOMY

The gills are the site of gas diffusion. Carbon dioxide is released into the water and oxygen is collected by red blood cells. Ammonia is shed by the gill tissue. Essential salts are absorbed by the gills. Water enters the body through the gills.

Sound waves in the water are detected by the swimbladder and amplified by a series of modified backbones, linking them to the inner ear of the koi, enabling it to hear.

The paired kidneys conserve salts in the body and produce vast amounts of very dilute urine to remove water and maintain an osmotic balance in the body.

The swimbladder is a gas-filled buoyancy organ that allows the koi to remain at any depth in the water using the minimum amount of energy. The gas inside is mostly oxygen, as this is taken from the blood supply. When the koi wants to reach the pond surface to feed, gas is added to the swimbladder. When swimming to the bottom, gas is removed.

Koi have very good eyesight.

Brain

Backbone

Barbels (two pairs)

The three-chambered heart (atrium, ventricle and sinus venosus) pumps deoxygenated blood to the gills. The muscular section of the heart, the ventricle, receives oxygen-rich blood from the coronary artery.

Food is digested in the intestine through the action of enzymes and absorbed by the rich blood supply. Remaining solid waste is void as feces.

The spleen stores immature red blood cells and produces cells of the immune system.

The vent describes the area of the body where the intestine opens at the anus and where urine from the kidneys is released and eggs or sperm (milt) are shed into the water through the urogenital opening.

In koi, the liver is a very large organ. All food digested in the intestine passes to the liver for storage or distribution to the tissues. The liver breaks down unwanted proteins into ammonia, processes damaged or old red blood cells to form bile and breaks down any poisons or toxins.

The gonads, or reproductive organs, are situated on either side of the body. The ovaries produce eggs and can be very large. The testes produce sperm (milt).

The digestive system

Instead of teeth in the jaws, koi have paired pharyngeal bones inset with a number of large, molar like teeth and located just behind the gill arches. The pharyngeal teeth grind food against a cartilaginous pad at the base of the skull. Koi do not have a stomach; the esophagus simply grades into the intestine. Food is digested in the intestine and absorbed through the lining before being transported by the blood to the liver. In koi, the liver is a large organ with a number of functions, but it is the main processing plant for all food and it is here that the components are further refined and sorted before being distributed to the tissues or stored. The liver also receives all the waste products from the tissues, breaking down damaged blood cells to produce bile, and unwanted proteins into ammonia. Any toxic substance accidentally ingested is also broken down by the liver.

Water and salt regulation

In fish, water and salt regulation — also known as osmoregulation — is a very important physiological process. The body fluids and cells of koi contain water and salts in specific amounts and it is important to maintain these

FRESHWATER OSMOREGULATION

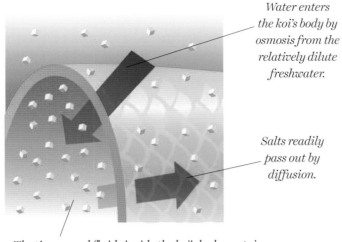

Water enters the koi's body by osmosis from the relatively dilute freshwater.

Salts readily pass out by diffusion.

The tissues and fluids inside the koi's body contain more salts than the surrounding water.

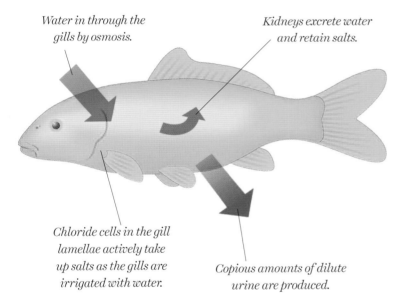

Water in through the gills by osmosis.

Kidneys excrete water and retain salts.

Chloride cells in the gill lamellae actively take up salts as the gills are irrigated with water.

Copious amounts of dilute urine are produced.

concentrations on a continuous basis. The principal salts are sodium, potassium, calcium, magnesium, chloride and sulphate. The body actually contains more salts than the surrounding water, and the problem is that water readily enters the fish through osmosis. (Osmosis describes the movement of water from a weaker solution into a more concentrated one through a partially permeable membrane.) The surrounding water represents the weaker solution, the skin and gill tissues of the koi are partially permeable membranes, and the salt content of the blood and other body fluids represents the concentrated solution. This

means that there is a tendency for water to enter the koi's body continually, primarily through the gill tissue, and for salts inside the body to leach into the surrounding water by diffusion. (This situation is helped to a certain extent by special cells on the gills called chloride cells that actively extract salts from the surrounding water.) Koi are able to overcome this problem because their kidneys extract and retain salt from the blood, while removing excess water by producing copious amounts of dilute urine. Because water freely enters the body, koi do not need to drink.

There is also a compromise between the amount of gill tissue that the fish must "expose" in order to respire efficiently and the "danger" of exposing too much, thus allowing water to enter the body too freely. Forced exercise, such as that caused by continuously netting the pond, can cause a koi to absorb so much water that its body swells into a state of dropsy (see page 122), simply because it is using such a vast area of gill tissue to respire and letting in water during the process.

Gill structure and function

The gills are the principal organ of respiration and are of necessity very delicate, since they allow oxygen to pass from the water, through the tissue and into the blood, and waste carbon dioxide gas to be released. Koi are remarkably efficient at extracting oxygen from water. The gill filaments, or primary lamellae, have a large surface area that is extended by outfolds of tissue, known as the secondary lamellae. The blood is in intimate contact with the water at the gills, the two being separated by a single layer of epithelial cells. In order to extract the maximum amount of oxygen from the water, the blood flow through the gills is in the opposite direction to the water flow, a so-called countercurrent system. Finally, as the blood cells pass through the secondary lamellae, they are literally stretched to increase the surface area and allow the maximum amount of oxygen to be transferred to the red respiratory protein hemoglobin.

The gills are an important site for excreting nitrogenous waste, with 82 percent being eliminated as ammonia and 8 percent as urea. The remaining 10 percent is excreted by the kidneys as urea in the form of dilute urine.

The fact that blood is in such intimate contact with the water at the gills means that it is either cooled or warmed, depending on the ambient water temperature. The oxygenated blood flow leaving the gills is divided into two

branches, one to the brain and the other to the body tissues via the dorsal aorta, a large artery that runs beneath the vertebral column and therefore along the centerline of the body.

The swimbladder

The swimbladder is a gas-filled sac that lies at the top of the body cavity, just beneath the vertebral column. In koi, the swimbladder is a two-chambered structure, with the posterior kidneys lying astride the constriction between the chambers. The primary function of the swimbladder is to control buoyancy and allow koi to remain at any depth in the water using the minimum amount of energy. In koi, the swimbladder primitively retains a connection to the gut and, indeed, the fish can top up the gas content of this organ by gulping air at the water surface. More usually, the gas content of the swimbladder is controlled by a number of blood vessels.

In koi (as in many other fish), the swimbladder fulfils a secondary role in amplifying sound and transmitting it to the inner ear via a series of small bones.

Health care

Keeping koi is a rewarding and enjoyable hobby, but whenever large numbers of animals are held in a captive environment, there are occasions when one or more becomes sick. It is very common to encounter outbreaks of disease as a consequence of poor water conditions and stress. Good pond management means testing the water regularly, ensuring that the pond and filters are free of organic detritus, observing the koi, watching and learning their normal behavior patterns and offering a good-quality feed (see pages 150–155). In the event of any fish becoming sick, or even dying, it is important to determine the cause in order to effect an appropriate course of action.

In the event of any health problem, your immediate course of action should be to test all water quality parameters, if only to eliminate them as the cause of the problem, and to add supplementary aeration, providing symptoms of gas bubble disease are not indicated (see page 77). Increasing the aeration

HOW THE GILLS WORK

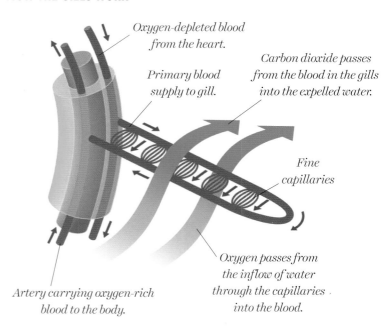

Oxygen-depleted blood from the heart.

Carbon dioxide passes from the blood in the gills into the expelled water.

Primary blood supply to gill.

Fine capillaries

Oxygen passes from the inflow of water through the capillaries into the blood.

Artery carrying oxygen-rich blood to the body.

Above: The drawing reveals how blood flow in the capillaries of the gill lamellae and water flow over the gill filaments allows gaseous exchange to take place.

has two effects. The first is to make more oxygen available to the koi, which is important if they are stressed. Second, as the air passes through the water, it collects any volatile contaminants such as free ammonia. These are released into the atmosphere as the bubble bursts at the water surface.

When searching for the underlying cause of a health problem, look for a pattern in the numbers of koi affected. For example, if large numbers of fish of mixed sizes are affected, this may be an indication that there is a water quality problem, most commonly because of high levels of ammonia or nitrite, or low levels of dissolved oxygen. Outbreaks of infectious disease, such as those caused

Left: Stress is a contributing factor in outbreaks of koi herpes virus (KHV). Transportation is very stressful and can lead to the koi becoming vulnerable to infection.

do you risk injuring the koi, but they will also be continuously stressed and subject to opportunist infections (see page 141).

There are situations where it becomes necessary to treat either an individual koi or even the entire population, but if in doubt, it is sensible to consult someone with experience in fish health matters, such as your koi dealer or a veterinarian.

Environmentally related disease

Poor water quality is the biggest cause of disease and mortalities in the pond and, unless the environmental conditions are improved through partial water changes, the koi are unlikely to recover. Exposure to poor water quality over a period of days to weeks causes koi to become increasingly stressed and subject to secondary disease and infections.

Dissolved oxygen

Oxygen is an essential requirement for koi, and in summer, when this vital gas is at a premium due to higher water temperatures, it can drop to critically low levels (see page 20). The minimum requirement for healthy growth, tissue repair and reproduction is 6 mg of dissolved oxygen/l of water. Although koi will tolerate a drop to 3 mg/l for a short period of time, this does cause considerable stress.

In a koi pond, it is quite common during the summer months to find that the water has a consistently low dissolved oxygen level, which causes koi to become lethargic and cease feeding. It is frequently assumed that koi will come to the water surface and gasp if the oxygen level is low, but this really is a last resort. Fish gasping at the surface means that the situation is extremely critical and you must implement massive aeration immediately.

As we have seen on page 22, it is not only fish that use up the oxygen in the water, but also plants, algae and bacteria. When the oxygen level crashes overnight, it is common to find the largest or most active koi dead in the morning and others breathing heavily at the water surface, even though they previously appeared to be in good health. Irrespective of whether the oxygen level has been at a continuously low level or drops rapidly overnight as a consequence of algae or submerged plant growth, the koi will become stressed.

Gas bubble disease

In winter, when air is readily soluble in water, you may encounter gas bubble disease. The physiological effects of this condition closely match nitrogen narcosis, or the

Above: *If the dissolved oxygen level in the water begins to drop, the koi will become lethargic and stop feeding. At critically low levels, they will move to the aerated area of the pond and will be seen gasping at the surface. At this stage, extra aeration is vital.*

by parasites, bacteria or viruses, tend to affect only a few koi initially, but the numbers increase steadily over a period of time.

Where only a single koi is affected and the problem does not appear to be spreading to any others in the pond, physical injury is the most likely cause. Most injuries to koi are incurred through poor or repeated netting and handling, so avoid routinely catching the fish in order to examine them. Not only

"bends" suffered by deep sea divers, and, indeed, the affected koi suffer cramp-like spasms of the lateral musculature of the body. Basically, the water becomes supersaturated with air, which means in effect that the air is in solution in the water. Air is primarily composed of nitrogen gas, which under conditions of air supersaturation means that the water is saturated with dissolved nitrogen and a small amount of other gases. It is the dissolved nitrogen content of the water that causes the symptoms of gas bubble disease, hence the similarity to nitrogen narcosis. As the koi breathes the water supersaturated with air, the dissolved nitrogen readily enters through the gills and into solution in the blood. Once inside the blood circulatory system, the changes in blood pressure allow the nitrogen to come out of solution as a gas, creating air bubbles in the blood flow, called "air embolisms." These collect in the filaments of the fins and sometimes around the eyes, between the bony rays, the gill tissue and membranes lining the mouth. Occasionally, air may become trapped between the epidermis and dermis, and when the pressure becomes too great, it simply lifts the entire outer layer of skin.

In most instances, once the problem has been diagnosed and remedied, the affected koi gradually recover without further treatment. You can deal with water affected by supersaturation of air by splashing it vigorously, say by pumping it against the wall of the pond or a solid object temporarily placed in the pond. The splashing action increases the water surface area, allowing the excess dissolved air to escape back into the atmosphere.

The effects of ammonia poisoning

When ammonia concentrations begin to increase in the water, the initial response of koi is to produce more mucus on the body surface and gills. If the ammonia level in the water continues to increase, the cells of the gills begin to swell and then proliferate, giving rise to a condition called lamellar hyperplasia. In the early stages, the tips of the gills are affected and the condition is often called clubbed gills. If the exposure to ammonia persists, whole areas of the gill filaments can become fused together. This causes the koi respiratory distress, osmoregulatory failure and dropsy.

Left: When adding salt to the pond, dissolve it first in a bucket of water, rather than to add large volumes of neat salt crystals to the pond, which could burn delicate koi skin.

Where the water is free of ammonia pollution, koi can readily shed ammonia from the body at the gills. Whatever the concentration of ammonia recorded in the water, the koi has the same amount in its body and tissues. Where the water quality has deteriorated and become polluted with ammonia, the koi can only excrete ammonia in excess of the concentration found in the water. An accumulation of ammonia alters the pH of the blood, reducing the fish's ability to absorb oxygen from the water and use nutrients effectively, and reduces growth rates.

The toxicity of ammonia can be reduced by adding cooking salt (sodium chloride) or pond or aquarium salt (sodium chloride packaged for the aquatic trade) to the pond water. This converts free ammonia to the ionized form, which is less harmful. It is important to understand that the concentration of ammonia in the pond water must be reduced through regular, partial water changes. The volume and frequency of the water changes needed depend on the amount of pollutant present. Certain mineral substances, such as zeolite

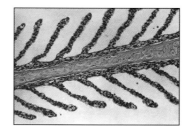

Left: The normal structure of the gills is very delicate and the tiny, fingerlike lamellae that allow the blood to come into intimate contact with the water can be clearly seen here.

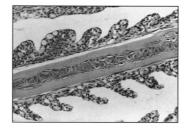

Left: Exposure to ammonia causes the structure of the gills to break down. The cells proliferate, causing the lamellae to become and short and thickened — a condition known as lamellar hyperplasia.

and ion-exchange resins, can be used to reduce ammonia levels by adsorbing the ionized form (see also pages 25–26).

The effects of nitrite poisoning

Nitrite is the secondary breakdown product of ammonia via the nitrogen cycle (see page 26) and is also poisonous to koi. Because nitrite is a skin irritant, it causes koi to rub and flick repeatedly on hard surfaces. This behavior may be mistaken for a parasite infection and treated inappropriately. Nitrite poisoning may also be called "brown blood disease," as nitrite binds with the hemoglobin in the red blood cells to form methemoglobin, which prevents oxygen from being absorbed and gives the blood a dark brown appearance instead of the characteristic red color. Nitrite is a potent relaxant of smooth muscle and a vasodilator (it causes the blood vessels to expand) and these effects can lead to failure of the heart and blood vascular system. Finally, there is evidence that nitrite acts as an immunosuppressant (reduces the effectiveness of the immune system), and chronic exposure can lead to secondary infections, such as bacterial gill disease.

The effect of temperature on koi

Generally speaking, adult koi are tolerant of temperatures in the range 3 to 25°C (37–77°F), although as carp originated from southern Europe, the preferred temperatures are probably between 15 and 22°C (59–72°F). In recent years, there has been a trend in Japan to overwinter koi in their first and second years in fish houses, where the water temperature is maintained at a minimum of 16°C (61°F) and more usually at 18°C (64°F). This means that juvenile koi are very sensitive to low temperatures and will develop symptoms of thermal stress when water temperatures drop below about 14°C (57°F). When exposed to low temperatures, young koi become lethargic and often lie on their sides, but will swim away if disturbed. Usually the integrity of the skin is affected, rendering the fish susceptible to fungal infections. Providing young koi are introduced into the pond during the summer months in temperate regions, they should adapt to the gradual reduction in temperature as autumn progresses.

The immune system of koi is influenced by water temperature and is most effective in the warmer summer months. This is followed by a gradual decline in efficiency through the autumn and early winter and is largely ineffective during the coldest months. Traditionally, spring is regarded as the most difficult time for koi and this is probably because the fish are largely immunosuppressed, while the moderate increase in temperatures at this time of the year promotes the activity of parasites and other pathogens. The immune system is also affected by the nutritional status of koi and, given that they are largely unfed through the winter, this can also have a further impact in the spring months.

Koi will usually tolerate a rapid drop in temperature more readily than a rapid rise, although water temperatures may fluctuate by as much as 10°C (18°F) during a 24-hour period. Temperature increases can lower the dissolved oxygen levels in the pond (see page 20), but the immune system of the fish takes time to catch up with any rise in temperature. However, many parasites and bacteria can take advantage of the warmer conditions, and thrive.

Above: *At temperatures of 18°C (64°F) and above, the immune system of young koi will be at its most responsive to invading parasites and bacteria. Once the water temperature drops below 10°C (50°F), the immune system is not particularly effective.*

Netting and handling koi

If you believe that your koi are suffering from any of the health problems discussed later in this book, you will probably need to take one or more fish out of the pond for closer inspection. This could be in order to take a skin scrape, a mucus swab, to move the fish into quarantine or simply to take a closer look at the fish before deciding on the next course of action. When moving or examining koi, you must do so in such a way as to cause the minimum stress or injury to the fish. Bad netting and handling can itself be a large stress factor, which could lead to future health problems, and many physical injuries are caused by careless netting.

A sock net

A pan net

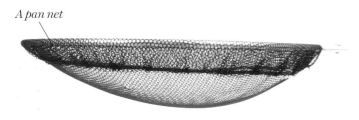

Catching your koi

Before making any attempt to catch a fish you must have the right equipment:

- a pan net suitable to accommodate the largest fish in the pond
- a viewing bowl
- a sock net

A pan net is very shallow, which reduces the risk of the fish becoming entangled in the netting. In fact, this net should only be used as a guide and under no circumstances should you ever lift the net out of the water with the fish in it. You are basically trying to use it to shepherd the desired fish into a viewing bowl. Ideally, get a helper at this point to submerge one side of the bowl so that the fish can simply swim from

NETTING A KOI SINGLE HANDED

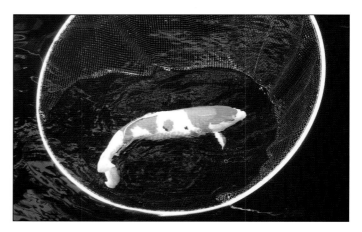

1 Catch the koi to be inspected in a suitably sized pan net.

2 Guide the koi to the bowl with the net, then use the edge of the net to tip one side of the bowl below water level.

3 Gently tip the net to transfer the koi from net to bowl.

NETTING A KOI WITH A HELPER

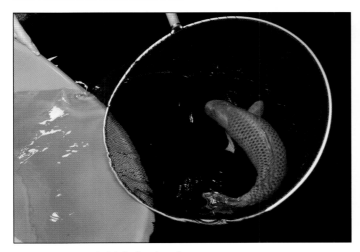

1 Ask a helper to hold the bowl as shown.

2 Move the net toward the submerged edge of the bowl.

3 Gently tip the net so that the koi swims into the bowl.

4 To prevent jumping, keep the water level quite low.

the net into the bowl. If you have to work on your own, float the viewing bowl and half fill it with water. Once the fish is caught, bring it to the surface and lift one side of the net so that it hooks over the lip of the bowl. Then force one side of the bowl down into the water and simultaneously tip the fish from the net to the bowl. The diameter of both the net and the viewing bowl must be wide enough to accommodate your largest koi. It is advisable to opt for a floating bowl, otherwise you may find you are spending more time lifting the bowl from the bottom of the pond than you are catching koi.

When trying to catch a fish, follow a few simple rules. These will make it easier for you to catch the koi and reduce the risk of damaging it. Ideally, leave the bowl and the koi in the water. The bowl is heavy and the water creates a suction force when lifted. There is a risk of serious back injury to the koi-keeper.

1 Turn off all air pumps and water features so that you can see what you are doing.

2 Move the net so that its edge slices through the water. This reduces drag and allows you to move the net much more quickly.

USING A SOCK NET

1 Pull the sock net through the water to make it wet.

2 Coax the koi head-first into the sock net.

3 Hold each end of the net and lift it out of the water.

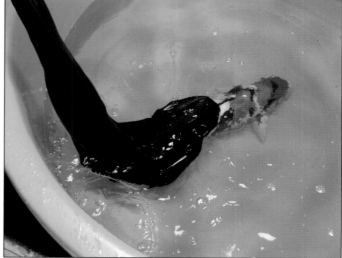

4 Pull the sock net through the water to release the koi.

3 When bringing a captured fish to the surface, avoid any underwater returns. The pressure of the water returning to the pond from these could force the koi into the net and cause it physical damage.

4 If you are trying to catch small koi or the pond is very large, you may find it hard to catch the fish with one net. Rather than chasing around the pond and risking accidentally bumping the fish with the net, try one of two tactics. Either ask someone to help you and give them another net so that they can keep the fish at one end while you try to catch it. If this is not possible, lower the water level, thus reducing the area in which the fish can swim.

5 If the pond is very large, netting a particular koi may prove too stressful to both yourself and the fish. In such a case it may be advisable to get a custom-made seine net for your pond, which allows all the koi to be caught easily without undue stress. Then you can simply remove the ones that need to be inspected and place them into a viewing bowl before allowing the others to return to the pond.

6 If a koi really is too difficult to catch, switch the pumps and aeration back on and try again, either after a few hours, or the following day.

Once you have a fish in the bowl, you may wish to move it or to inspect it more closely. There are two ways of moving fish without causing it stress and damage.

Using a sock net

Sock nets are available in various sizes. Ensure that the one you are using has a large enough diameter for the fish in question, and that it will hold the full length of the fish in the sock. First make sure that the whole sock is wet. Then hold the sock net in one hand under the water in the bowl and use your other hand to persuade the fish gently into the sock head-first. Once it is fully in the sock, hold the end of the sock in one hand and grasp the handle in the other. The sock net can then be lifted out of the water. Keep the net as straight as possible. To release the fish from the sock, simply immerse it in the water and let go of the end of the sock. Then lift the sock from the water by the handle; if done correctly the fish will swim out.

Using a plastic bag

If a sock net is not available, a plastic bag can be used in much the same way. The only difference is that as the bag is sealed at one end, you will have to tip the fish from the bag.

Spinning the fish

If you need to handle a koi that is behaving in a lively fashion, you could employ a tactic called "spinning." Simply spin the fish gently with your hands for a minute or two while it is in the bowl. The causes the fish to become disoriented, which in turn makes it easier to handle without the need for a sedating agent.

Above: *Using your hands, gently spin the koi with a circular motion, always working in the same direction. After a minute or two the koi should be quite calm.*

USING A PLASTIC BAG

1 Put the plastic bag in the bowl, half-fill with water, then coax the koi into it.

2 Hold the top and one of the bottom corners of the bag.

3 You can now lift the bag and move the koi as desired.

Using a microscope

A microscope is an essential piece of equipment for the correct identification of diseases. It allows koi-keepers to identify parasite infections. Many koi-keepers cite the price of a good-quality microscope as the reason they do not own one, but this is false economy. If you can identify parasites and treat them early, you can stop the spread of an infection before it becomes a real concern and leads to potential losses or physical damage to high-quality koi. A good-quality

This is a binocular microscope with its own light source.

Above: A microscope is an essential tool for the koi-keeper to aid in the identification of many diseases. You can buy used ones to save money.

microscope is also a sound investment, and if you no longer need it, as long as it has been well-maintained you will easily be able to sell it. There are various factors to consider when choosing the best unit for your budget and intended use.

Styles of microscope

First, do you want a binocular (using two eye-pieces) or a monocular (single eye-piece) microscope? This choice is largely influenced by budget and personal preference. Another decision that is often influenced by budget is whether to buy a microscope with its own light source or not. A microscope with its own light source generally needs electricity to light a bulb in the base of the unit. The advantage of this is that the microscope can be set up in one location and used at any time simply by turning on the power supply. The intensity of the light can normally be controlled, allowing greater flexibility. The other — generally cheaper — option is a microscope without its own light source. Instead it has a mirror located in the base, which you turn to reflect rays of light onto the subject being examined. The disadvantage of this system is that you are dependent upon an external light source, and the intensity of this light may not be controllable, which can affect the brightness of the image.

Lenses

There are two lenses to consider when buying a microscope: the eyepiece lens and the objective lens. Most microscopes feature more than one objective lens; usually there are three, each with different powers of magnification. These lenses sit on a revolving turret so that the magnification can be easily changed simply by turning a dial, which will move to the next lens. A microscope mainly intended for parasite identification should be equipped with lenses of the following power — 10x, 20x and 40x. The eyepiece lens is what you actually look down, and its magnification will affect the overall magnification of the image. These are easily interchangeable and thus allow you to achieve different levels of magnification. The typical magnification of the eyepiece lens for parasitic identification is normally 10x or 15x. By using a 10x eyepiece lens with an objective lens of 40x, you achieve a magnification of 400x (10 x 40 = 400). A 40x lens is really the greatest magnification you will need for identifying fish parasites, which are usually wet mounts. The higher magnification lenses are designed for use with fixed, permanent mount, histology slide preparations.

Key:

1 Monocular eyepiece lens
2 Tube
3 Focusing knob
4 Revolving turret of three objective lenses
5 Clips to retain slide
6 Stage
7 Mirror to reflect light up through slide

Above: *A classic compound light microscope, so-called because the magnification is a compound of the lens power in the eyepiece and objective lenses.*

Mounting a slide

Having taken a slide for examination (see pages 86–87), it must be correctly placed on the microscope so that it can be viewed. Place the slide on what is known as the stage, which may be either fixed or move up and down. In some microscopes the stage moves up and down to bring the slide into focus, while others work by moving the lens and eyepiece with a focus dial. The slide is held in place by a slide clamp. The sample on the slide is normally covered by a small square of thin glass called a cover slip.

Viewing the slide

Once it is firmly in position you can view the slide. To prevent damage to the lens, it is better to focus away from the slide. If you move the lens toward the slide you may overfocus and crash the lens onto it, which can both break the slide and, more importantly, damage or scratch the objective lens. There are typically two controls on a standard microscope for controlling the focus. Use the first one to find the object quickly and focus on it roughly. The second control allows for fine tuning of the focusing by moving either the tube or stage just a fraction each time you turn the fine focus dial.

Unless you know exactly what you are looking for and at what magnification it will be found, always start at the lowest magnification, then increase it once a full scan of the slide has been achieved. To ensure that you see all of the slide, view it in a methodical manner making either left to right or front to back passes, before gently moving on to view the next sector. The slide is moved by using the controls situated underneath the stage. There may also be additional controls for finer movement, which allows for exact positioning over a specific area.

The basic microscope uses a mirror to beam light through the specimen and lenses. Traditionally, daylight was considered the best light as it is very white. These days, most microscopes have an integral light source, which is much easier to use and emits white light. The majority of microscopes have a unit underneath the stage, which is the condenser, the function of which is to focus the light on the specimen. To focus the condenser, start with it in the lowest position. Place a small object, such as a needle tip, on the stage and slowly raise the condenser until the object is in sharp focus, at which point the condenser is focused.

Taking a skin scrape

If your koi are not behaving in their normal way, but all the water quality parameters, including the oxygen level, are acceptable, it is worth taking a skin scrape. This involves scraping a sterile blunt instrument or (for the more experienced) a slide over a fish's skin to collect some of the mucus that covers its body. You can then examine the mucus sample under a microscope and identify any parasites present within the pond that may be affecting the behavior of the koi. Typical behavioral changes include koi hanging in the water, swimming with fins clamped to their sides, rapid gill movements, fish congregating in areas of enriched oxygen such as water returns and airstones, fish that are isolated and not mixing with other koi in the pond, loss of appetite and flicking or rubbing against any surfaces in the pond as if the fish were trying to relieve an irritation. If you do not own a microscope to examine the skin scrape, a nearby koi dealer can help, but they must be able to view the scrape quickly, ideally within 30–60 minutes of it having been taken. It may be more appropriate to contact a fish health professional or experienced member of a local koi club to assist with examining skin scrapes.

To take a skin scrape you will need a sterile blunt instrument and some slides and cover slips handy. If you are taking a sample from a large koi, it also helps to have someone to help you. To take a skin scrape from a large koi, it is better to sedate or lightly anesthetize the fish to reduce stress and prevent injury. These sedatives have little effect on clinical parasite infections.

How to take the skin scrape

Begin by placing the koi in a viewing bowl. Then tip out some water so that just enough remains to cover the koi. When dealing with small koi, you may be able to hold the fish in one hand while taking the scrape with the other. For larger koi it is far easier if you have an assistant who can hold the koi against the side of the bowl while you take the scrape. It is sometimes necessary to apply quite a bit of pressure to the koi while holding it to stop it from jumping about and damaging itself. To calm down the koi, quickly and safely, you can employ a tactic known as spinning, which is described on page 83.

Once the koi is firmly held, take the blunt instrument or slide and run it along the fish's body. Do this from head to tail in the direction of the scales. Never take a skin scrape in the other direction as this may result in scale damage.

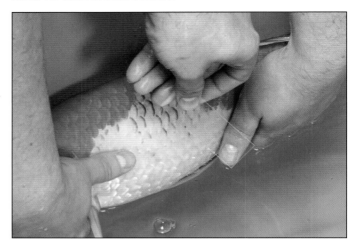

1 Take a blunt instrument or slide, as shown here.

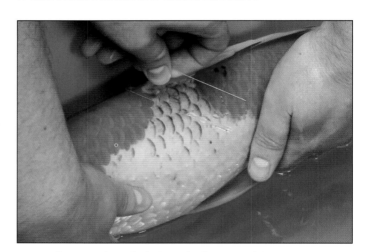

2 Gently run it along the body in the direction of the scales.

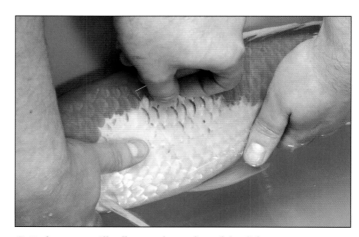

3 Body mucus will collect on the surface of the slide.

Now examine the slide under your microscope. If you find nothing, it pays to take scrapes from other koi in your pond.

Only consider taking scrapes when signs of parasite infection become obvious. Remember, parasites will always be present but in low numbers; it is only when koi become stressed that these numbers increase and a problem results. As you learn how to view and interpret a scrape, you will be able to spot any increase in parasite levels and, hopefully, identify and treat the problem before it gets out of control.

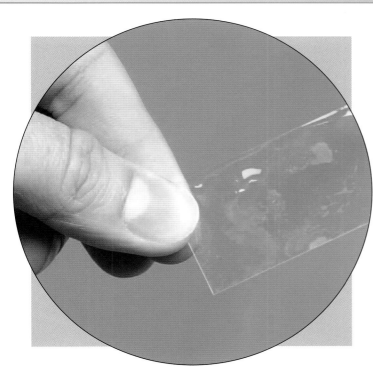

4 A collection of mucus will be deposited on the slide or blunt instrument used to take the scrape.

You may need to apply light pressure while taking the scrape, and perhaps make more than one pass to get enough mucus for the sample. A skin scrape can be taken anywhere on the koi, but do take note of the symptoms that your koi is displaying. For example, if it is gasping for air, take a scrape as close to the gills as you can. The amount of mucus required is quite small and as long as an area of the slide can be seen to have mucus on it, you will have enough to examine it successfully. If using a blunt instrument to take the scrape, transfer the mucus onto the slide once you have collected it.

Once you have taken the scrape, you can put the koi back in the pond. Normally, a scrape done correctly will not have any adverse side effect on the koi.

Prepare your slide for examination under the microscope by taking a cover slip, and using this to move the sample of mucus to the center of the slide. Put a drop of pond water (not tap water) on the slide to dilute the mucus sample, then drop the cover slip into position. Gently ease it onto the slide, allowing the mucus to spread out underneath it. If you do not have any cover slips, you can use another slide and sandwich the mucus between the two pieces of glass.

Below: Having taken your sample, you can now examine it. To prepare the slide, place a cover slip over the mucus. Then position the slide on the microscope ready for examination.

HOW TO TAKE A SWAB

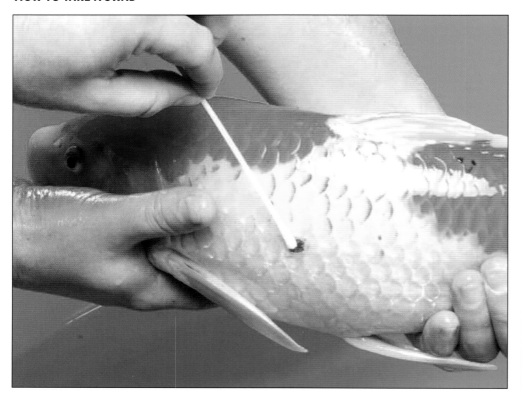

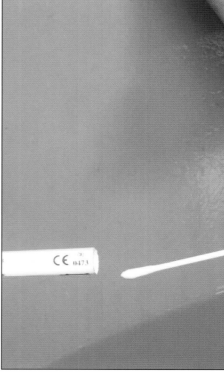

1 Remove the swab from its protective sterile packaging and rub it over the area to be tested.

2 As soon as you have taken the sample satisfactorily, place the swab back into its sterile protective casing.

Taking a swab

It may be that your koi are looking off-color, perhaps afflicted with ulcers, sores and areas of infection. If the water quality is fine and a skin scrape has not revealed any obvious cause for their condition, it is worth taking a swab and sending it away for analysis to check if a bacterial infection is causing the problem.

Unlike a skin scrape, which can be examined at home, a swab needs to be processed by a qualified laboratory. Your local koi specialist should be able to assist you to take a swab by supplying the necessary equipment and either sending it away for you or advising you on how to do this yourself. The results may also be sent back to your local dealer or veterinarian and they can then advise on the correct course of treatment. Try to take and send swabs to a laboratory at the start of the week, unless otherwise advised by the laboratory itself, or by your local dealer or veterinarian. If you take a swab on a Friday but the laboratory is closed over the weekend, work will not start on it until Monday at the earliest. By this time, the levels of bacteria on the swab may have decreased or increased, giving a false reading.

How to take a swab

Make sure you have all the necessary items both for taking the swab and getting it in the mail immediately. Generally, you need the swab, a request form completed with your details and details of where and how the swab was taken, a prepaid envelope, and a biohazard bag.

Now catch the koi and place it in a viewing bowl. It may be easier to lightly sedate the koi to avoid causing it further stress or injury when taking a swab from an infected area or open ulcer. Tip water from the viewing bowl until only enough is left to cover the chosen koi.

It is far easier to carry out this step with two people. One of you should hold the koi against the side of the viewing bowl so that any areas that look infected are easily visible. Some pressure may be required to hold the koi

3 *Now complete any necessary paperwork and despatch the package without delay.*

still, but this will cause less harm than if the koi is simply left to thrash about in the bowl. If the koi is particularly lively, try "spinning" it to calm it down (see page 83). Once the koi is held firmly in position, the other person can take the swab from areas of ulceration or sites of physical damage on the fish, as it is these areas that will produce the most accurate diagnosis of what is actually present.

Only open the packing when you are ready to take the swab. Do not remove the swab from its container until the koi is secure in the bowl. This will reduce the risk of any airborne bacteria getting onto the swab and giving false readings. A swab is basically like a large cotton swab. To take a sample, simply roll it back and forth over the area to be tested.

When you have obtained the sample, immediately place the swab back into its container, again to prevent any contamination. Write any necessary details on the container for identification purposes. You can now release the koi back into the pond — it should suffer no adverse effects.

Once labeled, and with all the required paperwork completed, place the container in the biohazard bag. This goes into the addressed envelope, which should be mailed immediately, unless you have arranged to return it to your koi specialist or veterinarian instead.

Despatching the swab
Make sure you use the quickest postal service available — many laboratories will supply prepaid envelopes. The quicker the swab gets to the laboratory, the sooner you will have the results that will provide a more accurate picture of what your problem is. As most of the work in processing the swab is done by a specialist laboratory, there is usually a charge to pay. Do not let this deter you, as the information you will get back is priceless when treating your koi. Taking swabs should only be undertaken when there is an indication of infectious disease. However, be aware that all koi have bacteria associated with them, and routine swabbing can become misleading, leading to unnecessary treatment.

Transporting koi

There may come a time when you need to transport at least one, or maybe more, koi to a veterinarian or a koi dealer for further examination to allow an exact identification of a disease to be made, or for extra treatment. Although it is always better to treat a sick koi on site, rather than put it through the extra stress of being moved, this is not always possible. To minimize the stress of transportation, it is vital that the koi are handled and packaged correctly.

Before attempting to transport any koi, assemble all the necessary equipment, including suitably sized plastic bags for carrying the koi. Make sure you have enough of these so that each bag can be doubled up, i.e., one bag placed inside another. This helps to prevent leaks occurring. A supply of air or oxygen will be required to inflate the bag once the koi is placed inside it. Ideally, you should use oxygen, but most people do not have access to an oxygen bottle. A viable alternative, which is suitable if the fish will not be traveling for more than 60 to 90 minutes without the bag being opened and resealed, is to inflate the bag with a normal air pump. This is a standard piece of equipment for most koi-keepers. You will also need rubber bands to seal the bags and a suitably sized box in which to place them.

Bagging koi for transportation

Once the koi in question are in the viewing bowl, decide on the correct size of bag and how many koi can be placed in each one. Plastic koi bags are generally available from your local koi dealer and if you tell them the number and size of the koi that you are intending to move, they will be able to supply the correct size and quantity of bags. Expect to pay for these bags as they are manufactured from thicker plastic and generally have a double seal to make leaks less likely. They are available in numerous sizes, but the most common are:

- 30 x 60 cm (12 in x 24 in) suitable for small koi measuring up to 13–15 cm (5–6 in)
- 40 x 75 cm (16 in x 30 in) suitable for a number of small koi or individual koi measuring 25–30 cm (10–12 in)
- 60 x 100 cm (24 in x 39 in) suitable for a large number, say up to 30, small koi under 15 cm (6 in) or three to four koi of around 25–30 cm (10–12 in)or individual large koi up to 71–75 cm (28 to 30 in)

Larger koi will require a bigger bag, which your koi dealer may not carry as a stock item and may need to order for you.

BAGGING A KOI

1 Take a fish bag of a suitable size for the koi to be moved.

2 Decant a small amount of water into the bag.

3 *Place the bag containing the water inside a second bag.*

4 *To prevent water from becoming trapped between the two bags, roll the tops of the bags down.*

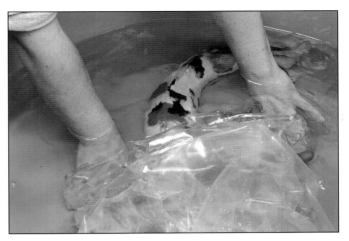

5 *Coax the koi into the bag adding water while doing so.*

6 *With the correct amount of water in the bag, unroll the top.*

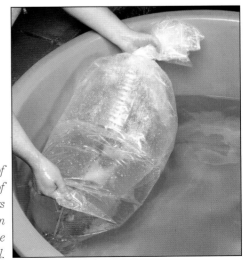

7 *Hold the top of the bag and one of the bottom corners securely and then lift it out of the viewing bowl.*

Select the correct bag size and add about 2.5 cm (1 in) of water to it. Drop this bag inside another bag of the same size. This process is known as double bagging. Before continuing, it is a good idea to roll over the top of both bags a couple of times to prevent the gap between them filling with water. You are now ready to transfer your koi to the bag.

Lean over the bowl, take the bag in your hands and gently lower it into the water. Now coax the selected koi into the bag. You will find that the bag starts to fill with water at the same time. Once the koi is in the bag, lift it from the water and check if it has the correct amount of water in it. For smaller koi the bag should be about one-third full of water, allowing for two-thirds air when inflated. When dealing with larger koi try to ensure that when the bag is laid on its side the water level is high enough to cover the gills.

When there is sufficient water in the bag, inflate the bag. If you are travelling a short distance, use an air line from your air pump. For longer journeys, use oxygen. Once the bag is inflated, secure the neck with two rubber bands in case one should break. Make absolutely sure that both the inner and outer bags are sealed.

Place the bagged koi inside a suitable box ready for transporting. Lay the bag horizontally in the box, rather than upright. The box should be a good fit for the bag to prevent it from rolling around. If the box is too big, pack the space with suitable material; spare plastic bags inflated with air are a good choice.

When placing the box in your car, position it lengthways across the vehicle. This prevents damage to the fish if you have to brake suddenly. If the box was positioned the other way around, the koi would smash into the ends of the box. This is a particularly important consideration when transporting larger koi. It is also sensible to place the box out of direct sunlight to avoid sudden changes in temperature.

If you are transporting your koi over a very long distance, you might consider using polystyrene boxes, as these will help maintain a more stable temperature within the box. If it is very hot, consider adding ice packs inside the boxes to help maintain cool conditions throughout the journey.

When releasing koi after transportation, check the temperatures of the bag water and the pond water. If they are significantly different, allow the bag to float on the pond for 30 to 60 minutes out of direct sunlight before releasing the koi back into the water.

INFLATING A PLASTIC BAG

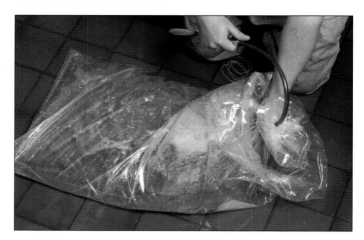

1 *Hold the top tight while inserting the air/oxygen hose.*

2 *Inflate the bag until only enough plastic is left to tie it off.*

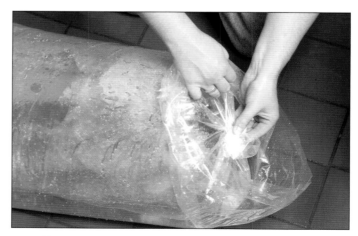

3 *Seal both bags separately with rubber bands.*

4 Take a suitably sized box and place the bag in it.

5 Seal the lid securely prior to transportation.

Above: *On arrival at the final destination, float the bag on the pond for 30 minutes or so to help stabilize any temperature differences. During this time, be sure to keep the bag out of direct sunlight to avoid the risk of the fish overheating.*

If you need to move a large number of koi, it is worth discussing the situation with your local koi dealer, who may have access to transportation tanks that can be put on the back of a truck or trailer. They can also aerate the water in the tank with pure oxygen, which is fed from an oxygen bottle on the vehicle via a special airstone in the tank. Koi moved this way can be both lifted into the tank and, on reaching their destination, transferred using a sock net.

Conditions caused by parasites

The most commonly encountered clearly visible parasites of koi — anchor worm and fish lice — are crustaceans. This group of parasites is very injurious to koi and it is vital to eradicate any infestation quickly, before it can become established in the pond system. Any treatment for anchor worm and fish lice must take into account the water temperature and the length of time it takes for the young to develop.

The gills and area around the eyes are susceptible to parasite infestation.

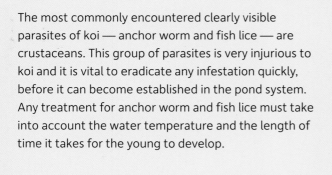

Parasites such as leeches and anchor worm may be seen attached to a fish's body.

Many skin parasites may also be found on the fins.

Some parasites, such as tapeworms, live inside the fish and so are not visible externally.

Parasite infections of the skin can lead to heavy mucus production.

Anchor worm   96

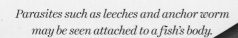
***Apiosoma*   98**

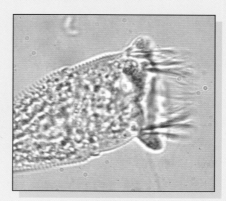

***Argulus*   100**

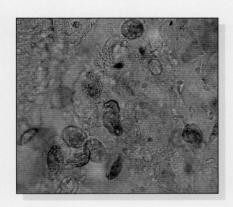

Chilodonella **102**

Costia **103**

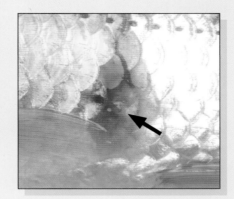

Epistylis **104**

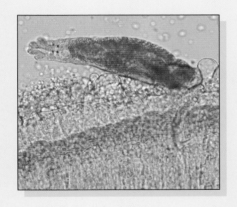

Gill and skin flukes **106**

Leeches **108**

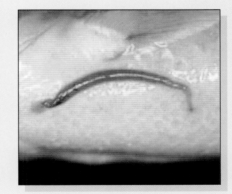

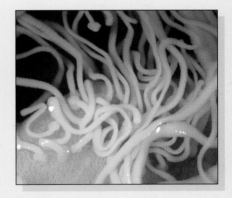

Tapeworm infestations **110**

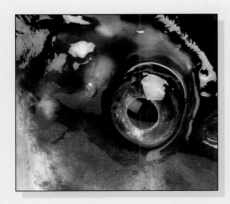

Trichodina **112**

White spot **113**

Anchor worm

Anchor worm (*Lernaea cyprinacea*) has a rather complex life cycle. Only the female is parasitic. Her thin, threadlike body, often with a pair of egg strings at the rear end, protrudes from beneath a scale on the affected koi. The eggs are shed into the water, and the rate at which the young hatch depends on the water temperature. Juvenile anchor worm stages bear no resemblance to the adult and are free living. At the point of sexual maturity, males and females congregate on the gill tissue, where mating takes place. The males die, but the female moves onto the body and searches for a suitable site, usually around a scale, to burrow beneath the skin.

Once in place, the female undergoes the most amazing transformation, with the head growing into an anchor device that will hold her in place for several months. During the time the anchor worm is attached, she feeds continuously on the blood and tissues of the host fish. It is very common to find ulcers developing at the site of attachment.

ANCHOR WORM LIFE CYCLE

The anchor worm is a crustacean but looks like a worm, hence the common name.

After mating, the female anchor worm crawls beneath a scale and burrows her head into the skin, where she transforms into the parasitic stage, held firmly in place by the anchorlike appendages.

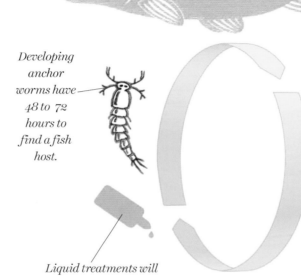

Developing anchor worms have 48 to 72 hours to find a fish host.

Remove adult anchor worms entirely with a pair of tweezers.

Egg sacs develop and are shed into the water, where they release the hatched eggs.

Liquid treatments will kill juvenile anchor worms.

The juvenile anchor worm goes through a series of metamorphic changes before achieving adulthood.

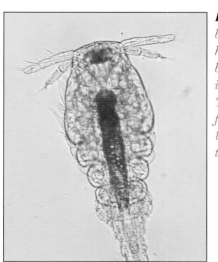

Left: *An anchor worm before mating. Notice how the four appendages by the head are already in the anchor shape. These will harden to form the familiar anchor. Unmated females die at this stage.*

Right: *Dead anchor worms that have been removed from a fish. The larger end is the part that attaches to the koi.*

Right: *An anchor worm's attachment organ fixes itself by penetrating under the fish's scale.*

Below: *The anchor worm can be removed with tweezers. If none are available, you can push the anchor worm out with your fingernail, but make sure that it comes out whole and that no part is left still attached to your koi.*

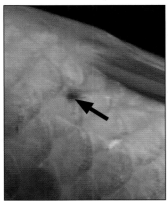

Left: *Although very faint, a small anchor worm can be seen here attached to the underside of a koi, close to its pelvic fins.*

Right: *Unfortunately, removing the worm is not the end of the story. The attachment site often requires treatment. This is an example of anchor worm damage.*

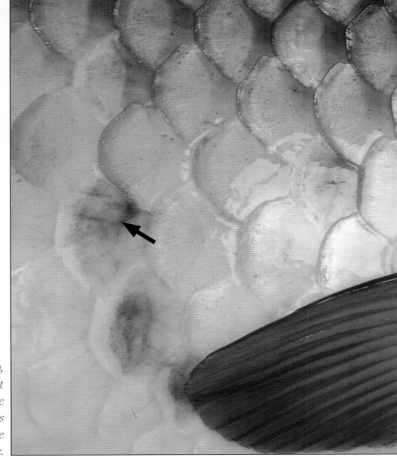

Apiosoma

Apiosoma is found on the gills, skin and fins of koi. Strictly speaking, it is not a parasite as it does not feed on the koi tissues or body fluids. The ring of tiny hairs known as cilia on the top of the organism beat continuously, wafting bacteria and other organic detritus into the oral cavity in the center. Because Apiosoma feed on bacteria, they can often be found in large numbers around the edge of an ulcer or open wound on the koi, where they feed on the micro-organisms. Apiosoma can cause mortalities in fry and juvenile koi simply because of the large numbers that are attached to the gill tissue, which passes food-laden water to the Apiosoma as the fish breathes. These tiny organisms remain in one place for their entire life, adhered with a drop of "glue" secreted from the stalk-like base. It is this sticky chemical that irritates the koi and causes it to rub and flick. The symptoms of infection with Apiosoma are very similar to those caused by Trichodina and Chilodonella. Taking a skin scrape and examining it under a microscope makes it possible to establish an accurate identification and apply the correct treatment.

Identification

External signs of an Apiosoma infestation include the production of excess mucus, which results in the skin looking opaque. In severe cases the actual skin color may disappear, as the mucus becomes so thick that the body actually looks white. Infected fish may start to hang in the water with their fins clamped, and spend more time in areas of heavily oxygenated water, such as around water returns and airstones. This will especially be the case if the gills are affected. If an extremely large quantity of Apiosoma are present, your koi may flick their heads from side to side to try to relieve any irritation caused. Over time, infected koi will stop feeding and become emaciated. A telltale sign of a heavy infection is when the body of the koi looks disproportionately small in relation to the head. As illness takes hold, secondary infections may occur, not only because of the damage done by the Apiosoma, but as a result of any flicking that may have occurred when the koi attempted to relieve skin irritation. This secondary infection may take the form of fungus or, more seriously, bacterial infections, and these should be treated as soon as they are noticed.

Prevention

As with many parasites, Apiosoma are not a problem in a well-maintained system. It is only when environmental conditions deteriorate that a problem arises. To avoid an outbreak of Apiosoma, maintain good water quality at all times. Carry out regular maintenance on filters to avoid the buildup of sediment and mulm within the pond and filter system. When doing this work, it is important to condition replacement water. Using untreated tap water may result in more stress to the fish, which could be a trigger for the problem itself. In addition, avoid high

Above: Apiosoma is not visible to the naked eye, so a microscope is required to make an exact identification of this protozoan.

One of the characteristic physical symptoms of Apiosoma is emaciation.

stocking levels, as this parasite will thrive in heavily stocked ponds. Maintaining a constant water temperature will also prevent undue stress being caused to the fish as a result of temperature fluctuations. A pond heating system will provide a regular and constant water temperature.

Treatment

Less severe cases of Apiosoma can be easily treated with a proprietary antiparasite medication or by using malachite green and formalin — the dose rate will depend upon the concentration of the mix. Alternatively consider using potassium permanganate at a dose rate of 1.5 g/ 1000 l (220 gal). This can be repeated every 5 to 7 days over a period of 3 weeks (allowing you a maximum of three such treatments).

Salt can also be used as an effective treatment, either as a bath or a pond treatment. If the infection has become severe, the chances are that there will be numerous sites of secondary infection on the fish and these will need to be topically treated with propolis. Although treatment will normally result in complete eradication of the parasites, a severe gill infestation may cause gill damage. Further losses of fish may therefore take place, even after the problem with the parasite has been eliminated.

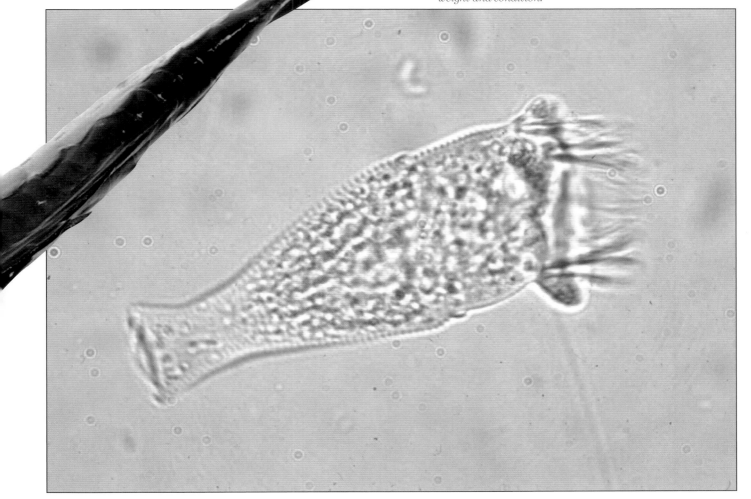

Below: *Massive numbers of* Apiosoma *sp. can attach to the gills of young koi. This affects the fishes' ability to breathe, which can reduce their appetite. As a result, they quickly lose weight and condition.*

Argulus

Fish lice (Argulus japonicus) are saucer-shaped parasites about 1 cm (0.4 in) in diameter when adult. The young are miniature versions of the adults. All stages of fish lice will feed on koi, puncturing the skin to suck blood and juices, using a mouth that closely resembles a hypodermic needle. Unfortunately, this invasive method of feeding also means that fish lice can readily transmit bacterial and viral infections. When the fish louse bites a koi, it also injects a substance that is an attractant to other lice, which feed at the same site. Over a period of time, this results in open lesions and ulcers.

Prevention

The only way of introducing fish lice to the koi pond is with an infected fish. Many years ago, it was quite common for

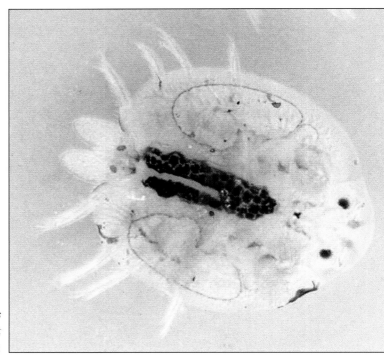

Below: *Here, two* Argulus *(fish lice) can be seen attached to the dorsal fin of a koi.*

Right: *To see* Argulus *in this much detail you need to view it under a microscope.*

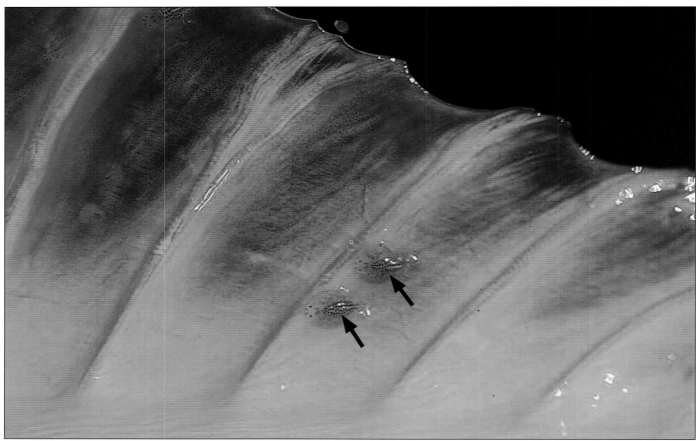

FISH LOUSE LIFE CYCLE

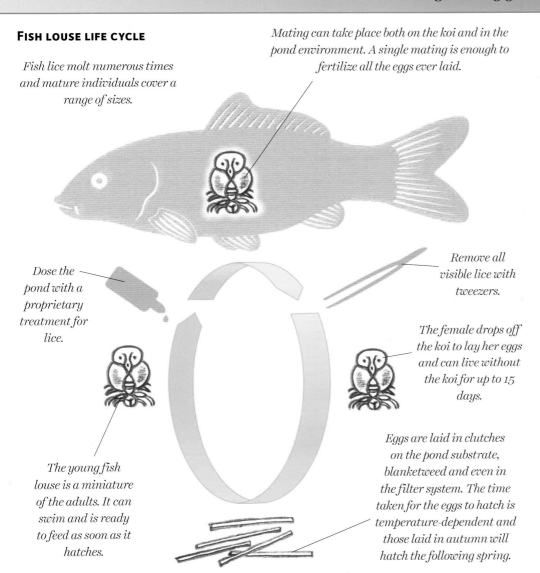

Fish lice molt numerous times and mature individuals cover a range of sizes.

Mating can take place both on the koi and in the pond environment. A single mating is enough to fertilize all the eggs ever laid.

Dose the pond with a proprietary treatment for lice.

Remove all visible lice with tweezers.

The young fish louse is a miniature of the adults. It can swim and is ready to feed as soon as it hatches.

The female drops off the koi to lay her eggs and can live without the koi for up to 15 days.

Eggs are laid in clutches on the pond substrate, blanketweed and even in the filter system. The time taken for the eggs to hatch is temperature-dependent and those laid in autumn will hatch the following spring.

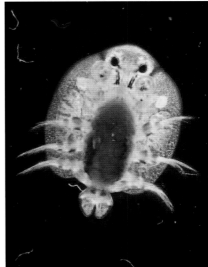

Above: *The fish louse is very adept at swimming, although it prefers to remain on the koi to feed, holding itself onto the body surface by the two large sucker discs just below the head. The mouth is formed into a needlelike projection, which is used to pierce the host's skin. Then the fish louse sucks blood and fluids from the koi.*

imported koi to be infected with fish lice, but these days it is an extremely rare occurrence, as most countries of origin have eradicated this parasite from the farms. Wild fish are frequently infected with native species of fish lice, so it is common sense not to introduce them into a koi pond.

Treatment

If you spot a koi in your pond with fish lice, the chances are that a number of your koi will also be affected. Check all the koi for adult lice and remove any specimens you find with a pair of sterilized tweezers. Once removed, spray the area with propolis to prevent secondary infection. Emamectin benzoate is a very effective treatment for fish lice and is available as a pond treatment in Europe, but only on veterinary prescription in the United States.

Female fish lice prefer to lay their eggs on pieces of vegetation and debris. It can help to reduce numbers of fish lice in the pond by tying pieces of plant or even twigs into bundles and the females will lay their eggs onto them. Every week or so, remove and destroy the twig bundles, thus gradually reducing the numbers of fish lice hatching. At temperatures of 16°C (61°F), it takes approximately 6 weeks for fish lice to hatch, so the rate at which the bundles of plants or twigs are removed depends on water temperature.

Chilodonella

Chilodonella cyprini is a heart-shaped parasite that is found to infect all freshwater fish, but tends to be a nuisance in the koi pond in the spring months. It thrives at water temperatures of 5 to 10°C (40–50°F). In common with costia, chilodonella feeds by puncturing the skin cells and sucking out the content, which may lead to skin lesions, secondary infections and compromise osmoregulation.

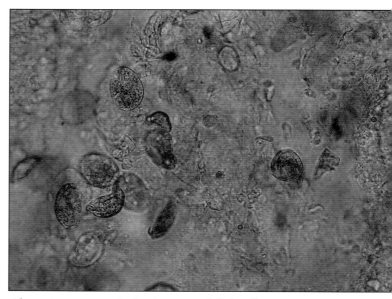

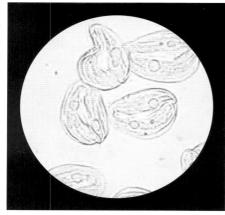

Right: An exact identification of the protozoan Chilodonella *is only possible using a microscope.*

Below: Koi infected with Chilodonella *may flick against the side of a pond, incurring physical damage such as this.*

Above: A mucus sample showing many Chilodonella *parasites.* Chilodonella *tends to infect koi at lower temperatures and damages the skin as it feeds. Infected koi rub, flick and jump in response to the irritation caused by this parasite.*

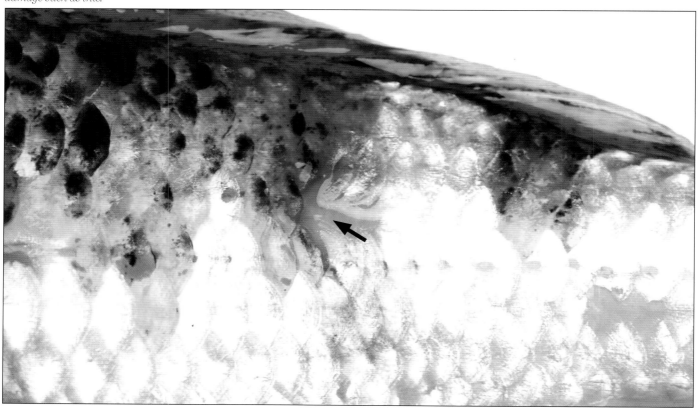

Left: Ichthyobodo necator, *or costia, causes intense irritation as it feeds on the skin. Infected koi may have a gray bloom due to the excess mucus produced as a response to the feeding costia, and a stressed "bloodshot" appearance.*

Costia

Costia (*Ichthyobodo necator*) is perhaps the smallest skin parasite of koi, being roughly the same size as a red blood cell. Costia is bean- or comma-shaped, with two hairlike flagellae of unequal length that enable the parasite to swim. It survives in a range of temperatures between 2 and 30°C (35–86°F), but prefers the cooler part of that range. Costia feeds by puncturing the cells of the skin and gills and sucking out the content. In large numbers they can cause considerable damage, weakening koi and allowing secondary infections of bacteria and fungi to take hold. The irritation caused by costia feeding may cause koi to increase the amount of mucus on the body, giving it a gray appearance. Stressed koi tend to be particularly prone to infection with costia.

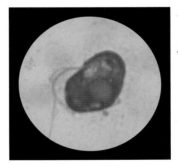

Left: It takes a well-practiced eye to spot the shape of the costia parasite under the microscope.

Below: As with most parasite infections, flicking will occur when costia is present, which may result in physical damage occurring to the skin of the fish, as can be seen here.

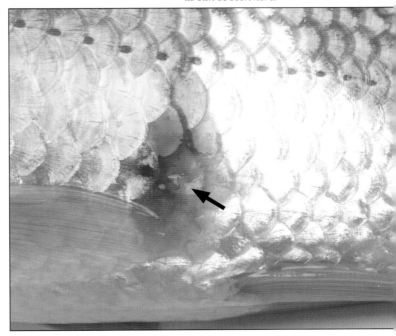

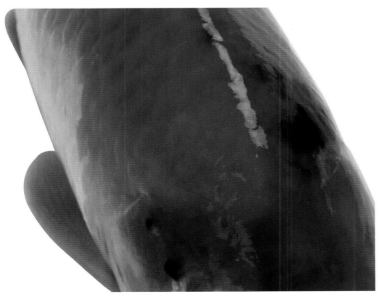

Left: A telltale sign that costia may be present is the presence of a milky haze over the skin, most noticeably on the head and shoulder region of the koi.

Epistylis

Epistylis is a ciliate protozoan that is not visible to the naked eye, so to make an exact identification you must examine a skin scrape under a microscope. When viewed like this Epistylis looks bell-shaped, with a long "handle" connected to it. Tiny hairlike cilia on the end of the bell shape may be visible. Cilia are used for feeding, and for wafting bacteria and bits of organic debris into the mouth, located centrally under the ciliary ring. Epistylis may also be seen in its contracted form and in this instance it will simply look circular.

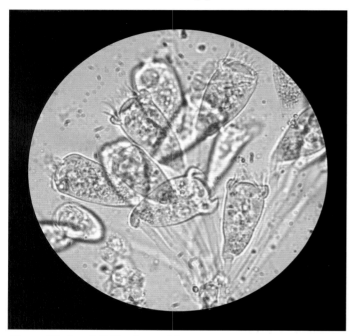

Above: *The long bell-like shape of the protozoan* Epistylis *is visible under the microscope, but it takes a practiced eye to identify it accurately.*

Identification

In the early stages, koi infected with Epistylis may show no external visible signs, but you may observe behavioral changes, such as flicking or hanging in the water. At this point, examining a skin scrape under a microscope is the only way to make an exact diagnosis. As the infection worsens, small white patches may appear on the skin. These may develop in size up to 5 mm (0.2 in) or so. At first these may be limited in number, but as they become larger they will spread and more will become apparent on the body of the infected koi, as well as on the gills. As these small white patches spread, the skin will become redder and this eventually leads to scales lifting

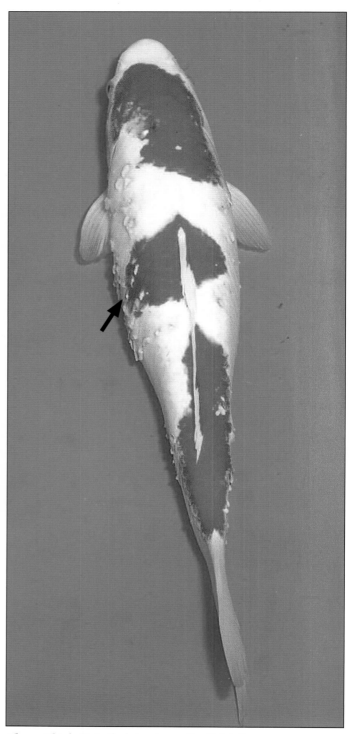

Above: *This koi is in the later stages of an* Epistylis *infection. The white patches on the skin are turning into areas of redness, and scales may be lost as the infection develops.*

Above: *This fish exhibits the early stages of* Epistylis. *If treated at this stage, the loss of scales may be prevented.*

and (if not treated) falling out. This leaves the affected area susceptible to secondary infections from bacteria or fungus.

At this stage of infection it is vital to check regularly for other parasites, as these will quickly take advantage of the situation and worsen the problem. As the Epistylis infection spreads, it is quite common to see ulceration caused by bacteria attacking the areas where scales have been lost. As the situation worsens, badly infected fish will stop eating and start to look emaciated. There will be spells of inactivity when the koi simply hang in the water with their fins sometimes clamped to the sides of their bodies. Losses may occur. Koi that survive infection may have lost scales, but providing the underlying skin is intact, the color will not be affected and the scales will be replaced. Epistylis infections are very unlikely to occur when the pond temperature is below 12°C (54°F), but as the temperature rises the level of infection will increase. Water temperatures of over 20°C (68°F) lead to high levels of parasite activity.

Prevention

As with most diseases, improved husbandry and system maintenance can reduce the likelihood of infection and Epistylis is no exception. Outbreaks of Epistylis arise because there is a high organic load in the pond water, comprising bacteria, sloughed mucus and fecal material from the koi. Mechanical filtration is designed to remove this, so the best means of preventing an outbreak of Epistylis is to ensure that this part of the filter is cleaned regularly. If spotted early Epistylis should not cause a major problem, but if allowed to reach an advanced stage, it will leave infected koi highly susceptible to other infections. If Epistylis is experienced, be sure to check for the presence of any other infections that might move in and create a whole new set of problems.

Treatment

Epistylis can be treated with an off-the-shelf parasite treatment, or alternatively with malachite green alone. Dose rates will depend on the concentration of the solution. Alternatively, use salt as a bath at the dose of 100 g of salt/4.5 l (3.5 oz/gal) for 10 minutes, accurately timed. Repeat this for three consecutive days. Secondary infections will generally need specific treatment, either via topical treatment with propolis alone, or malachite green and propolis in more severe cases. Fungus is also common and in most instances this will need to be treated topically with malachite green and/or propolis.

Gill and skin flukes

Two main categories of fluke are associated with koi: skin and gill flukes. Heavy infestations of either indicate husbandry problems such as poor water conditions, including excessive amounts of organic material and low dissolved oxygen levels, or overcrowding in the pond. Flukes feed on the delicate epidermis of the skin and gills, causing irritation and excessive mucus production. For this reason, severe infestations of skin fluke are often called "gray slime disease." The rear ends of both gill and skin flukes are equipped with a pair of large hooks, like grappling hooks, plus a rim of tiny hooks. The hooks cause considerable damage to the skin and gills as the parasites move around and anchor themselves to feed. Heavy fluke infections may damage the koi's skin, giving rise to secondary bacterial infections. Heavy infestations (in excess of 30 individuals in a single mucus sample) should be regarded as serious.

Gill flukes (*Dactylogyrus* sp.) are characterized by the presence of four tiny eyespots at the head end. Adult flukes attach to the gill tissue and reproduce by laying eggs, which

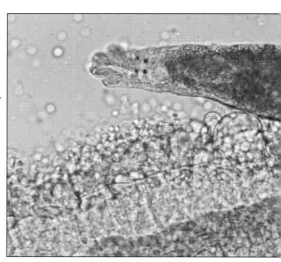

Right: *A gill fluke viewed under a microscope. Take a skin scrape to make a definite identification of flukes. When taking the scrape, try to take the mucus sample as close to the gills as possible.*

are shed into the water as the gills are irrigated during respiration. The speed with which the eggs hatch depends on the water temperature, but the larval fluke is very active and quickly seeks a koi host to invade. It is quite common to find these larval flukes close to the operculum on the body of the fish. Heavy infestations of gill fluke cause the tips of the gill tissue to grow into trunklike appendages.

Skin flukes (*Gyrodactylus* sp.) are usually found on the body and differ from gill flukes in that they have no eyes and give birth to live young.

Below: *The skin fluke gives birth to live young. Here the "baby" is visible in the central part of the body. Usually, large numbers are present feeding on the koi, which responds by producing more mucus, giving a bloom to the appearance, commonly termed "gray slime disease."*

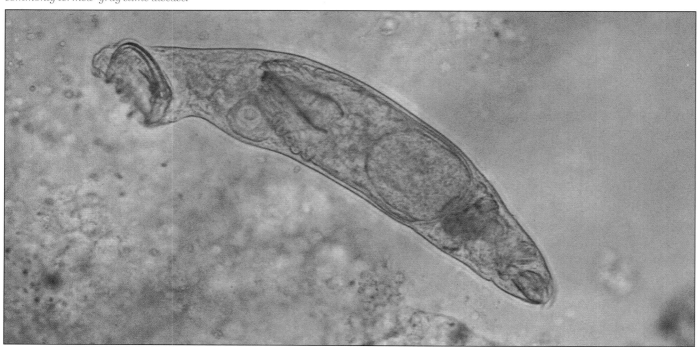

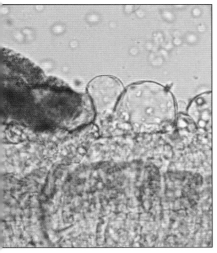

GILL FLUKE LIFE CYCLE

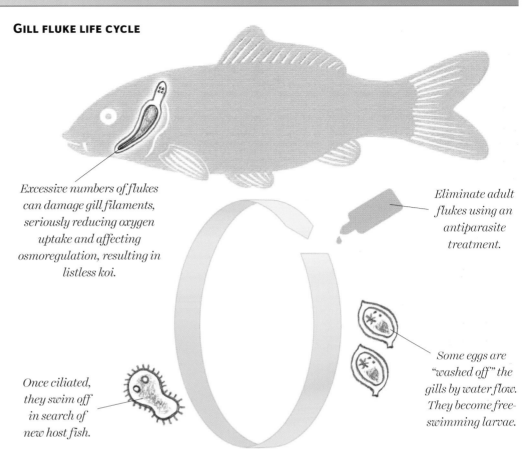

Excessive numbers of flukes can damage gill filaments, seriously reducing oxygen uptake and affecting osmoregulation, resulting in listless koi.

Eliminate adult flukes using an antiparasite treatment.

Once ciliated, they swim off in search of new host fish.

Some eggs are "washed off" the gills by water flow. They become free-swimming larvae.

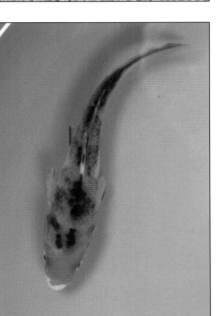

Above: *A small koi with a heavy fluke infestation. As the infection takes hold, your fish may become emaciated and exhibit a milky color due to excess mucus production.*

Right: *Skin flukes may cause fish to rub against the side of the pond to relieve the irritation. This can lead to lesions and scarring when the wound heals.*

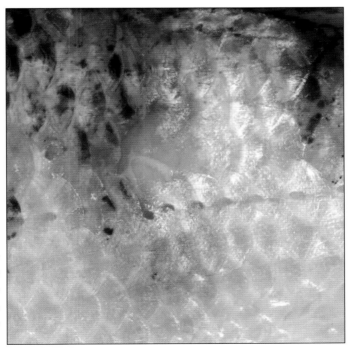

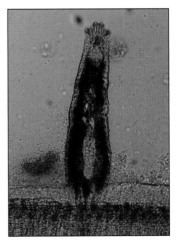

Above: *Gill flukes attach themselves to the tissue with hooks on the "foot," or haptor, and stretch out among the gill filaments to browse in the mucus.*

Leeches

Leeches can be a problem in the koi pond, especially one with plants, as the leeches will sway from the leaves and stems to catch a passing fish. Plants are an ideal site for the leeches to lay their eggs, which are deposited in tough leathery cocoons that are resistant to most treatments. Piscicola geometra is the only leech that is entirely parasitic on fish and it can only be introduced if the koi pond is stocked with a fish carrying one or more leeches. Other leeches, mainly parasites of frogs and toads, can be introduced in the spring when the amphibians use the koi pond to breed. These amphibian leeches will attempt to feed on the fish, but generally are more of an unsightly nuisance than harmful to koi. Leeches can live without a host for a considerable time.

Prevention

In the past, plants were always cited as a source of introducing leeches to ponds. Thirty or 40 years ago they were a likely source of introduction, as pond plants were cut from native rivers, lakes and canals. Plants from these sources certainly did carry any wildlife found in the water and this was then transferred when the plants were sold to the customer. Today, plants cultured for the pond or aquarium are an extremely unlikely source of leeches, as cuttings and seedlings are carefully grown and nurtured in polytunnels and greenhouses in the absence of any wildlife. Birds

Right: Leeches should not pose a particular threat unless they are found physically attached to your koi.

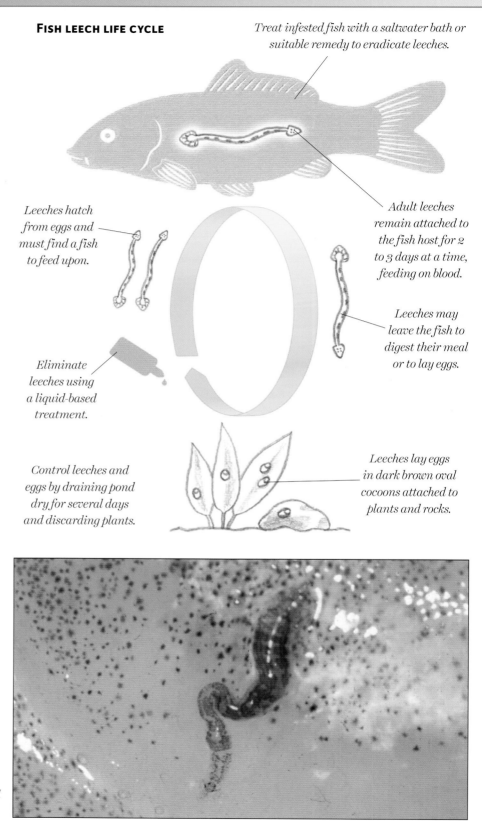

FISH LEECH LIFE CYCLE

Treat infested fish with a saltwater bath or suitable remedy to eradicate leeches.

Leeches hatch from eggs and must find a fish to feed upon.

Adult leeches remain attached to the fish host for 2 to 3 days at a time, feeding on blood.

Leeches may leave the fish to digest their meal or to lay eggs.

Eliminate leeches using a liquid-based treatment.

Control leeches and eggs by draining pond dry for several days and discarding plants.

Leeches lay eggs in dark brown oval cocoons attached to plants and rocks.

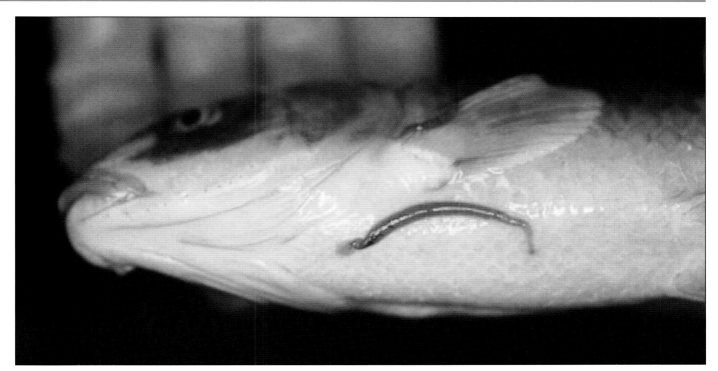

Above: A leech can be seen attached to the underside of a koi. This should be carefully removed, ensuring that the attachment organs are not left embedded in the fish.

and waterfowl have also been blamed for introducing an assortment of fish parasites, including leeches, but they are entirely innocent. Amphibians can certainly introduce some species of leech, so perhaps the solution is to create a small pond or bog garden dedicated to the frogs and toads, which will keep them away from the koi pond. Since the fish leech Piscicola geometra can only be introduced on infected fish, prevention is simple: never stock your koi pond with any fish from the wild.

Treatment

Eradicating leeches is a problem for several reasons. First, leeches lay their eggs in tough, leathery cocoons that are impermeable to any chemical treatment. The hatching rate of the young leeches depends on the water temperature; in cold weather it may take several months for the embryos in the eggs to develop and they may take several months to hatch. During the summer months, when the pond water is warmer, it may take only a few weeks for the leeches to hatch. Any effective treatment must take these factors into consideration. In the past, organophosphates, which are powerful nerve poisons, were used to control leeches, but these have been withdrawn following safety concerns and their impact on the environment. There are some medications available that purport to control leeches, but take into consideration the temperatures and rate at which the leeches hatch when using them.

The natural method of controlling leeches is to remove and destroy all pond plants and vegetation, as this is where the adult leeches will have laid their eggs. Remove the koi to a temporary pond and examine each one. If any leeches are attached, physically remove them. Make sure that any temporary accommodation can comfortably house the koi for as long as the remedial work on the pond takes place. There must be adequate aeration in the temporary system. Monitor the water quality carefully, undertaking partial water changes if the water becomes polluted with ammonia. Koi have a habit of jumping when transferred to a new pond, so take precautions to ensure that they cannot jump out of the temporary pond or the main pond when they are returned to it. Drain the water from the koi pond and thoroughly clean all pond surfaces to remove any remaining adult leeches and cocoons. Refill the koi pond and return the koi, but take the opportunity to check again that all leeches have been removed from the koi.

Tapeworm infestations

There are numerous species of tapeworm, but the main species that affects koi is Bothriocephalus acheilognathi. Tapeworms seldom prove a threat to koi and can be almost impossible to detect. They are present in the intestines of the koi, so external signs of an infestation are hard to spot until the later stages. As the worm develops in the intestine, the host koi may appear very thin and undernourished. In extreme cases you may see the parasitic worm exiting the vent of the koi. Obviously, when buying koi, avoid any individual showing these signs of an advanced infestation.

Life cycle

Bothriocephalus are parasitic worms that in their adult stages attain lengths of 15 to 23 cm (6–9 in) and a body width of 3 mm (0.1 in) within the intestine of a koi. They have a white ribbon-like appearance, but are generally only seen when a fish undergoes a postmortem. Before they reach this size they must complete a complex life cycle. First, a fish already infected with a tapeworm excretes waste containing eggs of the internal worm into the water, and after a time they turn into free-swimming larvae. These newly hatched larvae must then find a host in which to develop further. This host is often a copepod which may simply eat the larvae, which triggers the next stage of development. A copepod is a free-living crustacean (and hence is related to anchor worms and freshwater fleas), which may be naturally present in any body of water, but in a pond they are generally introduced on plants or live food. If the copepod happens to be eaten by a koi harboring the larvae, there is chance of infection.

Prevention

The best preventative measure is to avoid introducing any koi already infested with Bothriocephalus sp., but as there are seldom external signs of infection, in reality this can prove very difficult. The next step is to ensure that the copepod host is not present. This is also difficult because copepods may just suddenly appear. However, you can take steps to keep their numbers low to prevent such an event. Avoid adding plants to your pond, and steer clear of live food, as both may harbor copepods. If you do favor plants and live food, make sure that you disinfect them first. Improved maintenance of your pond, resulting in a decrease in the organic matter present, may also help. This means improving the discharges of your filters to remove fish waste.

Treatment

In a well-maintained pond, the hosts needed to complete the life cycle of tapeworms are not always present, so treatment is not needed. If a newly purchased koi is infected with a tapeworm, your other koi are very unlikely

TAPEWORM LIFE CYCLE

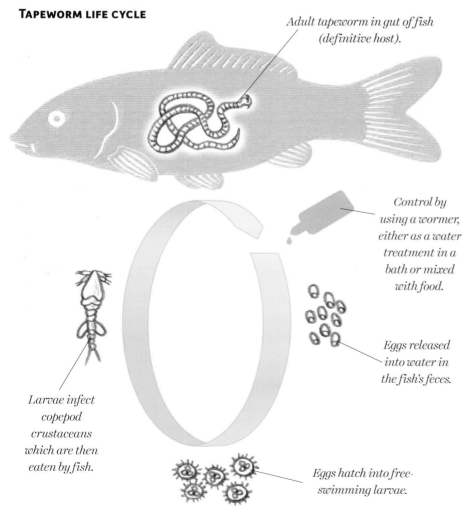

Adult tapeworm in gut of fish (definitive host).

Control by using a wormer, either as a water treatment in a bath or mixed with food.

Eggs released into water in the fish's feces.

Larvae infect copepod crustaceans which are then eaten by fish.

Eggs hatch into free-swimming larvae.

to become infected, as long as copepods are not present. After a time, the internal worm in the infected koi will die, and thus reinfection cannot occur. Overall, these worms are a minor threat to the average pondkeeper as long as the system is clean and well-maintained. They are more of a problem for the fish farmer and breeder.

Should you feel that treatment is required, you may wish to use a proprietary worming treatment, either as a water treatment at the rate recommended by the manufacturer, or mixed with the food — in this case seek expert advice.

Some wormers are available as an injectable solution, which may prove more effective on larger koi. Such an injection should be given intra-muscularly. Seek assistance from your veterinarian or local koi health specialist, who will determine the dose rate for the koi in question and administer it.

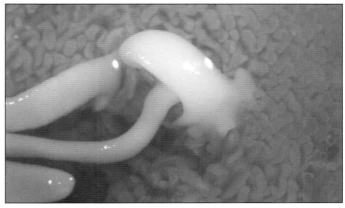

Above: *Tapeworms in koi can reach up to 23 cm (9 in) in length inside the intestine of the fish. They do not pose a major threat to "hobby koi."*

Below: *The typical koi hobbyist will be very unlikely to see a tapeworm. Generally, they are only observed when a postmortem is performed.*

Trichodina

Trichodina is a single-celled organism, or protozoan, that feeds on bacteria and any organic detritus that becomes trapped in the koi's mucus. This means that *Trichodina* thrives in ponds where the filters are badly maintained and, as a consequence, where large quantities of organic detritus are found in the water column. It is often mistakenly thought that organic material in suspension is visible, but in fact it has no effect on the water clarity. Trichodina can also be a free-living organism living in the pipe bends and congested filters.

Identification

Trichodina is only visible under the microscope. In side view, it is shaped rather like a flying saucer, but from underneath it is circular, with a fringe of tiny hairs called cilia and a calcified structure. This structure is a series of interlocking hooks whose only function is to support the otherwise soft body of Trichodina. The Trichodina use the cilia in a beating motion to move around the mucus of the koi, as well as using the cilia to waft the minute pieces of organic debris on which it feeds into its mouth. In ponds laden with organic material, the detritus also becomes trapped in the mucus of the koi and is a valuable

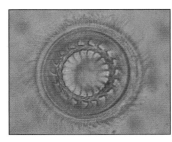

Left: *The characteristic appearance of* Trichodina, *with its inner ring of calcified teeth that support the structure of the parasite. The tiny hairs that* Trichodina *uses to move around are just visible around the outermost edge.*

food source for the Trichodina. The Trichodina irritate the koi, which produce more mucus in response, and this in turn traps more organic material, encouraging the tiny organisms to thrive and thus the problem becomes self-perpetuating. Ultimately, the skin cells which are overproducing the mucus to reduce the irritation become exhausted and unable to keep pace with the increasing numbers of Trichodina. At this stage, the skin of the koi feels dry to the touch and often there are secondary bacterial or fungal diseases which complicate treatment. The initial indication that something is wrong is generally flicking and rubbing as the fish tries to relieve the irritation caused by these parasites.

Below: Trichodina *irritates the koi, making it flick, jump or rub, which may lead to physical injuries and secondary infections, such as seen on the eye of this koi.*

White spot

White spot (Ichthyophthirius multifiliis) parasites cause infected koi to break out in white spots, hence the common name. This parasite probably kills more captive fish worldwide than any other true fish disease. The visible white spots are the mature stage of the parasite, and actually located beneath the epidermis. The mature white spot parasite ruptures its way through the delicate epidermis, leaving the skin literally peppered with tiny puncture wounds. In heavy infections, this entire layer of skin sloughs off. The wounds created by white spot parasites make it difficult for koi to regulate their water and salt balance and leave them vulnerable to infection by opportunist bacteria and fungi.

Above: A common carp with a heavy infection of white spot, even visible on the eye. The larger parasites are mature and ready to rupture. The fish is sloughing mucus in response to the white spot.

WHITE SPOT LIFE CYCLE

Adult parasites develop into the characteristic white spots.

The tomites must find a fish host within 24 to 48 hours.

Parasites break out of "white spots" on the skin and fall to the pond floor.

Up to 1,000 tomites can emerge from the cyst when it ruptures.

Break the cycle here using a proprietary treatment to eliminate free-swimming parasites.

Each parasite forms a cyst around itself and reproduces by splitting.

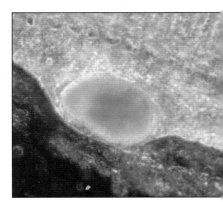

Above: White spot also infects the gill tissue. Here an individual is surrounded by the delicate epithelium. The lesions created as the white spot ruptures out of the skin of the gill tissue reduce oxygen uptake and affect osmoregulation.

Conditions caused by bacteria, viruses and other disorders

Bacteria, usually including those species responsible for some disease in koi, are present in every aquatic environment. Preventing bacterial infections through careful management and good hygiene is far better than trying to cure a problem once it has arisen, but infections can occasionally arise, even in the best systems. In most instances, only an isolated koi may be affected by a bacterial infection. Sometimes, koi will respond to proprietary brands of antibacterial medication, but it is also possible that an antibiotic or antimicrobial treatment is necessary for the fish to make a full recovery. It is important that antibiotic and antimicrobial medications are only used as prescribed and when absolutely necessary, as bacterial resistance to these drugs is becoming a severe problem in both human and veterinary medicine. Since antibiotics and antimicrobials will only be effective if the immune system of the koi is functioning, the use of these drugs is inappropriate at low temperatures (when the immune system is at a low ebb). Finally, it is important to realize that antibiotic and antimicrobial drugs are not selective in the bacteria they target. They not only damage bacteria that cause disease, but also beneficial bacteria that may fend off other disease-causing species.

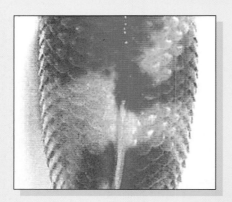

Aeromonas   **116**

Skin lesions are often the result of flicking to relieve the irritation caused by skin parasites.

Bubbles in the fins are an indication of gas bubble disease. Fins are also vulnerable to fungal rot.

Conditions such as dropsy cause external lifting of the fish's scales so that it resembles a pinecone.

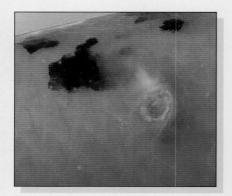

Ulcers   **116**

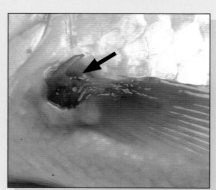
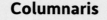

Columnaris   **119**

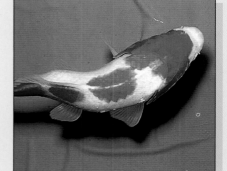

Curvature of the spine   **120**

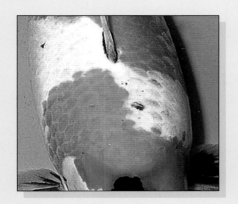

Dropsy   122

Egg retention   124

**Fungal
infections   127**

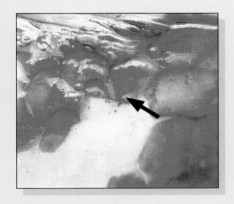

Hi-Kui   128

Viruses   130

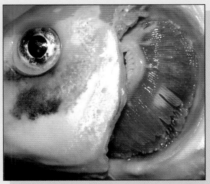

**Papilloma
and carp pox   132**

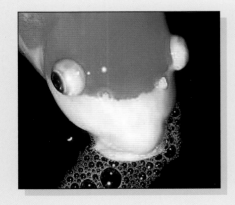

Popeye   134

**Swimbladder
disorders   136**

**Other health
problems   138**

Aeromonas

One of the most commonly encountered bacterial infections is caused by *Aeromonas hydrophila,* an opportunist pathogen that usually takes advantage of injured, sick or weakened koi. It causes open lesions and severe ulceration. In recent years, it has become increasingly resistant to antibiotic and antimicrobial drugs and it is not uncommon to find it resistant to all drugs used in veterinary medicine.

Ulcers

Koi have three natural defenses against bacterial infection: mucus, skin and scales. If any or all of these are breached, opportunist bacteria such as *Aeromonas hydrophila,* which are present in all ponds, will begin to attack the flesh. Left unchecked, a hole will develop and bacteria enter the bloodstream, causing popeye (exophthalmia) and/or dropsy. Ultimately, the fish will die. Ulcers result either from a parasitic infection or poor water quality and can be prevented by paying close attention to your fishes' behavior, regularly testing the water for nitrite and ammonia content and taking the appropriate action if anything is wrong. Given the value of many koi collections, it is sensible to invest in a microscope to check for parasites, as the majority cannot be seen with the naked eye (see pages 84–85).

Treating ulcers

When you first notice an ulcer, you must begin treatment at once, especially if the water temperature is above 15°C (59°F), as the problem will spread very quickly. The only way to carry

TREATING A KOI WITH PROPOLIS

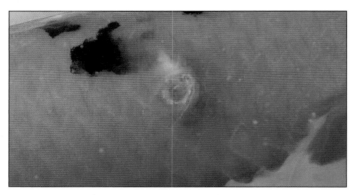

1 A typical small wound or ulcer on a koi. Once you spot a lesion or ulcer, it is vital to start treatment right away.

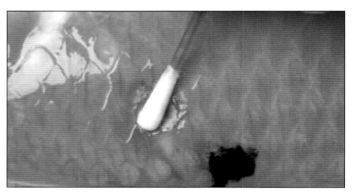

2 Anesthetise the koi and wrap it in wet toweling. Then carefully clean the affected site with a cotton swab.

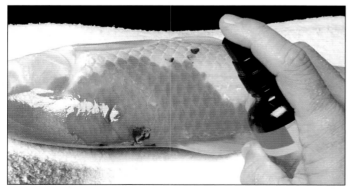

3 Treat the cleaned area with propolis spray until fully covered. This will absorb into the surface tissues, not only disinfecting the area, but also stopping bacteria further penetrating the tissues.

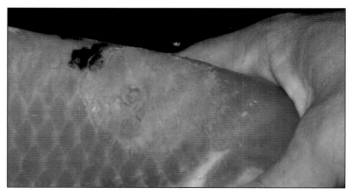

4 Allow the propolis to dry, forming a protective coating over the area, before replacing the koi into the pond. Repeat every 2 to 3 days or when needed. If problems persist, consult a koi health expert.

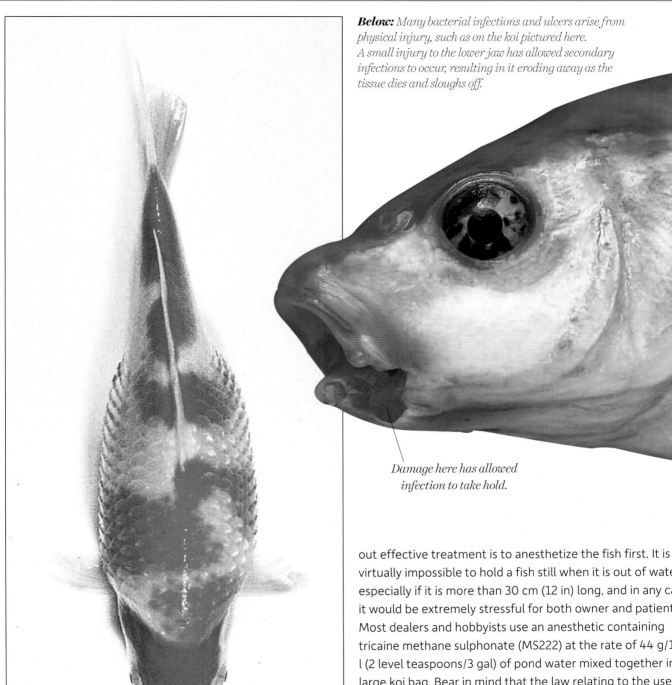

Below: *Many bacterial infections and ulcers arise from physical injury, such as on the koi pictured here. A small injury to the lower jaw has allowed secondary infections to occur, resulting in it eroding away as the tissue dies and sloughs off.*

Damage here has allowed infection to take hold.

Above: *This koi has a severe case of* Aeromonas *that has resulted in lifting of the scales, which in turn may be an indication of bacterial dropsy.*

out effective treatment is to anesthetize the fish first. It is virtually impossible to hold a fish still when it is out of water, especially if it is more than 30 cm (12 in) long, and in any case it would be extremely stressful for both owner and patient. Most dealers and hobbyists use an anesthetic containing tricaine methane sulphonate (MS222) at the rate of 44 g/10 l (2 level teaspoons/3 gal) of pond water mixed together in a large koi bag. Bear in mind that the law relating to the use of this and other suitable chemicals may vary around the world.

Net the fish into a floating basket and transfer it into the mixture using a koi sock to prevent further damage. After a few minutes the fish will roll onto its side as the anaesthetic takes effect. Gently lift the fish out of the water, but do not remove it from the bag until you are sure it is completely sedated, because you do not want it to come around while

TREATING AN ULCER

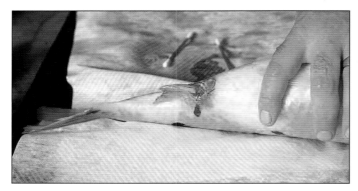

1 Once the koi has been anesthetized, place it on wet toweling to prevent any further damage to the skin. Usually the head and eyes are covered by the towel, which reduces the likelihood of the koi suddenly flapping, but leaves the ulcerated area exposed.

2 Examine the area for any evidence of large parasites, such as anchor worm or fish lice, which might have caused the ulcer. Using a cotton swab, apply gentle pressure to remove dead tissue and clean the area. Remove any dead scales with tweezers.

3 Once the area has been cleaned, apply an antiseptic solution. This can be covered with a thin layer of waterproof gel to seal the wound and help prevent further secondary infections.

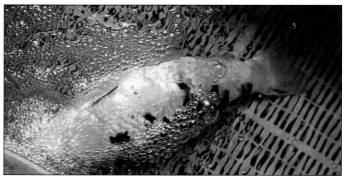

4 Gently place the koi into a floating basket and provide aeration to help it recover from the anesthetic. It should soon be swimming normally, but monitor it during the recovery period.

you are carrying out the treatment. Transfer the fish onto a wet towel and cover its eyes, which will help to pacify the koi.

Using a cotton swab, apply pressure gently but firmly to the scales around the ulcer, following their direction from nose to tail. Dead scales will come away readily, allowing the surrounding tissue to regenerate. Work a cotton swab under the live scales around the ulcer to remove the bacteria, then dry the area with a tissue or paper towel. Clean the wound with an antibacterial product and apply an antiseptic solution to the affected area. Now apply a sealer over the antiseptic, otherwise it will wash off as soon as it comes into contact with water. The sealer should be capable of adhering to a mucous membrane; there are creams formulated for mouth

sores in humans that are ideal for this purpose and these should remain on the fish for 3 or 4 days. When the treatment is complete, return the fish to the floating basket and put an airstone close to its head to speed its recovery.

It may be necessary to repeat the treatment after a week or so, depending on the severity of the ulcer. However, you should give the fish a chance to repair itself. If you notice a white skin starting to develop over the wound, leave it alone, as this means that the koi is recovering. Stubborn ulcers that do not heal may require more specialist treatment with the aid of antibiotic injections, but this should only be undertaken by an experienced professional.

Columnaris

Flavobacterium columnare (previously known as *Flexibacter columnaris*) is a bacterium that can cause a number of conditions in koi. It is important not to confuse columnaris with a fungus infection as often the two can appear very similar, but a different course of treatment is required for each. The easiest way to identify this bacterium is to take a swab from the affected area and send it away for analysis (see pages 88–89).

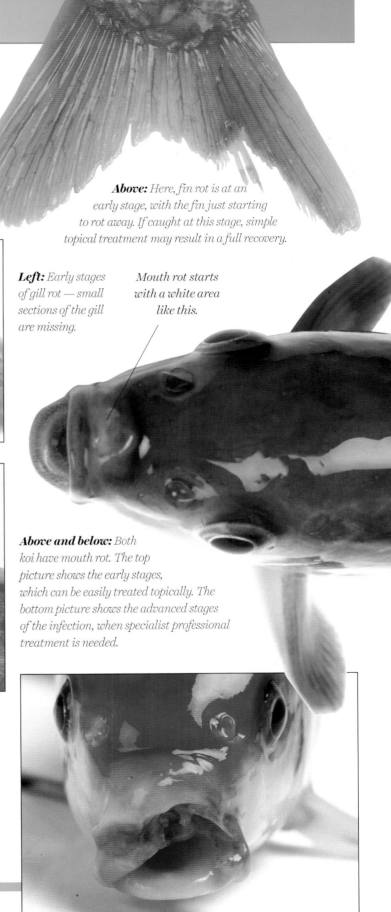

Above: Here, fin rot is at an early stage, with the fin just starting to rot away. If caught at this stage, simple topical treatment may result in a full recovery.

Left: Early stages of gill rot — small sections of the gill are missing.

Mouth rot starts with a white area like this.

Above and below: Both koi have mouth rot. The top picture shows the early stages, which can be easily treated topically. The bottom picture shows the advanced stages of the infection, when specialist professional treatment is needed.

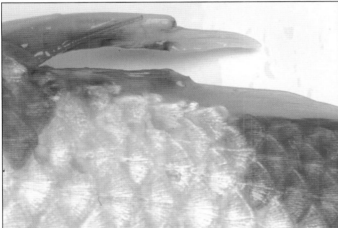

Above and left: Advanced stages of fin rot are shown here on the dorsal fin and on the pectoral fin.

Curvature of the spine

In most instances, curvature of the spine in koi is a physical problem rather than a true disease, although mycobacteriosis, popularly known as tuberculosis (TB), can also cause the spine to become curved. Many koi-keepers encounter the condition, especially if their ponds are not stocked exclusively with koi, but also contain varieties such as orfe. Orfe are susceptible to spinal problems following the use of certain antiparasite chemicals. This may also be a problem for the koi-breeder and one not exclusively limited to curvature of the spine. Other deformities, such as deformed eyes, missing fins, missing gill plates, etc., may also become apparent. When breeding koi it is vital to identify the correct brood stock. Avoid selecting closely related koi, such as brother and sister or parent and offspring. The environmental conditions in which the eggs are kept during development are also critical to the proper development of the young. If these are not ideal, developmental problems may occur, especially if critical factors such as water quality are not correct.

Identification

This is an easy condition to spot, as a koi will appear to have a kink or bend in its spine, normally between the dorsal fin and the tail. In extreme cases it may not be limited to just one kink or bend; koi may have a number of these, creating a Z-shaped appearance.

Prevention

Often, koi have been infected with TB for a number of years before the symptoms, such as curvature of the spine, become apparent, so prevention is difficult. Usually this condition occurs in mature koi for the following reasons: overdose of medication or use of a particular medication; electric shock; lightning strike; malnutrition. Here we consider each in turn.

Until comparatively recently, organophosphates were used to treat a variety of parasites, such as leeches, fish lice, anchor worm and flukes. These chemicals are nerve poisons that kill the parasites by disrupting the entire nervous system, but they were withdrawn on safety and environmental grounds. Although koi seemed to tolerate exposure to organophosphates, other species, such as rudd and orfe, proved to be extremely sensitive and the damage to the nervous system resulted in kinking or bending in their spines. These misshapen elderly orfe and rudd may still be seen in some ponds.

Above: *Even a koi with quite severe curvature of the spine may well continue to live a normal happy life. As there is no treatment for this condition, in such cases the fish should just be left alone.*

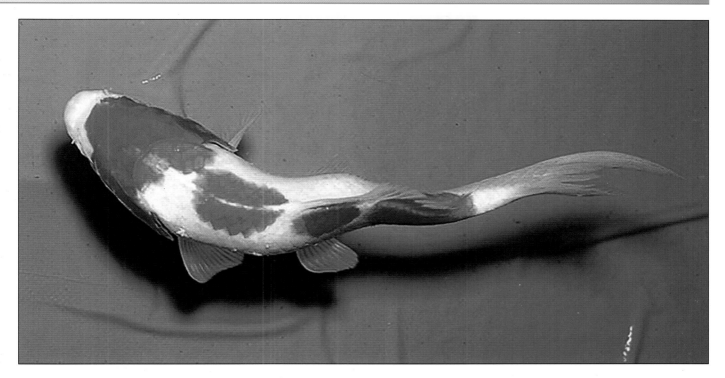

Above: Curvature of the spine, as shown here, may be caused by numerous factors, such as electric shock, lightning strikes, malnutrition or overdosing with certain medications.

Orfe, rudd and baby koi can prove sensitive to commonly used treatments, particularly if overdosed, and these may also affect the nervous system, resulting in unsightly curving of the spine. It is therefore important to measure any pond treatment accurately and to be sure of the volume of water in your pond before adding any medication, otherwise an accidental overdose may occur. The best way to determine the pond volume is to use a flowmeter when filling the pond for the first time. You can buy or rent a flowmeter from your local koi retailer. Bear in mind that there will always be slight variations in the pond volume as a consequence of flushing drains, filters and, in hot weather, through evaporation.

Problems with electrical items within the pond, such as pumps or UV units, can also cause curvature of the spine. An electric shock may affect the fishes' central nervous system, resulting in kinking or bending. The best way to avoid this risk is to run all electrical items from a GFI unit. A GFI will switch off electrical items as soon as a fault occurs. Nowadays, it is normal to run all outdoor electrical items from a GFI, particularly when using equipment in conjunction with water. Another factor that may cause curvature of the spine

is lightning strikes, which cause koi to flex violently, risking spinal damage as a result.

Physical deformities such as curvature may also be caused by malnutrition and supplying an incorrect feed, especially in the case of newly hatched fry and juvenile koi. It is important to choose a suitable high-quality feed at all times, and to provide mineral and vitamin additives appropriately. If the food is of a suitable quality, additives are not necessary. Poor handling techniques may also result in a koi being dropped and injuring its spine. Certain internal bacterial infections have been linked with spinal damage, but these are relatively rare.

Treatment

TB has never been successfully treated in koi (see also page 139). Once a koi exhibits a bent or kinked spine, there is very little that can be done to correct the condition. A koi with a bent spine may live a normal life without any adverse effects other than aesthetic ones, as its appearance is affected. However, in some severe cases, an affected koi may start to lose the ability to swim correctly, which can result in it not being able to feed. In such circumstances, or if the affected koi appears to be in distress, it may be necessary to consider euthanasia to prevent prolonged suffering.

Dropsy

In a koi pond, it is usually only a single koi that develops dropsy. On rare ocasions, large numbers of koi may develop dropsy if a viral disease has accidentally been introduced with a new fish. Unfortunately, dropsy has numerous causes, but the vast majority in freshwater fish are not infectious. Female carp, and therefore koi, are very prone to cysts and tumors. Often these are not visible, but as they increase in size they compress either vital blood vessels, soft tissues or urinary ducts, which causes fluid to build up in the tissues. Other causes can simply be major organ failure, or even heart and circulatory conditions. Without knowing the underlying cause, dropsy is very difficult to treat and the prognosis is usually poor. Even if it were possible to identify the cause of dropsy, it remains impossible to treat koi for many of the underlying physiological causes of the condition.

In advanced stages of bacterial dropsy reddish areas may appear on the body.

Identification

Early signs of dropsy include swelling of the body and protrusion of the eyes. Following these early symptoms the body continues to swell, resulting in the scales on the affected koi lifting, causing the fish to take on a pinecone appearance. In these advanced stages the koi may also lose its ability to maintain correct balance in the water because its swimbladder is under abnormal pressure caused by the accumulation of fluids within its body cavity. If you suspect that dropsy may be the problem, you may also notice a decrease in appetite, plus a tendency for the affected koi to remain at the water surface and close to areas of high oxygen, such as water returns and outlets from the pond.

Prevention

You may have the most advanced, well-maintained pond, but still experience dropsy, as it is hard to prevent this disease completely. The only obvious precautions to take against dropsy are to supply a well-balanced and healthy diet at all times, to provide good water quality and to heat the water. Ensure that basic husbandry procedures are maintained to the highest level. When buying new koi, avoid any that exhibit any of the early symptoms of dropsy Unfortunately, even this may not prevent dropsy from occurring, as sometimes it just strikes without any explanation — organ failure due to old age, for example.

Treatment

When you spot the symptoms of dropsy, you should isolate the affected fish. However, the practicalities of doing this depend on the size of the koi and also the size of the quarantine facilities you have available. It is pointless isolating a 60 cm (24 in) koi in a 100 cm (40 in) tank, as the stress caused will outweigh any advantage obtained by moving the infected koi in the first place. The first treatment for dropsy should be to introduce salt, applied at the level of around 5 to 6 kg/1000 l (11– 13 lb/220 gal) of water for at least 3 to 5 days, or until there is an improvement. By isolating the affected fish in a temporary holding pond,

Left: *Dropsy is easily spotted by the swelling of the body. In advanced stages, reddish areas may appear on the body.*

you avoid subjecting all your fish to salt and thermal stress, especially as many types of dropsy are very hard to cure. Slowly increase the water temperature in the treatment pond to over 25°C (77°F) — and perhaps even as high as 30°C (86°F) — at the rate of 1°C every day or two.

To this salt treatment you may wish to add a good antibacterial medication that is safe to use with salt, such as acriflavine. Whatever medication you choose, follow the directions and complete a course of treatment before reassessing the situation. One of the most distressing things about dropsy is that although it can sometimes be cured, in most cases it proves fatal. This is generally because by the time external symptoms are spotted, irreparable internal damage and/or infections have occurred, mainly to the kidneys, and these are beyond treatment. For this reason you should constantly assess the treatment, and if the symptoms seem to be worsening after 5 days or so, it may be kinder to consider euthanasia.

Right: *The raised pinecone scales and protruding eyes are typical symptoms of bacterial dropsy.*

Egg retention

Occasionally, a koi may develop an unusual physical characteristic, such as a swollen abdominal area or a growth on a fin. These can be caused by a number of factors; some are hereditary, others are induced by changes in the environment or the presence of a bacterial or viral infection. If you find a tumor, nine times out of ten it will prove to be harmless. If it is internal, little can be done, other than careful monitoring of the affected koi. If the growth is external, it may be possible for a veterinarian to remove it surgically, but the chances are that it may return once removed. There is also a risk that the area from which it is removed may become infected. Generally, the best approach is to leave suspected tumors alone and just monitor the affected fish. Consider taking action only if the koi appears in distress and loses its ability to eat. Then euthanasia should be considered as the humane option.

A female koi is presumed to be egg-bound when she fails to spawn and the abdomen may be very distended. Female carp — and therefore koi — can carry eggs for many years without actually shedding them and it causes them no harm.

Generally, female carp/koi will resorb eggs and use them as a nutrient source during periods of starvation or when, as a consequence of illness, they have ceased feeding. This condition is known as "atresia." Healthy female carp do not resorb eggs, even in cold periods during the winter. The final maturation and release of eggs for spawning is very rapid and presumed to be due to the release of an enzyme into the ovaries. Sometimes most of the eggs are shed, but a number remain in the ovary postspawning. Over time, these eggs become encapsulated in a fibrous tissue and over a period of years are probably responsible for the tumors and cysts that are common in females of this species.

Females may become egg- or spawn-bound if the eggs have been released into the ovaries and the spawning fish are disturbed, say, by the appearance of a predator. In this situation, if the males stop chasing the females and spawning stops, the eggs are not shed and the females die, presumably through bacterial contamination.

Below: A dissected koi which is egg-bound. Mature female koi can produce up to 200,000 eggs, but these may be carried for several years without spawning. Maturation of the eggs requires a good-quality protein diet and environmental triggers of daylight and temperature.

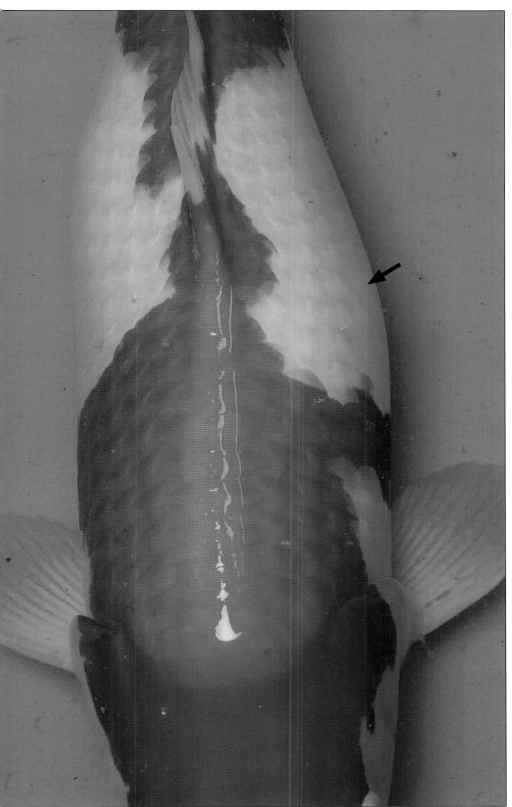

Identification

Both male and female koi can suffer from a variety of internal swellings and tumors, which appear to deform the body. It is very common for female koi to suffer from cysts and tumors within the ovaries and these do lead to the body becoming visibly swollen. In order to identify the condition, first confirm that the fish is female. A koi needs to be around 30 cm (12 in) or longer to sex. It is possible to identify a female koi by comparing body shape and fin size. Female koi tend to be broader across the shoulders and fuller-bodied, with a cigar shape, whereas male koi tend to be more slender and torpedo-shaped. The fins on a male koi may be larger and less rounded at the ends. However, the most reliable method of sexing is to inspect the vent area. A female koi will have a line running from head to tail in the vent area, crossed at one end with another line running from side to side to give the appearance of a T. A male koi will simply have a line running from head to tail. Having determined that the koi is female, gently feel the swollen area; if it is soft to the touch, but not too fluid, it could possibly be unreleased eggs. If the area feels hard, it could still be eggs, but is more likely to be a tumor. However, without invasive surgery, which is normally ineffective, it is impossible to make an exact diagnosis.

Left: This koi has an internal tumor (the arrow shows the abnormal bulge). It may be of the ovaries, although only a postmortem will allow an exact identification to be made.

Prevention

Just because you have a pond containing male and female koi, it does not mean that the females will spawn. Generally, however if the environmental and dietary conditions are right, female koi will produce and store eggs each year. These are generally released during spawning, which takes place when the water temperature reaches 20°C (68°F) or higher. Unless you are a koi-breeder, it is best to maintain a constant temperature throughout the winter of around 16°C (61°C).

In order for koi to spawn, feeding regimes play an important role. In the weeks leading up to spawning, the koi should be offered a high-protein diet to enhance the maturation of both eggs and milt. Providing there is suitable spawning material, the koi should spawn. In the wild, carp and, therefore, koi prefer shallow marginal areas in which to lay their eggs, but most formal koi ponds tend to be deep and steep-sided, following the traditional Japanese style. Once the water temperature in the pond reaches about 18°C (64°F) in early summer, it may help to introduce spawning mats or brushes and sometimes this can induce the koi to spawn.

Treatment

As female carp, and therefore koi, can carry their eggs for several years without spawning, the abdomen may become very distended. Even though a koi is extremely healthy, the condition can cause the koi owner great anxiety. Although these koi usually do spawn eventually, often the reason they fail to do so is because the conditions are inappropriate.

It has been advocated that female koi that appear egg-bound should be either hand-stripped or given hormones to induce spawning. It is important to realize that unless the eggs are mature and have been released into the body cavity, any attempt at hand-stripping the koi will only result in internal injury and possible death. If a koi is ready to drop her eggs, applying the gentlest pressure on the abdomen will cause a stream of eggs to be released from the vent. In this instance, continue gently massaging the abdomen in the direction of head to tail until all the eggs have been released. Although many koi-keepers view pituitary extract or synthetic

Right: This koi has a suspected tumor of the reproductive organs. In some cases it can be difficult to determine if a koi has a tumor or another condition such as dropsy, which can cause similar physical symptoms.

Determining the sex

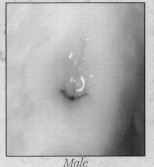
Male

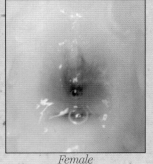
Female

One possible way to sex a koi is to examine the shape of the vent. Female koi have a line running from head to tail, with another line running across it at the tail end. Male koi do not have this cross-piece. Instead, they have a simple line running from head to tail. However, this difference is not easy to distinguish — you need an experienced eye to do it accurately. Another technique is to gently feel between the pelvic bones of the fish. In female koi, the two pelvic girdles are distinctly separate to allow the abdomen to expand as the eggs mature. In male koi, the pelvic bones are fused in the center; in juvenile koi the pelvic bones are located close together and it may be difficult to differentiate between the sexes.

Fungal infections

Koi with a suppressed immune system generally tend to be more susceptible to fungal infections, although damage to the body surface — perhaps caused by water conditions, parasite damage or physical injuries — may also lead to infection. Stressed koi are also susceptible to outbreaks of fungus because the integrity of the skin breaks down, thus allowing fungal spores to invade. Once a koi has become infected, the fungus appears as a cottonwool-like growth, often a dirty brown color as it traps pieces of dirt and detritus. In some ponds fungal growth can appear green, as microscopic algae become trapped in the fibers. Fungus spreads extremely rapidly and very invasively, entirely coating a koi within 24 hours and reaching deep into the muscle tissue.

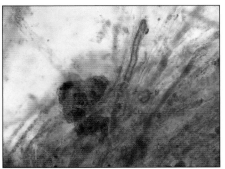

Above: *Under the microscope, fungus has a rather fibrous appearance, as it grows with fine, interconnecting branches known as "hyphae."*

The fungus will spread over the entire body surface of the koi, even infecting the eyes.

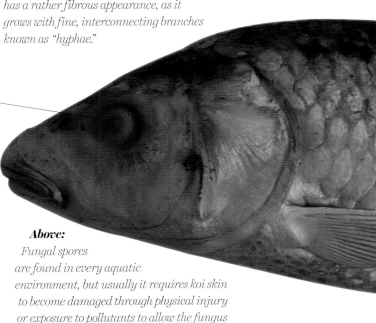

Above:
Fungal spores are found in every aquatic environment, but usually it requires koi skin to become damaged through physical injury or exposure to pollutants to allow the fungus to become established.

equivalent hormone injections as the panacea for koi that retain their eggs, these will only have an effect if the female is within 24 hours of spawning naturally.

If a koi is genuinely egg-bound — where spawning has been interrupted and the males have lost interest and are no longer inducing the female to shed her eggs — then hand-stripping should be undertaken right away. Once the eggs have been released from the ovaries and the koi does not spawn, peritonitis sets in as the eggs disintegrate and the female will die within a few days.

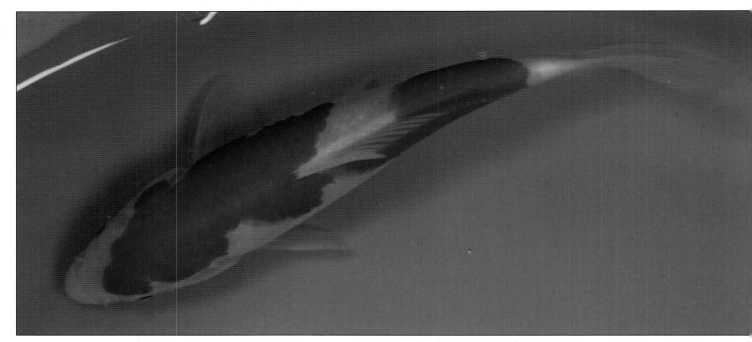

Above: Hi-kui disease generally only affects higher-grade koi with red pigmentation, such as Go Sanke varieties.

Hi-kui

Hi-kui is a disease that only attacks the skin of koi with red pigmentation, especially Go Sanke varieties, i.e., Kohaku, Showa and Sanke. The term Hi-kui is composed of two elements: *hi* means red and *kui* translates as eaten, so Hi-kui can be simply described as a disease that eats the red areas of pigmentation on koi. Hi-kui is widely used to describe several conditions, although the actual cause could in fact be a number of things. Hi-kui may be used to describe complaints such as localized, minor skin conditions, which can normally be treated easily using the methods described below. At the other extreme it may be used to describe complaints such as skin cancer, which require examination by your veterinarian or koi health specialist who will advise on a suitable treatment regime. It must be said that skin cancer in koi is not widely experienced, although if in doubt, always seek specialist advice. Hi-kui only tends to affect good-quality koi with stable areas of red pigmentation. Lower-quality koi whose red pigmentation may be unstable are seldom affected.

Identification

Hi-kui disease may show itself in a numbers of ways. You may notice a small discoloration of an area of red pigmentation, causing the red pigment to look faded compared to the rest of the red on the koi. This area may also look matt and sunken and lack the same sheen as the rest of the fish. Alternatively, an area of red pigmentation may take on a brown haze and look raised compared to the surrounding area. Third, small dark brown areas may appear with a diameter ranging from a pinhead up to the size of a small coin.

Whatever symptoms your koi exhibit, the problem is caused by a thickening of the overlying epidermal tissue, which may be triggered by a number of factors, the most likely being overexposure to sunlight resulting in sunburn. Excessive sunlight can trigger tumors of red pigment cells by damaging the cells' DNA. Poor husbandry and system maintenance may make attacks of Hi-kui worse, as dirt and waste within the system can attract anaerobic bacteria that view these affected areas as an ideal site for secondary infection.

Prevention

As overexposure to sunlight is one of the main causes of Hi-kui disease, shading the pond is a good idea. For this reason many keepers believe that koi kept in green water are less likely to get Hi-kui, although this is not an attractive solution for the typical hobbyist who wants to view their koi in clear water. Good system maintenance and regularly discharging collected waste will all help. They do not necessarily stop Hi-kui from occurring, but they do help to prevent other infections taking hold. It is also essential to maintain optimum oxygen levels at all times, especially when temperatures are high. These periods usually coincide with high exposure to sunlight. Despite these precautions it may be impossible to stop an outbreak of Hi-kui, as it can simply appear through no fault of your own. Unfortunately, it tends to occur more readily on high-quality koi with strong and stable hi (red), and if your collection contains fish that fall into this category, be warned that it might just happen!

Treatment

Hi-kui is not contagious and in real terms it has no effect on the overall health of the koi, as long as the system in which they are kept is of a suitable standard and well-maintained. The main effect of Hi-kui is cosmetic — it degrades the appearance of your fish, and in the case of high value koi, it may devalue them. Whether you decide to treat it or not is a matter of personal choice. If you do decide to seek treatment,

the koi in question will need to be sedated before any surgical treatment can be carried out. Having sedated the fish, a veterinarian or koi health specialist will scrape away the area of Hi-kui with a clean sterilized scalpel until the raised parts of Hi-kui are gone, or at least reduced in size if a large area is affected. Then a suitable topical treatment may be applied to the area to stop secondary infections, such as fungus. Propolis is a good treatment to apply, although malachite green or a similar remedy will do.

The koi can then be returned to the pond, but the treated area of skin must be monitored on a regular basis to ensure that no secondary infections occur. It may be necessary to repeat the topical treatment on a regular basis until the area is healed. An alternative, less drastic treatment is to apply a steroid-based cream to the affected area for a number of weeks, applying the cream several times during the day. This approach is generally preferable as a first step before resorting to surgical removal, which may leave your koi open to secondary infections.

Below: *This fish is showing advanced stages of Hi-kui — the red pigmentation and skin tissue is breaking down.*

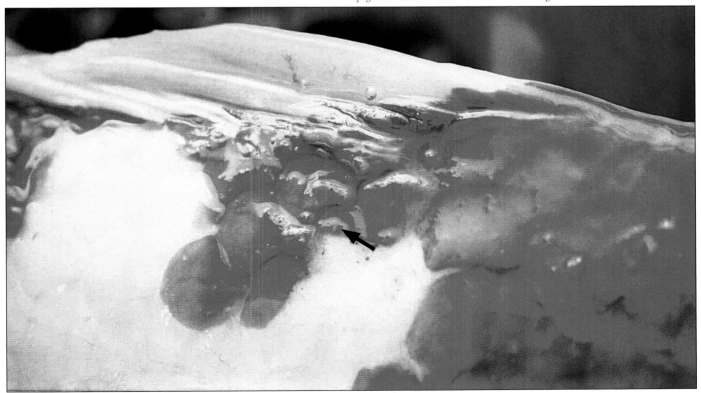

Viruses

There is no cure for a viral infection. Although spring viremia of carp (SVC) virus is a serious disease that can affect carp, koi must be in contact with infected fish to become infected themselves. As spring viremia of carp predominantly affects wild carp, it is unlikely that most koi-keepers will encounter the disease, unless fish are taken from rivers or lakes to stock the pond — a very unwise strategy and illegal in many countries.

Above: KHV is highly infectious. It causes gill erosion, often accompanied by sunken, cloudy eyes, as seen on this koi.

Koi herpesvirus

Koi herpesvirus is what is termed an emerging disease It first appeared in 1996, although the causative agent was not identified until 2000. Koi herpesvirus, a serious disease, causing significant mortalities among koi and carp, spread worldwide within a matter of years. In 2006, the World Organisation for Animal Health, known as Organisation Internationale Epizootique (OIE), included KHV on the list of Notifiable Diseases. The disease has occurred among wild carp populations in the UK and since 2010 it has been classified as Notifiable in the UK and Europe. Research into KHV is very much a work in progress, with strong evidence that goldfish, grass carp and ide, and even some freshwater aquatic invertebrates, can carry the virus. The virus is spread in the feces and mucus, and is known to survive for at least 4 hours outside of the host. What is apparent is that the virus is highly infectious and it requires exposure of just a few minutes

for the disease to spread to an uninfected koi. The symptoms of KHV include a rapid onset of disease and mortalities, usually within a temperature range of 18 to 25°C. The breathing rate as seen by movements of the gill covers is rapid, the koi have a patchy, pimply white appearance on the skin and often the eyes are sunken into the head.

Examination of the affected koi may show erosion of the gills. Tissue samples of potentially infected koi are tested with polymerase chain reaction (PCR), where the virus is identified or enzyme-linked immunosorbent assay (ELISA), which reacts to antibodies produced by the koi in response to infection with KHV. In many instances the koi mortalities caused by KHV are between 80 percent and 100 percent, but in instances where the koi pond is well-managed the disease can appear chronic, without a rapid onset and mortalities of between 30 percent and 50 percent.

Prevention

In the hobbyist's pond, the disease usually occurs as a result of introducing latent KHV-infected koi, but it is important to regard nets and other equipment as a potential source of infection. Never share equipment with other hobbyists and keep equipment associated with any quarantine facility strictly for use with the koi in quarantine and separate from that used on the pond. (See also Quarantining koi pages 148–149.) Routine disinfection of equipment is important in preventing the spread of any disease, whether viral or bacterial. Finally, the most important management tool in preventing the spread of disease is to wash your hands between handling koi in any different holding systems.

Sometimes koi can become surplus to requirement; they may have lost color or some other reason has necessitated their disposal. It may be possible to find a new owner for these koi, in which case they should be subject to quarantine before being introduced to the new pond. Should it happen that the koi cannot be rehomed, then regrettably, they should be humanely euthanized. Under no circumstances should koi be introduced to any natural pond, lake or river where they may spread KHV to native stocks of carp.

The ability to ship fish worldwide and within hours has facilitated movements of live fish for ornamental and other purposes, such as sport and food, on a massive scale. A few years ago, it would have been unthinkable to transport carp from Australia to Europe, but this is now possible because of the speed of nonstop jet travel. Although there are benefits to the rapid movement of fish, it means there is a greater likelihood that introduced fish will infect native fish with new and emerging diseases that may be common in their country of origin. Without doubt, the ability to ship koi and carp so readily has lead to the rapid spread of this serious disease. The lesson we should take away from the KHV experience is that we must be prepared for other new and emerging diseases that can arise just as suddenly and with similarly devastating results.

Right: *Infection with KHV suppresses the immune system and infected fish may therefore develop a range of secondary diseases, including bacterial ones. The symptoms of bacterial disease are evident on the side and around the mouth of this carp, which proved positive for KHV using PCR.*

Below: *KHV targets the gills, where the virus "hijacks" the cells into producing virus particles. The viral infection often leads to cell death and dead tissues are then invaded by secondary bacteria, leading to erosion of the gills as here. This is regarded as a typical symptom of KHV infection.*

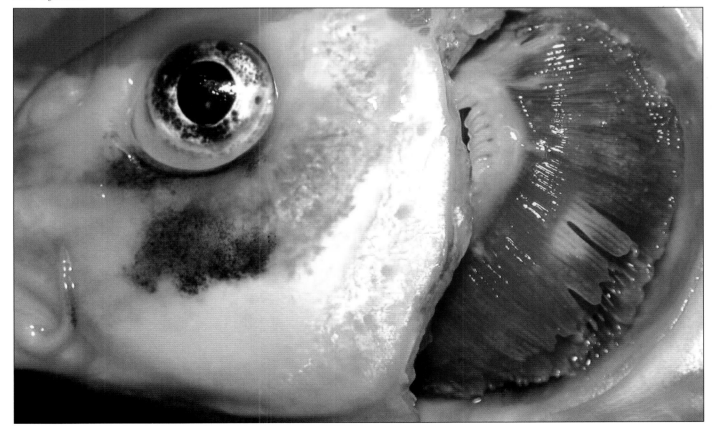

Papilloma and carp pox

Papilloma and carp pox are viral infections that tend to affect koi in periods of lower water temperature. At less than 1 year old, koi tend not to be affected by papilloma, and older koi sometimes seem to grow out of it. This is a relatively harmless disease and does not pose a major threat to koi. Carp pox and papilloma also have a very low level of infection, so one fish in a pond may show symptoms while the others remain healthy.

Identification

Carp pox is easy to identify by the hard, white, waxy lumps that appear mostly on the fins of the fish and occasionally on the head. On Doitsu or leather koi, carp pox may also be found on the body, as it tends to be found on areas lacking scales. Carp pox is often described by professionals and hobbyists alike as if a white candle had been lit and the hot wax allowed to drop onto the koi. Papillomas are similar in appearance to carp pox, with large areas appearing on the fins, especially around the hard leading ray. Elsewhere they tend to be smaller, with an average size of around 5 mm (0.2 in), and in some cases may be present all over the koi in quite large numbers. Like carp pox, they may have a white waxy appearance; however, you may also notice red or pink tumorlike growths.

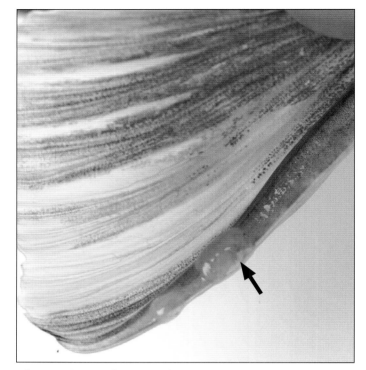

Above: A close-up of a pectoral fin showing a small area of carp pox. The fin areas are prone to carp pox.

Above: This fish has carp pox on the head and face, which is one of the most common areas for it to occur. Although unsightly, it seldom proves a serious health threat to your koi.

Prevention

Carp pox and papilloma are only a problem in cold water conditions, so if these can be avoided, you should not experience these diseases. Even if you do suffer an outbreak, it should not be any real cause for alarm as these viral infections are harmless. The worst effect is the koi's unsightly appearance while the virus is active.

Treatment

There is no cure for carp pox, but raising the water temperature may cause the virus to subside and the white waxy lumps to disappear. At a higher water temperature the koi is able to mount an effective immune response against the virus. An increase of around 10°C may be sufficient, but take care to implement this increase over a period of days and even weeks, making an increase of 1°C every 1 to 2 days. Avoid rapid temperature increases, which are very stressful for the fish and could result in other diseases occurring, especially parasite infections such as whitespot. The symptoms of carp pox may well disappear with this increase in temperature, but that does not mean that the koi in question is free from the disease. White waxy lumps may suddenly appear again in the future, generally during a period of lower water temperature.

Papilloma responds in the same way as carp pox: an increase in water temperature normally cures the koi. However, you may need to increase the temperature to over 25°C (77°F). Take the same precautions when increasing the temperature as described above. This measure should cause the growths on the koi to disappear over a period of 7 to 10 days.

Papilloma may reveal itself by the presence of tumors with a reddish to pink appearance. These may need to be removed surgically, a job that should be done by a veterinarian or your local koi health specialist. The areas from which these tumors are removed should be topically treated with, for example, malachite green and propolis. In extreme cases, when a large number are removed, secondary infection may occur that will require additional treatment. In this case, seek advice from your local koi health specialist.

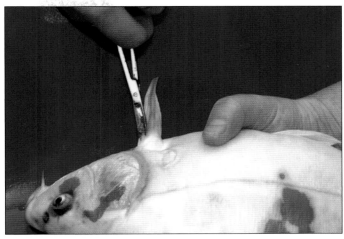

Above: *Only a veterinarian or koi health specialist should carry out this procedure. Do not attempt this yourself.*

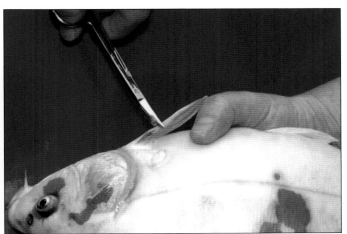

Above: *The papilloma is cut away using sterilized scissors.*

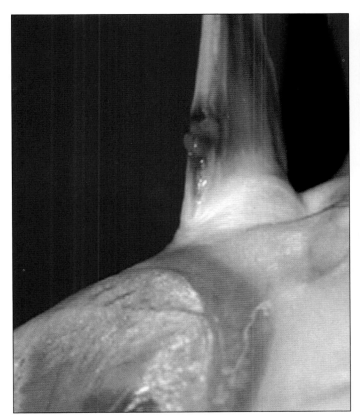

Above: *The pectoral fin of this carp has a papilloma growth, which has started to cause an infection on the front leading ray. The growth therefore needs to be removed.*

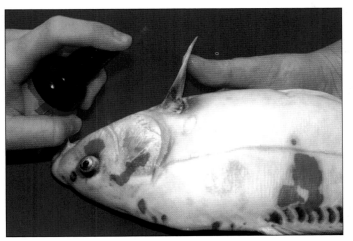

Above: *Following surgery, a topical treatment is applied.*

Popeye

This is a condition that affects either one or both eyes, causing them to stand out from the body as though they were mounted on stalks. If just one eye is protruding, the chances of a serious problem, and the resulting losses, are much less than if both eyes are affected. Such a case may suggest a more serious (and possibly internal) problem. Popeye can be caused by a number of factors, including parasitic, viral or bacterial infections, poor water quality, nutritional deficiency, internal problems and even physical damage.

Identification

Popeye is not usually a highly contagious condition and only one koi may show symptoms at any one time. However, the underlying cause will determine if the condition will prove infectious or not. The telltale signs of popeye are unmistakable: the eyes stand out from the body — in extreme cases by over 10 mm (0.4 in). Bear in mind that a koi's eyes normally protrude slightly from the body, so before assuming that a fish has popeye compare it with a known healthy koi. If it is popeye, it is vital to establish the cause of the problem. Stress is the most common trigger and poor water quality the main culprit. This should be the first avenue to investigate. If water quality proves fine, think about any changes that have occurred; even

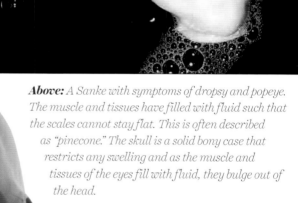

Above: A Sanke with symptoms of dropsy and popeye. The muscle and tissues have filled with fluid such that the scales cannot stay flat. This is often described as "pinecone." The skull is a solid bony case that restricts any swelling and as the muscle and tissues of the eyes fill with fluid, they bulge out of the head.

The eyes of this young koi are starting to stand out from the head.

Right: Popeye in its early stages can be hard to spot and may go unnoticed for a while. However, early identification can lead to more successful treatment.

events such as the introduction of one or two new koi can be enough to trigger popeye in some fish.

You may also find that a particular koi develops popeye at certain times of the year every year, and this may simply coincide with seasonal changes in water temperature. If you also notice that areas of scales are lifting, or if the koi has gone off its food, is starting to waste or there seems to be swelling, it could be that a bacterial or viral infection is causing the problem. It could also be linked to the onset of dropsy.

Internal problems are another trigger for popeye and these can be anything from a build up of fluid to organ failure or even a tumor. As these causes are internal, it is often difficult to identify them precisely. As long as they do not result in the onset of a more serious bacterial infection or even dropsy, the condition may still clear up of its own accord.

Prevention

Simple good husbandry is essential. If excellent water conditions are maintained at all times, and other stress factors are avoided, the likelihood of popeye developing are dramatically reduced. A pond heating system can also help in reducing stress, as it enables you to maintain a constant temperature throughout the year. Providing good-quality, well-balanced koi food will also help to prevent popeye, which can be triggered by a poor diet, especially if the vitamins A and/or E are lacking. When buying new koi, avoid any showing signs of popeye.

Treatment

As popeye is generally not contagious, it is not important to isolate the affected koi. In fact the koi generally improve faster if kept in their normal environment, as this will generally have better filtration and be more stable than most quarantine or isolation facilities. Try to establish the underlying cause. Often, a simple water test will show a high level of ammonia. Once this has been remedied via small water changes with conditioned, dechlorinated tap water, allied to a reduction in food levels until optimum water conditions are re-established, the condition will normally cure itself.

Left: This koi has severe popeye. At such an advanced stage it is easy to identify the condition, as one or both eyes protrude very noticeably.

Having ruled out this, and any other possible causes, such as poor diet, you may find that a bacterial problem is behind the outbreak. If it proves necessary to treat the affected koi with antibacterials, seek advice from a qualified professional regarding what medication to use, at what dose and how to administer it. In nonadvanced and localized cases, antibiotic eye drops may be suggested. In more severe cases, antibiotic injections will be required and the koi in question will need to be anesthetized to avoid undue stress during the treatment.

Usually only one koi will be affected with popeye, even if a bacterial or viral infection is responsible. However, if other koi start to show symptoms you may wish to treat the pond with an antibacterial medication such as acriflavine at the dose recommended on the bottle (as this will be dependent upon the strength of the solution mix). Alternatively, use potassium permanganate at the dose of 1.5 g/1,000 l (220 gal); or Chloramine-T at the dose of 1 g/1,000 l (220 gal); or an off-the-shelf product intended for bacterial infections. If both eyes are protruding and you notice scale lifting and swelling, the koi may have dropsy. In this case, follow the recommended treatments for dropsy.

Another option is to give the fish a salt bath of 100 g (3.5 oz) of salt/4.5 l (1 gal) of water for 10 minutes. This will help to release any fluid that may be causing internal pressure. This can be done once a day for three consecutive days.

Swimbladder disorders

The swimbladder is the gas-filled organ that allows the fish to maintain neutral buoyancy in the water, and any koi with a disease of the swimbladder has difficulty in swimming. Affected koi tend to remain on the bottom of the pond with the pectoral fins spread, occasionally swimming to the surface with a characteristic side-to-side rowing action in order to gulp air. Swimbladder disorders can occur for no apparent reason and the underlying health problem is difficult to diagnose. It may be caused by tumors, infections that lead to fluid displacing the gas in the chamber, fungal infections that damage the swimbladder or other noninfectious diseases that affect the secretion of gas from the blood into the swimbladder.

Koi belong to a group of fish known as "physostomes," as the swimbladder has a vestigial connection to the top of the throat. When koi larvae hatch, they undergo "swim up," rising to the water surface to take a gulp of air, which inflates the swimbladder for the first time. As the koi grow, blood vessels form an intimate connection to the posterior chamber and enable gas to be secreted into the swimbladder. Koi with a diseased swimbladder frequently rise to the surface to gulp air in an attempt to top up the swimbladder with atmospheric air. Koi that have traveled in bags for a period of hours also repeat this air-gulping in an attempt to top up the swimbladder, but in this case it is a perfectly normal behavior.

Identification

Koi with a swimbladder disorder will still be able to swim, but the effort required to do so may prove far greater than normal, and once stationary, the koi may simply float or sink back to its previous position. Koi may also swim with their tail-end higher, looking as if they are permanently in a nose dive position. Generally, a swimbladder disorder on its own is not a cause for any great alarm. In most cases an affected koi will survive quite happily, although it may maintain an unusual position in the water. However, if the fish is unable to take food or spends large amounts of time on the bottom and develops pressure sores that will prove susceptible to secondary infection, it may be necessary to consider euthanasia for the fish. If you suspect that air-gulping is the cause of the buoyancy problems, you should notice that the affected fish only suffers with these problems periodically. A true swimbladder problem will continue to affect the fish until it is rectified.

Prevention and treatment

It can be very difficult to determine why any particular koi has developed a disease of the swimbladder. There probably are some koi with a genetic predisposition to the disease and it occurs as the fish gets older. As koi rise naturally through the water, the blood removes excess gas from the swimbladder, preventing it from becoming overinflated. At the bottom of the koi pond, the water pressure is greatest and it will compress any gas in the swimbladder, effectively reducing its size and volume. As the koi rises, the volume of gas expands as the water pressure decreases and then the blood removes this excess gas. As physostomes, koi primitively retain an open duct between the swimbladder and intestine; they can either top up this organ by gulping air or releasing excess gas by belching.

Left: A koi with swimbladder problems may not just sink or float within the pond; it may also have trouble maintaining an upright position in the water, as shown here. For a conclusive confirmation that the swimbladder is the cause of this, a veterinarian may have to take an x-ray.

Above: *Here a large Chagoi suffering from a swimbladder disorder is unable to move below the water surface.*

Right: *Here, the skin of the swimbladder is thickened and inflamed. Inside is a mass of fungus instead of gas.*

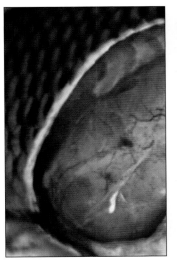
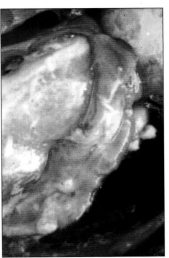

Prevention is always to ensure koi are raised in a slow, smooth operation and never snatched to the surface. In a situation where the swimbladder fills with excess gas or fluid, a veterinarian can aspirate the swimbladder. The difficulty is that without being able to diagnose why the swimbladder is affected in this way, removing the air or water is only a temporary fix and the condition will probably recur. An affected koi can be left in the pond as swimbladder disorders (unless they are the result of another infection) are not contagious.

Another measure to help the koi regain the correct function of its swimbladder is to lift it off the bottom and maintain it in a floating net or cage within the pond. This should be relatively shallow to keep the koi near the surface. Salt baths are another option, at a dose rate of 22 g/l (3.5 oz/gal) for 10 minutes. This can be done up to three times, giving the koi a bath on three successive days. Should bathing prove to be impractical, salt can be added to the pond at a dose rate of 3 g/l (0.5 oz/gal). However, be sure to test the salt levels and ideally reduce them to zero before using other medications, such as formalin. Formalin and salt work in the same way by stripping parasites and mucus from the koi's skin, and if you use both at the same time the fish may be burned.

Other health problems

Here, we consider some other conditions that koi-keepers may occasionally encounter.

Blood parasites

These are not often a problem for the general koi-keeper, and in fact the chances of them even being identified are slim, because a koi needs to go through an extensive postmortem for an exact identification to be made. Signs of this type of infection depend on the species of blood parasite, but may include anemia. Egg-laying species cause

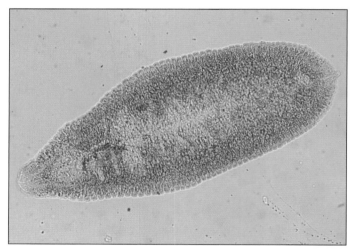

Above: Sanguinicola *is a blood parasite that is very rarely experienced as a problem by the average koi-keeper. Here it can be seen viewed under a microscope.*

damage to the gills and kidney. All these are common symptoms of numerous other diseases, which makes positive identification of these parasites even harder. If you want to research blood parasites further, the common culprits are Trypanosoma and Trypanoplasma, which can be spread by leeches in a pond. The other blood parasite that may be encountered is the bloodworm Sanguinicola. In its developmental stages, it needs an aquatic snail as an intermediate host, so eradicating the presence of all snails will help to prevent this parasite from causing problems. Blood parasites are extremely hard to treat. For a positive identification and advice on the best course of treatment, seek professional advice from your veterinarian, the laboratory that carried out the tests or a suitably qualified professional.

Herons and frogs

Herons stand patiently at the pond edge and stab at the koi, but they will also use their feet to scoop up fish close to the water surface. Herons have extremely good eyesight, so the koi in a pond stand out as an easy meal for a hungry bird. Usually heron start fishing at first light, which in the summer months is between 3 a.m. and 4 a.m. Although most herons are quite secretive and the only sign of a visit is missing koi or, sadly, one that has been stabbed by the bird. Sometimes they can be very persistent. It may be necessary to place wires around the pond to prevent the heron standing on the edge or to place a net over the pond to stop predation of the koi.

It has become increasingly common for frogs to become overamorous in the breeding season and for the males to attach themselves to an unsuspecting koi. Although in some cases the frog will realize its mistake and let go, it can cause physical damage that may require subsequent treatment. In some cases, the male frogs attach themselves around the head of the koi and the male clasps the fish so tightly that the gills are clamped shut. If the frog is not removed the koi will suffocate. Sometimes the hand of the frog actually depresses the eye of the koi and the bony socket, giving the

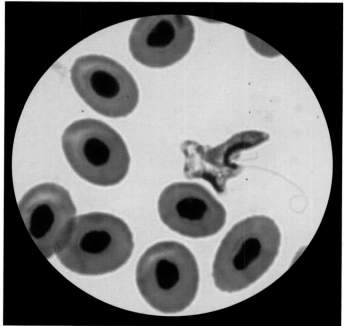

Above: *To be sure of making an exact identification of* Trypanoplasma, *contact a specialist. However, this parasite is seldom a problem for the average koi hobbyist.*

Above: *Improbable as it may seem, cases have been reported of overamorous frogs attaching themselves to unwary koi during the mating season. They usually let go without any human intervention being needed.*

frog an immovable grip. In these instances, the male frogs are almost impossible to pull off the unfortunate koi without causing injuries to either animal. The frog can be removed by anesthetizing the joined animals. Clove oil, tricaine methane sulphate (MS222) or 2-phenoxyethanol are suitable. As the frog is anesthetized, gently remove it from the koi without damaging either animal.

The common frog is declining in numbers and it may be that a shortage of breeding females is leading to this increase in the males making amorous advances toward the koi. Remember that the frogs are protected species and it is an offense to injure or kill them.

Fish tuberculosis (TB)

This is another disease (caused by mycobacteria) that the average koi-keeper is very unlikely to encounter. If it is identified, take great care when dealing with it, as this disease is a zoonosis, meaning that there is a chance of infection spreading to humans. Signs of a possible infection of fish by mycobacteria include rapid weight loss and the apparent wasting of the infected koi, combined with a drastic loss of

appetite. Again, symptoms include many other signs that are also indicative of other more common diseases, and in most instances these are more likely to be the culprits rather than fish TB. These symptoms include areas of reddening on the skin, which may then turn into small ulcerations, popeye, excessive periods of hanging in the water, clamped fins and, possibly, erratic swimming behavior. The only way of making an exact diagnosis is to send away a fish for testing. If you get a positive identification, seek advice from your veterinarian.

In the past, the recommendation was to cull infected koi, but this is probably rather draconian and it is better to manage the disease by ensuring koi are held in the best conditions and offered good-quality feed. It is important to remember that the disease can be transmitted to humans and it would be advisable to wear protective gloves when handling the koi or carrying out any maintenance work. Thankfully, TB in koi would seem to be rare.

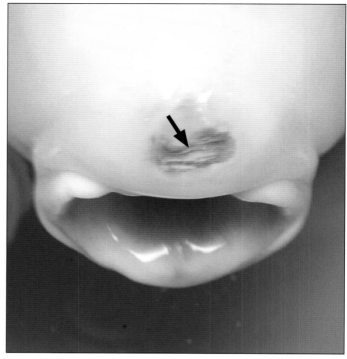

Above: This koi has damage around the mouth which may have happened either in transit (bag rub) or due to feeding around the edge of the pond and rubbing its face.

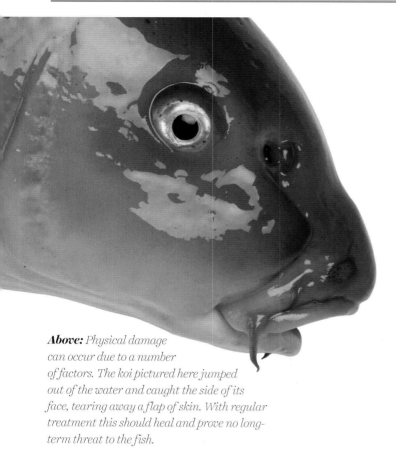

Above: Physical damage can occur due to a number of factors. The koi pictured here jumped out of the water and caught the side of its face, tearing away a flap of skin. With regular treatment this should heal and prove no long-term threat to the fish.

Physical damage

Koi-keepers are commonly faced with this problem amongs their fish, which can be caused by anything from koi bumping into sharp rocks, bad netting, spawning activity and poor transportation to attack by predators, such as herons, magpies or crows. The best step to take to avoid the occurrence of physical damage is to reduce the objects in the pond on which the koi can damage themselves. If predators such as herons are a problem, consider netting the pond or installing a suitable deterrent device. If spotted early, most physical damage can be easily treated with topical application of malachite green and propolis. However, if unnoticed for any length of time, bacterial or fungal infections may develop and these may need further treatment, possibly including the use of antibacterials and fungicides. Obvious signs of physical damage include missing scales, areas of reddening, split fins, and grazes on nonscaled areas, such as around the mouth or all over Doitsu koi.

Sleeping sickness of koi

In the last few years, the cause of sleeping sickness of koi has been identified as a virus, which has been formally named as carp edema virus (CEV). It is regarded as an emerging disease, although koi-breeders in Japan have been aware of it since the 1970s. This condition usually only affects young koi; koi over 2 years of age may not show any symptoms at all. Typically, the koi appear to be dead and simply lie on the bottom, showing no signs of movement. The low temperature has the effect of dramatically reducing their metabolism, so they may appear to be not breathing as the gill movement is so slight. When stimulated, the koi will move slowly but only for a short time before relapsing into their previous condition. This condition can be treated by adding salt to the pond and raising the water temperature to at least 21°C (70°F). If sleeping sickness is suspected, raise the temperature rapidly at a rate of 3 to 4°C every day or two, as prolonged exposure to low temperatures dramatically reduces the chances of recovery from this

Above: *Although they look dead, these fish are just suffering from sleeping sickness. As year-round heating becomes more popular with the serious koi hobbyist, outbreaks of this condition become less likely.*

increase and blood vessels to constrict. This is accompanied by the release of high-energy glucose to fuel muscles. The released hormones also stimulate ion exchange and gill perfusion, meaning that more of the gill surface area is in contact with the water, which is rapidly absorbed through the gills and could lead to dropsy. The overall effect of the hormones is to allow koi to respond rapidly to the cause of the stress and to escape.

Long-term stress, or a situation where a koi is subject to a variety of stresses, results in the release of the hormone cortisol. Cortisol induces the release of glucose and affects ion regulation, which under nonstressful conditions is primarily through the gills. However, stress causes the gut to become a site of ion regulation, and ions and salts are readily lost from the koi's body as a consequence of an increase in the production of urine. The main function of this hormone is to provide the long-term energy supply that enables the koi to survive the stress, but the side effects of its release are the suppression of the immune system, growth and reproduction. The effects of cortisol on the immune system are significant, as they render any stressed koi susceptible to secondary infections and disease, which can then prove difficult to control.

Interestingly, stress caused by handling or cold shock results in the release of both adrenaline and cortisol, which have a synergistic effect, meaning that each enhances the activity of the other.

Sunburn

Koi with areas of white pigmentation are susceptible to sunburn, and this is characterized by a reddening of the white pigment; in extreme cases blistering may occur. The best way to prevent this is to provide adequate shade over the pond. It is not necessary to cover the whole pond, but at least an area of it. Another approach is to build a pergola over the pond and use greenhouse shading or shaded polycarbonate to reduce the levels of direct sunlight reaching the pond. This will have the added benefit of reducing green water and blanketweed growth. If a koi does develop sunburn, do not apply harsh medications to the affected area as this may aggravate the situation. The simple application of propolis should be sufficient to clear things up. Keep an eye on the affected koi to ensure that no secondary infections occur, such as fungus or bacterial infections. Should these arise, take the necessary steps to treat them, i.e., further topical treatment or, in the case of bacterial infection, expert advice.

condition. While doing this, add salt at a dose rate of up to 6 kg/1,000 l (13 lb/220 gal). After 10 days, reduce the salt to a lower level through water changes. Although this condition is sometimes experienced by the hobbyist, it is more of a problem for farmers and breeders who keep vast stocks of young fish. Expect losses if not treated quickly.

Stress

Stress plays a very prominent role in outbreaks of disease in koi. How much effect stress has in rendering koi susceptible to outbreaks of disease depends on factors such as its severity, the period of time over which the koi is exposed to the stress, the overall condition of the koi, its reproductive status and age. The effects of stress are cumulative and therefore it is easy to increase the stress experienced by koi. A short-term stress, such as the attentions of a predator or netting the pond, induces a "fight or flight" response, where hormones such as adrenalin are released into the circulation, initially causing the heart rate to

Treatment table

Always take great care when adding any treatment to the koi pond. It is important to know the volume of water in the pond and filtration system. Follow the directions supplied with proprietary brands of medications exactly. When undertaking any calculations to obtain the required dose, always ask someone else to check the figures; it is easy to make a mistake with the decimal point! Always measure any medication accurately and never add any extra. It will not make the treatment more effective and could be harmful.

Many chemicals used as treatments also have an antibacterial effect, so it is important to monitor the water quality constantly during the period the pond is being dosed.

Above: Measure any medication carefully and never add it to the pond in concentrated form. Fill a plastic watering can with pond water, add the correct amount of medication and stir. Sprinkle onto the pond surface.

Acriflavine

Application: Treating parasitic, bacterial and fungal infections.
Dose: 5–10 mg/l, dissolved in water.
Possible problems: As a result of frequent use, many fish pathogens have become resistant to this chemical.

Chloramine-T

Application: treating *Ichthyobodo necator* (costia), *Trichodina* sp., white spot and skin flukes, skin and gill bacterial infections.
Dose: Dependent on water hardness, pH and water temperature.

pH	Soft water dose (mg/l)	Hardwater Dose (mg/l)
6	2.5	7
6.5	5	10
7	10	15
7.5	18	18
8	20	20

Possible problems: Chloramine-T can be toxic to koi in soft water. It is advisable to use an alternative treatment. Do not use where there are exposed metal surfaces. High doses may be toxic to koi. Always start with the lowest dose and increase if necessary. Do not use in conjunction with formalin or benzalkonium chloride (Roccal®).

Formalin

Application: Treating a range of protozoan and fluke infections.
Dose: 37–40 percent formalin 15–25 mg/l
Possible problems: Formalin reduces the oxygen content of the water and is a gill irritant. Monitor dissolved oxygen levels before and during treatment with formalin. It is a good idea to install additional aeration, both before and during treatment. Formalin is more toxic in soft, acidic water. At higher temperatures, formalin becomes increasingly toxic. Do not use if a white precipitate of paraformaldehyde is visible. Formalin forms paraformaldehyde at temperatures of 8°C (46°F) and below. Avoid using formalin if koi are stressed, such as following importation or transportation. If koi are ulcerated or have open lesions, use an alternative, less harsh medication. Aquatic plants are sensitive to formalin and may be adversely affected.

Leteux Meyer mixture

Application: Leteux Meyer mixture is a combination of formalin and malachite green. The effect is more potent when these two chemicals are combined than when either is used on its own. A very effective treatment for white spot and other protozoan parasite infections.
Dose: 0.1 mg/l malachite green with 25 mg/l formalin.
Possible problems: Leteux Meyer mixture will reduce oxygen levels in the pond and should only be used if the dissolved oxygen content remains above 5 mg/l. Increasing temperatures cause Leteux Meyer mixture to become increasingly toxic. In some countries, the use of products containing malachite green is prohibited.

Malachite green

Application: Used for treating white spot and fungal infections. Zinc-free malachite green must be used for koi treatment. This chemical has some unusual properties; in acid conditions it is green in color and water soluble, whereas in alkaline conditions it is colorless, insoluble in water but soluble in fats and oils. The use of malachite green in the aquatic environment is controversial, as this chemical is a known mutagenic (increases genetic mutations by directly affecting the DNA) and a possible cancer-causing agent. Its use has been prohibited for the food fish industry and some countries have banned the use of malachite green entirely. In others it is still available for use with ornamental fish.
Dose: 0.1 mg/l.
Possible problems: Malachite green is a potent respiratory poison for which there is no antidote and the effects are cumulative with regular, repeat treatments. The oxygen content of the water is reduced by malachite green; use supplementary aeration before and during treatment. As the temperature increases, malachite green becomes more toxic. Malachite green is more toxic in ponds with a low pH.

Organophosphate insecticides

Application: Used for the treatment of flukes, fish lice, anchor worm, gill maggots and leeches. In some countries the use of organophosphates for fish treatment is illegal.

Dose: Follow the manufacturer's recommended treatment advice.

Possible problems: Organophosphates are potent neurotoxins and some have been implicated as teratogens. The effects of treatment with organophosphates is cumulative, even if repeated doses are weeks apart. Certain fish species are very sensitive to organophosphates.

Potassium permanganate

Application: Used for the treatment of protozoan parasites and bacterial infections of the skin or gills.

Dose: 2 mg per liter.

Possible problems: Potassium permanganate is toxic in water with a high pH, forming a precipitate of manganese dioxide on the gills, so use it with caution. The presence of organic material in the filters and pond reduces the effectiveness of potassium permanganate. Do not use it in conjunction with either salt or formalin.

Quaternary ammonium compounds (Roccal®)

Application: Has been used for treating bacterial infections of the skin and gills and is of particular use where bacteria are multiplying within the mucus. After treatment, place the koi in untreated water.

Dose: 10 mg active QAC/l for 5–10 minutes.

Possible problems: Quaternary ammonium compounds are increasingly poisonous in soft water and with increasing temperatures.

Sodium chloride (common salt)

Application: Used for treating protozoan and fungal infections, as a mild bactericide and to reduce osmotic stress.

Dose: Short-term bath, 20 g/l for 10 minutes with aeration. For a prolonged immersion (pond treatment) use 3 g/l.

Possible problems: Salt does not break down or evaporate and is only removed by partial water changes.

USING A SALT DIP

Below: *It is very common for koi to become disoriented and lose their balance when first introduced into a salt bath. If the koi remains disoriented or becomes distressed, remove it from the salt bath immediately and return it to the pond. Always use aeration, as shown here, when using a dip treatment of salt.*

Right: *Use a salt tester — basically a hydrometer with suitable scales on it — to check the concentration of the salt solution. Aim for a strength of 20 g/l for a short-term dip.*

USING POTASSIUM PERMANGANATE

Above: *When preparing a potassium permanganate dip, measure the chemical carefully, ensuring any residues are fully dissolved before introducing any koi. Time any dip or bath treatment carefully and never add a few more minutes extra exposure time, as the chemical could be harmful to the koi.*

Above: *Once the koi has been placed in the potassium permanganate solution, monitor its progress continually. If the koi becomes distressed, return it to the pond at once and do not persist with the treatment. After treatment, place the fish in a vat or bowl of clean water to wash away the chemical.*

Buying koi

Buying koi is both a pleasure and a commitment, as all ornamental fish — whether inexpensive or very valuable — deserve the same high level of care. Buying and accepting losses of cheap koi before filter systems are fully matured is indefensible. When fish go into your pond, they should enjoy a stress-free environment from day one. And only when you are certain that you can provide these conditions should you start to build your own collection.

Buying koi is not as time-sensitive as it once was, thanks to improvements in shipping techniques and overseas holding facilities. And, if you heat your pond, you need no longer fear that newly imported koi will struggle to adapt to a change in climate. Options have widened in other directions; today, it is possible to fly to Japan to select fish at source from their breeders, or even to buy koi over the Internet. However, a visit in person to a reputable dealer is still the first choice for most koi-keepers. This chapter advises on choosing and buying your fish, how to get them home safely, and whether or not to quarantine them.

Country of origin

It makes sense to buy the best koi you can. Long-term, the cost of fish will be small compared to the outlay on their pond and the ongoing bills for food, medications and electricity.

Japanese koi are the finest in the world, and in real terms represent the best value for money. Fish from Israel, the USA, South Africa, China, Singapore and Cyprus all have their devotees. But only in Japan are experienced breeders able to capitalize on the long, hot summers and the unique mineral content of their mud ponds, essential to good growth and skin quality.

Even ordinary-grade Japanese fish compare favorably with the best koi from other countries and are a good choice for those who merely want a colorful display. As quality improves, the asking price rises, but balancing what you want against what you can afford is all part of the fascination of the hobby.

When to buy

The Japanese net their mud ponds in late October/ early November, and that is when the finest fish become available. Coincidentally, autumn temperatures best suit koi in transit, as cool water holds high levels of dissolved oxygen to sustain them through their flight. However, at other times of the year, sophisticated packing techniques and gradual temperature adjustment still ensure a safe journey in the aircraft's cargo hold.

It is common practice for dealers to travel out to hand-pick quality koi from the autumn harvest on behalf of their customers, or acquire a whole pondful of fish at favorable rates. Hobbyists in search of something really special can accompany these koi professionals to Japan. The fish they choose are either shipped back home or, for a fee, remain with the breeders for a further year or more to grow on. The risk is borne by the buyer, but the rewards can be great. Some dealers revisit Japan in the spring to buy the remainder of the koi from the autumn harvest. These

Below: A dealer and his customers buying koi in Japan. Their preliminary selections are netted and bowled, but will be whittled down when the fish are inspected at closer quarters.

Above: *It is important to view prospective purchases close-up, in a blue inspection bowl, and in good daylight. The customers may well like the fish, but not the price being asked by the koi farmer; in any event, this is not a procedure to be rushed.*

Where to buy

Reputable koi dealers may not always tell you what you would like to hear, or even sell you any fish until they are convinced your pond is suitable. Don't be put off by this. It means they care about their livestock and their responsibilities, and in the longer term they will be a valuable source of advice and assistance in return for your regular business.

If possible, buy koi only from specialist dealers — there are plenty to choose from. General aquatic outlets or pet stores are less likely to stock quality fish, or know much about keeping them. Long-established koi businesses pose the fewest risks, but new ones are being set up all the time. If you visit a new dealership, be guided by first impressions. Are the premises tiny and well laid out? Do the staff use separate nets for each pond or vat and disinfect them between use? Does the dealer stock all the necessary ancillary equipment as well as fish? The holding water should be well-filtered and clear, as much for the well-being of the koi as for ease of viewing. If any fish appear obviously diseased, in discomfort or unfit for sale — unless indicated as such and separately housed — go elsewhere.

Buying koi through the web

Many koi retailers worldwide now have their own website, or webpage. This usually features a description of the company, along with a list of available koi and associated products for sale by mail order. Now that the quality of photographs and

Below: *The Internet can give some idea of fish available for sale, but however good the images, this is no substitute for seeing the koi first-hand.*

represent real bargains. If Japanese holding facilities are available, fish can be released in batches to satisfy demand throughout the summer.

Ordinary and middle-grade koi tend to be handled more by wholesalers and buying cooperatives who know the overseas market well. They will offer guaranteed prices to breeders who can consistently supply colorful, healthy stock. These koi are available all year-round, especially in the smaller sizes.

Owners of heated ponds and quarantine tanks can safely buy koi at any time. For the rest, it is better to pay for selected fish and board them with the dealer until outside water temperatures stabilize above 10°C (50°F).

graphics on computers has improved, they have become a very popular form of communication with many of the larger retailers. Koi are described in detail, along with a picture, so that prospective buyers can make an astute choice, even though they have not seen a fish "in the flesh." It enables a would-be buyer to view a classic koi without having to make a long journey, only to be disappointed on arrival at the retailer.

Left: These koi have recovered from the traumas of shipment and are now well-acclimatized to the dealer's pond. They have also been properly quarantined. This is the safest, if not the most exciting, way of buying koi.

Below: The less koi are handled, the better. Here a fish is simply being lifted in the net for a customer — if she wants a closer look, it can be transferred to a viewing bowl or basket.

If the retailer has a known and trusted outlet, buyers may even accept what they have seen or read on their computer and acquire the koi over the web. The fish can then be sent via a courier service for immediate delivery. However, it is worth noting that even the best photographic images can give a misleading impression, so be cautious about buying koi without seeing them first.

With slightly more sophisticated computer technology, your trusted koi retailer can select a fish on your behalf while visiting Japan. Many dealers make seasonal buying trips to Japan and take close-up digital photographs of any exceptional koi they see while visiting a particular koi farm. The photographs are then downloaded onto a computer and emailed across the world to the retail outlet, or even directly to the customer to consider.

Choosing your koi

Until you gain experience, ask a seasoned koi-keeper to accompany you on buying visits. Allow yourself plenty of time and never feel pressured to make a purchase unless you see fish you really want. Even after a period of dealer quarantine, newly imported koi sometimes show minor abrasions and splits in the fins. With correct care, these fish will mend and can be a real bargain, but beginners should stay with unblemished koi.

Many newcomers to the hobby imagine they will save money by buying small koi and growing them. However,

Buying koi checklist

Plus points

- Good body shape and skin quality
- Well-distributed pattern the full length of the body (in varieties such as Showa)
- Clear, well-shaped head
- Fins in proportion to the body
- Bilateral symmetry
- Straight spine
- Good, lively deportment.

Minus points

- Badly split fins; missing fins (usually one of the pelvic fins)
- Reddened vent or raised, angry scales (both signs of bacterial infection)
- Scars or missing scales below the lateral line (not visible when koi is viewed from above)
- Anchor worm (Argulus) parasites
- Fungus
- Broken dorsal and/or pectoral fin rays
- Clamped fins
- Gills not working at the same rate, or too-rapid respiration indicating gill damage
- Damaged/missing eye(s)
- Eroded or reddened barbels
- Listless behavior
- Erratic swimming
- Head-up/head-down position in the water
- Excessively thin body, especially just behind gills
- Rough feel to body (indicating lack of protective mucus)
- Part-missing or outcurled gill covers.

General

Ask whether the fish is male or female (you do not want to pay for a female, only to find it is a male). Closely examine any fish, first in a bowl, then by holding up the bag to examine the underside and to check that all fins are present and correct.

---

although they cost more than babies, fish over 30 cm (12 in) long are hardier and represent a better investment. On a limited budget, it is wiser to buy one sizeable koi rather than three or four youngsters, and build the collection slowly.

When you spot a likely purchase, watch it for a while to see how it behaves. It should swim with an easy, fluid motion in the company of the other koi and not hang near the surface or in the bubbles of a venturi or filter return pipe. Check for slow, regular respiratory movements of the gill covers, and ensure they are both working at the same rate. Other things to look for at this stage are obvious wounds and blemishes, cloudy eyes, external parasites (such as anchor worm or fish lice), raised scales or holes.

Next, ask the dealer to "bowl" the fish for your inspection. Larger koi are gently encouraged to swim into a shallow pan net, then transferred to a tilted, floating bowl or soft-meshed holding net. Smaller ones can be dipped from a vat and bowled using a "koi sock," an open-ended mesh sleeve.

At closer quarters (and preferably in good daylight), double check for wounds and parasites. Ask the dealer to lift one of the koi's gill covers — the gills should be bright red, free of mucus and uncongested. From above, look for any skeletal deformities resulting in kinks in the backbone or tail root, and ensure that the fish deports itself well, using both its pectoral fins.

Ask the dealer about pattern (where this applies) and skin quality; for novices this is a difficult attribute to appreciate. Also find out the name of the variety if you don't already know it — there is no stigma attached to this, and plenty of time to learn.

No koi is perfect. A fish will exhibit good points and bad, although in top-quality koi the merits will increasingly outweigh the faults. However, in the final analysis — and provided the koi is healthy — it's what you like that matters.

Transporting koi

Having made your selection, ask the dealer to bag the fish for you. Before the bag is sealed, lift it up to the light and make one final check on the koi, paying special attention to the belly region. Examine the eyes and barbels, and satisfy yourself that there are no deformities of the mouth and jawbone, a common fault in Showa.

The double or triple bag should contain just enough clean transit water to cover the koi's back, with the remaining space inflated from an oxygen cylinder. For long journeys, the dealer will sometimes add a soothing, mildly antiseptic agent. The bag is then sealed with rubber bands.

Using a koi sock, an open-ended mesh sleeve, is a convenient way of moving koi.

BAGGING YOUR CHOSEN KOI

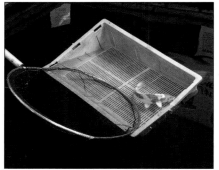

1 This Kujaku has been singled out as a possible purchase. It is gently tipped from a catching net into a floating viewing basket and brought nearer to the prospective buyer for a closer inspection.

2 From above it looks good — blemish-free, good skin and pattern, and it deports well in the basket. Ask questions if you are unsure.

The koi is upended by the dealer so that its underside can be checked, too.

3 When you are satisfied, the dealer will bag the koi, but before the bag is sealed check the koi once again to make sure that all is well.

4 The koi is double-bagged with just enough water to cover its back, while the remainder of the space is taken up by oxygen from a cylinder. It will now go into a polybox for, ideally, a swift journey to its home pond.

Once you have paid for your koi, it becomes your responsibility to get it home safely. Fish travel best in the dark, so wrap the bag in a black plastic bin liner and lay it on its side in a stout cardboard box or, better still, a large polystyrene container with a lid, as used to bring koi into the country. Your dealer may well give you one of these; it is a useful item to carry in the car at all times. The insulating properties of the polybox should maintain an even water temperature during the journey, but on very warm days, one or more coolpacks from the freezer, wrapped in newspaper or a blanket in order not to make direct contact with the polybag, will provide added protection.

If the koi are large, lay the wrapped bags or boxes lengthways across the trunk of the car or behind the front seats where they cannot shift around. That way, if the driver has to brake suddenly, the fish will not bang their noses. Do not carry the boxes in the front footwell or on a passenger's lap, where they will get too warm and be vulnerable in the event of an accident. Avoid unnecessary stops on the journey and drive smoothly, cornering gently and taking the most direct route home.

On arrival, open the bag, roll down the top to form a collar and float it on the surface of the pond or quarantine facility. This is to equalize water temperatures and should take no more than 20 minutes. Gradually adding more water to the bag in the belief that this will acclimatize the fish to any change in pH is pointless; to be of any benefit, this process would take weeks. Koi are far more likely to be damaged by being left too long in their transit water than by any small differences in water chemistry. Open the bag and carefully lift the fish out by hand or use a koi sock if it is too large to handle. Introduce the fish into the pond and discard the water in the bag.

If the fish go into a relatively low-volume quarantine vat, it is important to take an ammonia reading an hour or two later. Koi have a tendency to "dump" ammonia when they are moved from dirty into clean water, and you should perform a large partial water change through a purifier to dilute this toxin. Leave the new arrivals undisturbed, and on no account feed them for a couple of days. If possible, net over the pond or vat, as koi have a tendency to jump until they have become acclimatized to their new surroundings.

Quarantining koi

Before being shipped from Japan, koi are usually taken to special holding facilities near the airport where they are inspected, treated for parasites then rested and fasted for several days before being bagged and boxed ready for the flight. Fasting allows any food to pass through the koi before shipment, thus preventing the water in the transport bags being soiled with feces. Any treatment carried out at this stage will be in addition to any medication the koi may receive on arrival at their final destination. In the past, such treatment may have been deemed sufficient for the koi to be sold by the retailer, but times have changed. Although this may be regarded as a form of quarantine, in essence, it only prevents those koi that are unfit to travel from being exported and reduces the incidence of nuisance parasites, such as fish lice or anchor worm, being shipped with the fish.

Over the years, the issue of whether hobbyists should quarantine newly purchased koi has been hotly debated. Mostly, discussion centered around whether quarantine facilities were either appropriate or suitable and whether a further change in environment via a quarantine system was beneficial or created more stress for the koi. However, the emergence of koi herpesvirus has resulted in a drastic review of the need to quarantine any newly purchased koi. This serious disease has spread worldwide, causing significant mortalities of carp and koi that have come into contact with the virus. Koi-keepers have also been affected as a result of introducing an apparently healthy carrier fish that later infects all the koi in the pond, sometimes killing all of them. One of the problems is that survivors of KHV infection become carriers of the virus. If carrier koi become stressed, the virus can be activated, leading to clinical infection among the koi. Because it is impossible to know whether a koi is carrying the koi herpesvirus it has become imperative to quarantine all new koi, irrespective of how long they have been in the country or whether the retailer has previously quarantined them. In the past, many koi-keepers swapped or gave away koi without quarantining them. Because

KHV is such an insidious disease, this practice must now be regarded as high risk and any koi transferred from one pond to another should be quarantined at temperatures of 18 to 25°C before being introduced to its new home.

It is sensible to buy koi from a single source, but hobbyists are always tempted when a "must have" koi is at another site. Mixing koi from several sources has the potential to allow cross-infection of bacterial disease, such as ulcer disease, to occur amongs stressed fish. If all new koi are subject to quarantine before they are introduced to an existing koi population, it will reduce the risk of unnecessary outbreaks of disease.

Regardless of where koi originate or how expensive they are, there is always the potential for them to be carrying serious bacterial infections or viral diseases. There is no known treatment for any viral disease and bacterial problems are becoming increasingly resistant to antibiotics. Segregating new arrivals gives any latent pathogens time to show themselves. The quarantine period is up to the individual hobbyist; there is no guarantee that a problem will not emerge months or perhaps years later. Some koi-keepers hold fish back from their ponds for up to a year to minimize the risk, whereas others quarantine for just a few weeks. However, the length of quarantine is not the only factor; the care of the koi, the quality of their accommodation and other factors, such as water and temperature, all play a part.

A quarantine facility

The quarantine facility should provide an impeccable pond environment on a small scale — but not too small. Try to envisage the largest koi you are likely to buy and the volume of water you would need to accommodate this fish comfortably. The more swimming space the better. Avoid siting the facility in a garage that is regularly used for parking the car, as fumes from the vehicle are toxic. Beware also of the garage or shed where paints, wood preservatives and other chemicals are stored. These can also produce fumes that are dissolved in the water. Always keep equipment solely for use in the quarantine facility and mark it as such.

Left: *Until you gain experience, ask a seasoned koi-keeper to help you choose your new koi. Observe its behavior in the dealer's pond. It should swim with a fluid motion in the company of other koi.*

Feeding koi

In the summer months, when the pond water temperature is at its peak, there can be few greater pleasures for koi-keepers than to see their koi swarming toward them in their eagerness to feed. Koi begin to feed actively once water temperatures start to exceed 15°C (59°F). Watching the koi while they are feeding is an important part of routine management; observing them but not interfering with them, which might alter their behavior. As they feed, there is time to glance over the body and fins of each fish to ensure that there are no lesions, wounds, ulcers or large parasites, such as anchor worm and fish lice (see pages 96 and 100).

One of the early warning signs that a koi may be sick is a poor appetite at temperatures when others in the pond are hungry and feeding well. It is also important to check that all

Right: Koi are natural bottom-feeders, but giving them floating foods makes them easier to observe. The pectoral fins guide the fish into position. The upper and lower jaws of koi are protrusible and extend to enclose the food particle, which is seen as a sucking action.

the koi are feeding. Sometimes one fish may miss a feed, but eats with a voracious appetite next time it is fed.

A common reason why some koi do not eat is because the feed is too large for them. Always make sure the food is of a size that the smallest koi in the pond can easily swallow. Although the rate at which koi grow is dependent on feeding, other factors, such as temperature, water quality and stocking levels in the pond, can also have an influence. Under optimum temperatures and water conditions, koi in a lightly stocked pond will grow very rapidly.

The koi diet

Koi are omnivorous, which means they will feed on both animal and plant material, although they prefer aquatic insects and larvae. However, few koi ponds contain any planting, as the koi are the main focus of the feature and nothing should detract from them. This absence of plant life, combined with the numbers of koi, means that you must supply a manufactured feed to provide adequate food for all the fish.

The main component of any manufactured feed is protein. Good-quality feeds contain a large amount of protein derived from fish, but the problems of overfishing the seas have impacted on the availability and price of fish meal. It is therefore common to find protein from other sources, including plants such as soya, as well as animal products, incorporated into fish food. Although the protein content of the diet is very important for tissue maintenance, repair and growth, proteins cannot be stored by koi and any excess is

Above: The koi in this pond are greedily taking the food offered to them, and this is the perfect opportunity to check each one for wounds, lesions or larger parasites, such as fish lice or anchor worm.

PELLET FOODS

These large pellets are ideal for feeding to large adult koi.

Medium-sized pellets suit ponds with a range of koi of different sizes.

The smallest pellets are usually given to 1- or 2-year-old koi.

Pellets containing spirulina algae are high in protein and rich in vitamins, minerals and iodine.

excreted, mainly as ammonia, plus a small amount as urine. This is one of the principal reasons why you should feed sparingly. If the pond water is polluted with ammonia, the koi will be stressed by the poor water conditions.

Fatty acids, known more familiarly as "fats," are the second important component of fish food. Generally speaking, fats form an important energy source for koi, as well as helping them to absorb fat-soluble vitamins. Certain fats included in the feed are regarded as "essential," which means that if they were omitted the koi would suffer and show evidence of stunted growth, fin erosion, and liver and heart disorders.

Carbohydrates are also incorporated into the diet. Some may be used for energy, but koi can use the basic components to produce nonessential fatty acids.

Vitamins are essential to life, although they vary greatly in composition. They must be incorporated into the diet, as they are either produced in such small quantities as to be ineffectual or cannot be synthesized from raw ingredients.

Interestingly, some of the vitamins essential for the welfare of koi are produced by bacteria that naturally live in the gut. This is a very good reason to avoid using antibiotic and antimicrobial drugs unless absolutely necessary, as these will also affect the natural, beneficial microbial populations. Although only small amounts of vitamins are required, their absence in the diet — termed "avitaminosis" — leads to a range of diseases and even mortalities.

Many vitamins are rather unstable, and, furthermore, the processing required to produce koi pellets and sticks affects the natural vitamin content of the raw ingredients. To overcome this problem, manufacturers add vitamin supplements to the mixture to ensure that there is more than an adequate amount in the feed (see page 152).

Koi food also contains minerals, including calcium and phosphorus that are important components of bone, and elements such as magnesium, which is needed for metabolism. Sodium and potassium are essential for the normal functioning of nerves and, taken together with chlorine, for osmoregulation (see page 74). Finally, there is an assortment of trace elements, required only in minute

FLOATING STICKS

Wheat germ sticks are ideal for feeding at cooler times of year, such as in the autumn and spring.

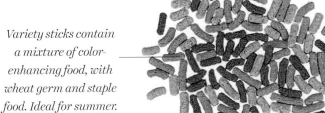

Variety sticks contain a mixture of color-enhancing food, with wheat germ and staple food. Ideal for summer.

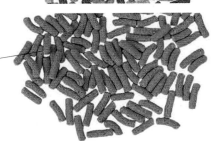

These floating sticks are a staple summer feed, with protein levels suitable for growth and reproduction.

FRESH AND TREAT FOODS

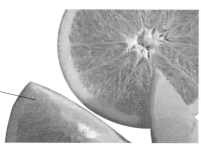

Orange is a good source of vitamin C, which helps to reduce stress and improves the immune system.

Garlic is a real treat for koi, which are attracted to any food coated in it. It can be used to entice them to feed by hand.

Some koi-keepers feed whole lettuce to their koi, which readily shred and eat this treat. It is a rich source of vitamin C and other nutrients.

Bloodworms are available live (the koi prefer these) or frozen (thaw before feeding). Offer bloodworms in summer.

Koi thoroughly enjoy prawns, a good source of protein. Feed these to koi in the summer, when the water temperatures are higher.

Brown bread is a good source of wheat germ and vitamins, but feed it sparingly, as it is rich in carbohydrate.

quantities but nevertheless essential. They include substances such as iron, copper, manganese, zinc and iodine. Although freshwater fish can absorb minerals directly from the water via the gills, the low concentrations of many minerals and trace elements in solution means they must be added to the diet.

You can choose from a range of proprietary koi foods, but when changing from one type of diet to another, always begin by mixing a little of the new food with the original one. Over a period of 7 to 10 days, gradually increase the proportion of new food, while reducing the original feed. Changing suddenly to a new brand or a different type of food often results in the koi refusing to feed.

Additives

Koi are prized for their beautiful color, and dietary additives can enhance the fishes' natural coloration. In summer, it is usual to mix color-enhancing feeds with the diet. These contain shrimp meal and extracts of the algae *Spirulina platensis*, which are considered by the Japanese to enhance the red coloration of koi. Bear in mind, however, that the red color patterns of koi are determined genetically and may not be stable. Although color-enhancing feeds will provide the raw ingredients for the red color, if the red fades, these additives will not have any effect.

Treats and supplements

Koi will relish many extremely beneficial treat foods that provide a source of fresh vitamins and minerals. Lettuce is a great treat for many koi. When you first offer it, shred the leaves and float them in the pond. It only takes a few minutes for the koi to start feeding. Within a few weeks, you can float a whole lettuce on the water and the koi will enjoy tearing pieces off it, leaving just a stub of stalk!

Oranges are another great favorite. Cut them into segments and put these into the pond with the rind left intact. The koi will busily tear away the flesh, leaving the rind. Both lettuce and orange are a valuable source of vitamin C, which is important for growth, tissue repair and reproduction. Once the fish have eaten the lettuce or orange, remove the stalk or rind. Bear in mind that feeding these foods can cause the water clarity to deteriorate for a few days.

Curiously, koi love garlic and a great treat is to coat their food in a little minced garlic! Other treats can include prawns, brown bread and, when available, live foods such as glassworms (insect larvae) and bloodworms. Avoid offering peas and corn, which are not easily digested by koi, and very rich in carbohydrate, which makes the fish excessively fat.

In recent years, there has been a great deal of interest in certain natural supplements that can be added to koi feeds. These are designed to boost the immune system and general health of koi. Some of these supplements are already incorporated into manufactured feeds, but new and more effective products are appearing in powdered form that you can mix with existing feeds. It will not be long before these, too, are incorporated into manufactured feeds.

Seasonal feeding

The amount of food that koi consume varies according to the season. In summer, when they are most active, they feed hungrily and will eat several times each day. With optimum temperatures and food availability, koi grow rapidly in summer, compared with the winter months, when they consume little and growth is very slow. This pattern of rapid growth in the summer and slower growth in the winter is reflected in the rings found on the scales of koi.

Below: These young koi are enjoying a segment of orange, eagerly tearing away the flesh to leave just the peel. Remove the remains of the peel from the pond when all the flesh has been eaten.

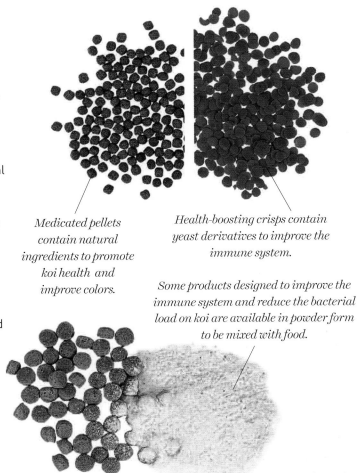

Medicated pellets contain natural ingredients to promote koi health and improve colors.

Health-boosting crisps contain yeast derivatives to improve the immune system.

Some products designed to improve the immune system and reduce the bacterial load on koi are available in powder form to be mixed with food.

Rather like growth rings on a tree, these can be used to assess the age of a koi.

Feeding in summer

The food consumed during the summer is used for energy, tissue maintenance and repair, growth, storage to help the fish through the winter and, in the case of adult koi, to produce eggs or sperm for spawning the following year. When water temperatures are between 18 and 20°C (64–68°F), koi are often fed on high-protein diets designed to promote growth. The efficiency with which koi use protein is dependent on temperature. At 15°C (59°F), they digest about 87 percent of the protein content of the diet, but at 20 to 25°C (68–77°F), they digest 89 percent. The digestibility of protein decreases rapidly under low dissolved oxygen concentrations.

Feeding in autumn and spring

As the water temperature drops in autumn, koi appetites gradually decline. At this time, reduce the amount of food offered to koi and gradually change from a high-protein feed to a wheat germbased diet. Koi digest wheat germ feeds more easily in autumn and spring, when the water temperatures are lower. At temperatures of less than 8 to 10°C (46–50°F), koi cease to feed altogether. Thus, during the coldest periods of the year, koi in an unheated pond will not feed at all. Depending on the water temperature in heated ponds, it is possible for koi to feed all year-round.

Once the water temperature creeps up toward 10°C (50°F)

ESTIMATING KOI WEIGHT

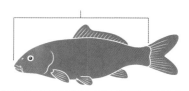

Use this graph to estimate the weight of your koi. Females full of eggs may weigh more than indicated.

Measure body length, not including the tail.

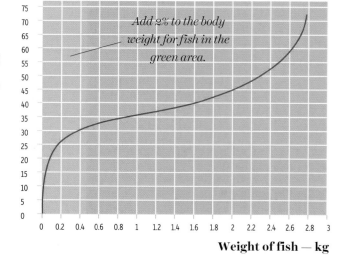

Add 2% to the body weight for fish in the green area.

Length of fish — cm

Weight of fish — kg

with the onset of spring, koi will again begin looking for food. Offer them wheat germ feeds, gradually mixed with the summer feed as the water warms up.

How much food is enough?

How much and how often to feed koi are common questions. Technically, baby koi (koi fry and fish up to 1 year old) will eat 5 to 10 percent of their body weight daily, when the water temperature is about 20°C (68°F). At these temperatures, juvenile koi consume about 5 percent, and sexually mature koi — as a guide fish that are 3 or more years old — will consume 2 percent of their body weight each day. This means that at 20°C (68°F), an adult koi weighing 1 kg (2.2 lb) should be consuming 20 g (0.7 oz) of food on a daily basis.

At low temperatures — 10–15°C (50–59°F) — koi will usually only require feeding once each day. As the water temperature rises, increase the frequency of feeding to two or three times a day at 20°C (68°F). Generally speaking, offer koi as much as they will consume within 2 or 3 minutes at each feed. When the feed is given, there is an initial surge of activity among the koi, but as they each get sufficient to eat, they feed more lazily. The point at which they begin to feed more casually is the moment to stop adding more food, and this really takes just a few minutes. It is better to feed sparingly but frequently, and to offer more food only if it is consumed very quickly, rather than to add too much. Excess food will not necessarily harm the koi, but it is not digested efficiently. It is simply voided as waste and places a burden on the filtration system. Remove uneaten food from the pond, otherwise this also becomes a source of ammonia pollution.

Below: These scales provide a quick way of working out how much your koi should be eating per day at 20°C (68°F). Simply compare the total koi weight with the feeding scale.

DAILY FOOD CONSUMPTION AT 20°C (68°F)

Total weight of fish — kg

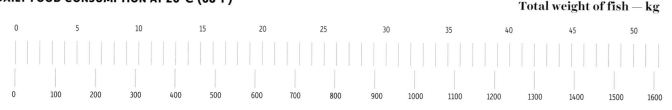

Weight of food per day — g

Many koi shows take place during the summer months and to prevent serious pollution problems in the show vat, it is a good idea to exhibit fish in a fasted state. Once again, in the 14 days leading up to the show, gradually reduce the amount of food offered until at 3 or 4 days before the event, the koi are not feeding on manufactured foods. However, they will continue to find insects, larvae and even blanketweed in the pond.

Feeding by hand

Many koi-keepers are very keen to encourage their koi to take food from their hand, but this requires patience and perseverance. Feed the koi from the same place each time and wait by the pond until they have finished feeding. Gradually approach them more closely until they associate you with feeding. Include a few treat foods, such as prawns or brown bread, and hold them very still in the water until the koi approach. On the first few occasions when they attempt to take the food from your hand, it is very likely that they will splash you in their eagerness to grab the treat. In time, the koi will associate you with feeding and become more relaxed about taking a treat or food from your hand. Certain varieties of koi, notably Chagoi and Ochiba Shigure, are renowned for being more "friendly." It can certainly speed the process if one koi is willing to feed by hand, as this encourages the others to do likewise.

Buying and storing feed

One of the commonest mistakes made with koi food is to buy in bulk and use the same batch of food for several months. Although food manufacturers go to great lengths to ensure a more-than-adequate vitamin content, once the bag has been opened and exposed to both air and light, the vitamins are rapidly lost. A bag of feed will lose almost half its vitamin content within a month of being opened and from then on, the vitamins deteriorate even more rapidly. In terms of providing koi with a balanced diet containing an adequate vitamin content, it is more economical to buy smaller amounts of food and use them within 3 or 4 weeks than to buy a single, large bag of food to last all summer. Similarly, you should discard any leftover wheat germ feed at the end of autumn or spring and buy a new supply when you recommence feeding with this diet.

Always store fish food in a dark, dry place and preferably in an airtight container, as this helps to reduce the vitamin loss. Damp food will encourage a range of molds to form, many of which are extremely poisonous to fish. Always discard any food that has come into contact with water.

Above: *Sometimes it takes the introduction of a variety such as Chagoi (shown here), which have a particularly amiable nature and are less wary, to start feeding by hand and it does not take long before the others are encouraged to follow suit.*

Vacation periods

Vacations may disrupt the feeding patterns of koi for a short period in the summer. Ideally, ask someone to check the pond on a daily basis to ensure that the pumps, filters and aeration systems are running. At the same time, they can feed the koi sparingly. If the visitor is not a fishkeeper, prepare daily rations for them to feed to the fish. Clearly, it is sensible not to disrupt feeding too much in the summer, but if this is unavoidable, take the following steps. In the 2 weeks before your vacation, gradually offer the koi decreasing amounts of food until the day of departure, when you offer no food. The koi will survive for 2 weeks. On your return, feed them sparingly at first and gradually increase the amount of food offered until you return to normal feeding levels.

Showing koi

Whether or not to show your koi is a decision that only you can make. On one hand, scooping an award at a major national event will confirm what you already suspected — that your fish can compete and win against the best in the country! Real satisfaction comes from knowing that your skills in choosing and then bringing koi into peak condition have been recognized by experienced judges. On the other hand, showing koi subjects the fish to the disruption of travel from home pond to show venue and back again. Furthermore, once the fish have been benched and introduced into their vats, responsibility for their welfare throughout the show is largely taken out of your hands. Problems do occasionally arise — with water quality, for example — and the mark of a well-run show is how quickly and effectively these are pinpointed and dealt with. Organizers understand that any question over the fish-health issue will keep exhibitors away and, as a result, show-running standards are probably higher today than at any time in the past.

Below: The public always like to pit their wits against the judges, but although they can get a good view of the fish, only the judges are allowed behind the barrier. In this "English" or "Western" show format, each competitor's koi are housed together in the same vat(s) throughout the event.

This chapter starts with a guide to preparing fish for a show to give them the best chance of success, and also covers transport to and from the event. The various types of show are also described.

Preparing for a show

The natural attributes of a show-quality koi can be enhanced or ruined by the way it is cared for. Judges are not only looking for koi that represent excellent examples of their variety, but fish that literally shine with health. There is no point in submitting a koi with any suspicion of disease, major damage, deformity or parasitic infestation; such faults will automatically disqualify it at the benching stage, and you will have had a wasted journey and gone down in the estimation of your fellow competitors.

Some koi never give of their best at shows. In their home pond they look fine, but subject them to the stress of netting and unfamiliar surroundings and their white skin reddens up as tiny capillary blood vessels rupture. Only experience will tell you whether any of your koi fall into this category.

However careful you are, large koi in particular can suffer minor damage in transit. This may take the form of a rubbed nose or a slightly split fin. Although the benching team will probably still allow the fish in, you should ask yourself whether that koi would be better off going straight back home. Remember, you have the option at any time during a show of withdrawing a fish you suspect to be in trouble.

Seasoned koi exhibitors may attend many events during the year, but do not necessarily take the same fish along to every one. It is better to have a "show pool" of likely candidates, so that while some are on the circuit, others are resting.

The size of a koi can boost or diminish its likelihood of success. For example, in UK shows run by the BKKS (British

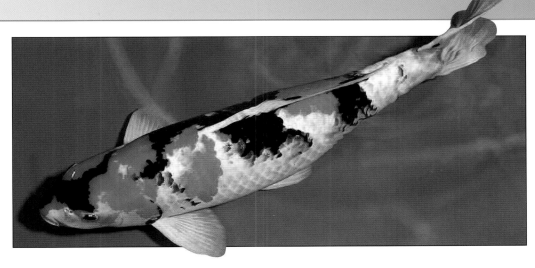

Left: It doesn't matter how good a koi may be, if it reacts badly to showing, there is little point in taking it along. This Showa, for example, has reddening of the white skin caused by stress-rupture of capillary blood vessels. Other koi may not deport themselves well, or their colors may fade.

Koi Keepers Society), there are seven size categories: Size 1: up to 20 cm (8 in); Size 2: 20 to 30 cm (8–12 in); Size 3: 30 to 40 cm (12–16 in); Size 4: 40 to 50 cm (16–20 in); Size 5: 50 to 60 cm (20–24 in); Size 6: 60 to 70 cm (24–28 in); Size 7: 70 cm (28 in) and above. This means that a koi measuring 53.34 cm (21 in), entered in Size 5 could well be up against fish almost 7.5 cm (3 in) longer than itself. Koi-keepers know to rest these "in-between" fish until they have grown enough to give themselves a realistic chance. Koi kept in heated ponds grow quickly, which for show purposes is a definite "plus." It means they will be eligible for entry into the larger size categories while they are only 4 or 5 years old and still retain the excellent skin quality of youth.

In the run-up period to a show there are several things (besides the obvious attention to good diet and water quality) that you can do to give koi that extra sparkle. Adding montmorillonite clay to food or directly to the pond replenishes essential minerals lost as water ages. Installing an automatic feeder to dispense regular small meals during the day optimizes growth and puts less strain on the filter than

When using montmorillonite clay, disperse it into a bucket of pond water before introducing it into the surface skimmer.

Below: *Regular meals of color-enhancing pellets delivered through an auto-feeder are a good preshow tactic. Follow this by a period of fasting (see page 155).*

Above: *Fresh "treat" foods, such as lettuce, may just give show koi that extra edge. In any event, it makes sense to offer them a varied diet, and something they have to "work for."*

one or two large offerings heaped in morning and evening. Top-grade color food, supplementing the normal rations 2 or 3 weeks before showing, enhances hi (red) and sumi (black), and some koi-keepers swear by natural food items, such as prawns, earthworms, lettuce and fresh orange segments, to get their fish "buzzing." All this will stand the koi in good stead for the fasting period leading up the show. This is essential if the fish are not to pollute their transit water or the vats in which they will be held.

Taking koi to and from shows

When you buy a koi from a dealer it is double-bagged with oxygen and taken home without delay. The same procedure applies with fish taken to a show, except that now you have to provide all the necessary equipment for the outgoing and return journeys. Luxury travel accommodation, sometimes offered by dealers (who will gain kudos if fish they supply win major awards), consists of a free-standing vat of soft opaque plastic with a zipped lid, and equipped with one or more shielded airstones fed from a regulated oxygen cylinder. The koi cannot damage themselves or jump out, and arrive unstressed at the show. Keen hobbyists can make their own version of this, but for most, the ubiquitous plastic bag is perfectly adequate.

Nets and baskets

There are a number of points to consider when choosing a net. The pole and head combined should be at least 90 cm (36 in) deeper than the pond, otherwise it will be very difficult to maneuvre in the water. The pole itself must be made from a strong but lightweight material, such as wood or aluminum. Plastic and carbon-fiber handles have a tendency to bend and can be difficult to handle at full stretch. Wooden handles are very easy to maneuvre, as they are buoyant in the water. Although aluminium handles are heavier, they have the added advantage of being telescopic and will extend from 1.8–3.7 m (6–12 ft), and the pole can be locked at any position in between.

The net heads are generally circular and available in 45, 50, 60 and 75 cm (18, 20, 24 and 30 in) diameters. The netting is made from nylon and should be reasonably fine so that a fish's fins do not get caught up. Choose a shallow pan net, as deeper nets tend to create "drag" and are heavy in the water.

A floating koi basket is useful for transferring a fish into, so you can examine it closely without it thrashing around in the net. The basket is supplied complete with a lid, which can be secured by a locking pin to prevent the fish escaping and injuring itself.

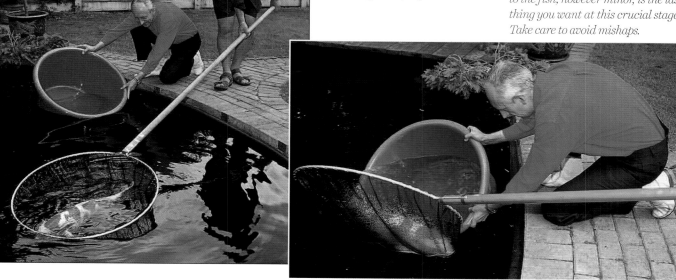

Left: *Having been selected to compete in a show, this large koi is gently netted. Some fish get used to the procedure and actually swim into the net. Others may resist; be patient.*

Below: *The koi is gently transferred from the net to a floating bowl for a final check before being bagged for transportation to the show. Damage to the fish, however minor, is the last thing you want at this crucial stage. Take care to avoid mishaps.*

Right: *Using a koi "sock" means that the fish is never directly handled. The koi is always released head-first through the open end of the fine-mesh sleeve, in order not to damage its scales or fins.*

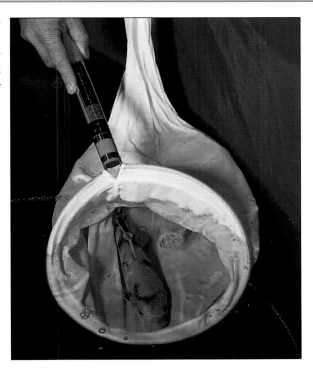

When you are ready to catch your fish, put a floating basket or bowl in the water and switch off all pumps so that you can get a good view. Once you lower the net into the water, the fish become very nervous and descend to the bottom to avoid being caught. It is important to move the net very slowly and avoid chasing the fish around, as you may inadvertently catch an innocent fish with the rim, resulting in an ulcer at a later date. Slowly tease the intended catch into an area from which it cannot escape, such as a corner of the pond or a shallow area. Gently move closer to the fish as it swims away from you toward the pond wall and just as it makes a turn, try to catch it in the center of the net. With the fish in the net, begin to raise the net to the surface and try to keep the fish's nose facing into the net. If it looks toward the rim, it will see an opportunity to escape and jump out. If this does happen, do not try to stop it escaping; let it go and try again, because all the thrashing around may cause an injury. Once the fish is near the surface, never lift it out of the water into the basket as it will flap around in the net and could lose scales or split its fins. Tip the floating basket or bowl with the rim of the net so that the edge is below the water level and coax the fish in. As you carefully remove the net, the basket will float up and the fish is safely landed.

Catch your koi as near to the time of departure as possible, so they spend the minimum time in confinement. Double or even triple bags are insurance against springing a leak. Unless the koi are very small, bag up each one separately. Various chemicals can be added to the transit water to calm the koi and neutralize ammonia excreted through their gills.

Add only enough clean pond water to cover the fishes' backs when the bags are laid on their side, then fill the rest of the space with oxygen. You will need to take your own cylinder along to the show, as you cannot rely on one being available there. Never blow into the bag to inflate it; instead of oxygen, the fish will have a suffocating layer of carbon dioxide above them.

Secure the bags with strong rubber bands, and make sure you have plenty of spares. Pack the koi securely in light-tight polystyrene fish boxes and make sure these will not slide around during the journey. Work out the shortest route to the show and make as few stops as possible on the way.

When the show is over and the debenching team has allowed you access to your koi, the bagging process is repeated. Take along your own koi sock to catch your fish from the net, rather than try to lift them bodily; both you and the fish will be tired by now, and accidents can happen when the ground underfoot is soaking wet.

On arrival back home, some koi-keepers give their fish a short salt bath, whereas others put them straight into the pond. Either way, watch the koi especially carefully for a few days after the show, notably for signs of white spot, which can be triggered by heating or cooling of vat water. Organizers try to maintain a steady temperature, but variations are bound to occur when water changes are made, or if vats (however well-shaded) are exposed to the sun. You should also test your pond for ammonia an hour or two after the show fish have returned, as bagged fish have a tendency to dump this toxin on their release.

Types of show

Interest in showing koi is usually kindled at club level, as it will indicate how well you are selecting and looking after your fish. Visiting other members' ponds will give you some idea, but there is a big difference between competition and mere speculation on your part.

Club shows can either be closed, with entry restricted to members' fish alone, or open to outsiders. Depending on

Left: A benching team at work. Koi are being transferred from their transit bags into the show vats and classified according to size and variety.

Below: Whenever a fish's eligibility for a particular size category is in question, the issue is settled by measuring it from nose to tail extremities against a scale marked on the side of the floating basket.

committee policy, or the association to which the club may be affiliated, the show can be Japanese or Western-style. The difference is described below. The organizers will decide which method to choose and advise entrants in advance. Size and variety classifications may also vary from show to show, taking into account the koi being put forward.

A typical Western-style show

The flagship koi show in the UK is the BKKS National, held annually in Western style. It is open to all koi-keepers, whether or not they belong to the Society. Entries must be booked several weeks in advance, so that the organizers can allocate vats and collect competition fees. On arrival at the venue, ideally on the Friday afternoon prior to the show weekend or, failing that, early on Saturday before the public are admitted, koi-keepers report to an official who checks their names off against the exhibitors' list and allocates a vat number. The fish are then carried in their unopened transit bags to the center ring and floated for up to 30 minutes in their vat until water temperatures have equalized. Then they are released.

On the first morning of the actual show, the benching team arrive to ensure that the fish are in sufficiently good health to compete, and then to categorize them according to size and variety. These volunteers play no part in the judging. The koi are measured in a floating basket marked with a scale. The process takes only seconds, with an experienced member of the benching team holding the koi gently against the scale. If a fish is a borderline case between size categories, the owner

has the right to ask for it to be remeasured. At the same time, the variety is noted down from a standard list of 13 possible show classes and the koi is cross-referenced to its vat number and photographed. These days, Polaroid cameras have been superseded by digital technology and the pictures are fed into a centralized computer that processes the results as they come through. The koi-keeper signs the benching form and keeps a copy, which is his proof of ownership of the fish.

With the benching completed, judging can begin. At a BKKS show, this is conducted by a team recruited and trained by the Judging and Standards Committee (JSC). Normally, one full and one trainee judge work in pairs, the more experienced of the two controlling the decisions. In the event of any dispute relating to variety or eligibility of a fish for showing, the final word rests with the senior judge on the day.

Initially, judges select first and second places in each of the seven sizes and 13 classifications, or as many as are possible from the entries — often there are gaps. From these are chosen first, second and third in all sizes, irrespective of variety. The next stage is to choose from this short list of up to 39 koi a Baby Champion (Sizes 1 and 2), Adult Champion (Sizes 3 and 4) and Mature Champion (Sizes 5, 6 and 7). These three are all possible contenders for the Grand Champion award, although in practice a baby koi almost never wins this, because it takes special skills to grow a koi on and still retain good body shape, skin quality and pattern. It is not "done" to talk to the officials while they are judging, but after the results are announced there is no harm in asking them how they arrived at their decisions.

As in Japan, the premier award tends to go to a Go Sanke (Kohaku, Sanke or Showa), which is no reflection on the quality of fish in the other 10 classifications. In some UK shows, additional awards may be made for Best Tategoi (koi with the most potential to improve), Best Home-bred Koi and Best Jumbo (the largest koi benched). The Jumbo award is the only one dependent on size alone.

Throughout the show, the vats should be continually tested for ammonia and falling pH, vacuumed to remove solids and part water-changed. A watch is also kept on dissolved oxygen levels, and spectators are discouraged from dipping their fingers in the water, kicking the vats or doing anything that might jeopardize the fish. Security vigils are mounted during the night, as many of the koi are extremely valuable.

On Sunday the results are known and posted and then the public can admire the winning koi. Prize presentations take place at the end of the day, after which competitors reclaim their fish, bag them up and take them home without delay.

Japanese shows

In Japanese-style shows, at whatever level, koi of the same size and variety are grouped in the same vat, irrespective of who owns them, and can be moved several times as judging progresses. This enables direct visual comparisons to be made between fish of very similar quality, which speeds the whole judging process and arguably makes for a fairer result.

Left: From the awards posted around the vat, this competitor's koi have fared rather well! Note the heavy aeration, which is only turned off briefly while the fish are being judged or for the benefit of photographers at the show.

Above: At a provincial English koi show, a senior judge works with a trainee so that the less experienced member of the team can be instructed and continuously assessed. Becoming a full judge can take 3 years or more.

Left: Booking in koi at the All-Japan Show near Tokyo is carried out with production line efficiency. Dealers help out with this task.

Right: Same size, but different varieties — the Japanese show format is easiest on the judges.

Right: Koi are taken to their show vats in wheeled trolleys such as this, and rarely is a drop of water spilled on the way.

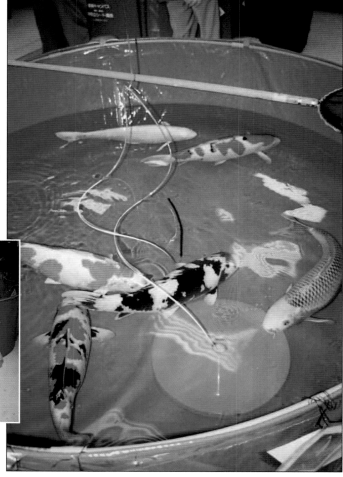

The All-Japan Show

This premier indoor event in the koi calendar takes place in January on the outskirts of Tokyo. Organizers are the All Japan Nishikigoi Dealers Association and the Zen Nippon Airinkai, who have affiliated chapters worldwide. The 5-day show is open to all koi-keepers, amateur and professional, but fish must be entered by the dealers, who also carry out benching duties and generally help out. Variety groupings are much the same as in the UK, except that the Japanese have separate categories for Doitsu koi and Goshiki. However, there are many more size groups and, in recognition of the physical differences between male and female koi, from Size 10 (55.88–60 cm/22–24 in) upward the sexes are judged independently of one another.

The judges, including dealer guests from abroad, select first and second in all sizes and varieties, the top fish joining others in their size in a separate vat. From these are picked the winners of each size, irrespective of variety. These koi are known as "Kokugyo." The penultimate stage is to award a Grand Prize in five size groupings — Baby Koi (Yogyo), Young Koi (Wakagoi), Adult Koi (Sogyu), Mature Koi (Seigyo) and Jumbo (Kyogoi). These then move to yet another vat, from which the Grand Champion is selected. To stand any chance at all, this fish must measure 80 cm (32 in) or more. Improving the growth rate and ultimate size of their koi is a primary aim of modern breeders, so more and more quality Jumbo-sized koi are in contention at the All-Japan Show.

Alternative show formats

The Japanese way does carry with it the slight risk of cross-infection of disease, hence the Western-style show. Here, all the koi belonging to one exhibitor remain in their own vat for the duration of the show. Western-style showing requires more vats, water reserves and a considerable amount of walking back and forth by the judges as they compare the koi. Following disease scares of spring viremia of carp virus (SVC) and Koi herpesvirus (KHV, page 130), more clubs are opting for the photographic show format.

Here, the koi never leave their home ponds, but a team of judges visits each entrant, bowls their koi, makes notes and takes photographs. Once all the ponds have been visited, the judges decide the winners. Internet koi shows allow hobbyists to compete directly with koi keepers worldwide, without the fish leaving their home. A koi club can host the entrants' pictures on a website and the judges can then view the pictures. Alternatively, the koi pictures are sent directly to the judges, who post their decision on the Internet.

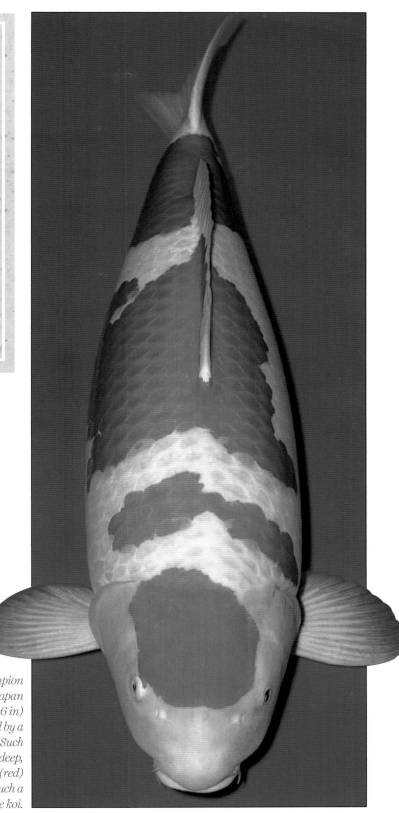

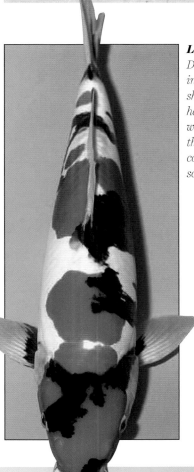

Left: *A 40 cm (16 in) Doitsu Showa entered in the 2001 All-Japan show. Doitsu fish there have their own classes, which is probably fairer than expecting them to compete against fully scaled koi.*

Right: *Grand Champion of the 2001 All-Japan show, a 90 cm (36 in) Kohaku owned by a Taiwanese hobbyist. Such youthful skin and deep, clearly-defined hi (red) are exceptional in such a large koi.*

Breeding koi

Breeding high-grade koi is a very complex subject that has intrigued breeders for centuries. In this chapter we enter the magical world of the famous Japanese breeders to find out how they perform miracles every season to produce bountiful selections of fantastic Nishikigoi. We then go on to see how we can put this knowledge into good practice to improve the breeding of the koi in our own ponds.

Left to their own devices and given the right conditions, koi will naturally spawn in late spring or early summer. The art of the professional fish farmer/breeder is to breed a particular variety of koi regularly and with consistent results. Hopefully, after successive spawnings over a number of seasons, a perfect specimen will have evolved. As in the case of many prized animals, such as cats, dogs and horses, a pedigree line is developed. This entails a broodstock of near-perfect males and females, brought together simply for the process of procreating and producing the perfect offspring. The same principles relate to the breeding of high-grade Nishikigoi.

Below: *A terraced mud pond in Japan. Similar ponds all over the Niigata region are infused with natural montmorillionite clay, allowing small fry and Tategoi to grow on at amazing rates in summer. Producing high-grade koi is a lucrative industry.*

Breeding Nishikigoi in Japan

Although koi are bred successfully in the Far East, Israel, South Africa, the United States and Europe, Japan is still the home of Nishikigoi, so we will examine the success story of the breeders there.

Several areas in Japan are important for the high-grade koi they produce, notably Hiroshima, Shizuoka, Saitama, Toyama and Kyushu, but the prefecture of Niigata remains by far the most distinguished. Here you will find many well-known resident Nishikigoi breeders and their fish. Kawasawa, Shinoda, Hosokai and Dainichi read like names from a "Who's Who" of koi-breeders.

Modern koi-breeders, even those following in their father's footsteps, have probably studied fish farming at university and traveled the world, learning the complexities of fish genetics and breeding methods. Fish farming in Japan does not only mean the breeding, subsequent spawning and growing on of a breeder's own fry. Some farmers just buy koi fry or even the eggs and grow them on in their own stock mud ponds. This is not cheating, but purely a practical answer to the lack of space for growing on prized koi from the top breeders.

Although the mud ponds are vast and hold enormous stocks of koi, they are only available during the summer growing period. The ponds are emptied during the October harvest and do not contain any stock until the following May. All stock is brought down to the breeders' winter holding facilities, which are usually located near their homes. The koi are then over-wintered in purpose-built, greenhouse-style facilities that contain many huge ponds for bringing on their prized new-season Tategoi (certain fish chosen by the breeder for their prospective potential) and their broodstock.

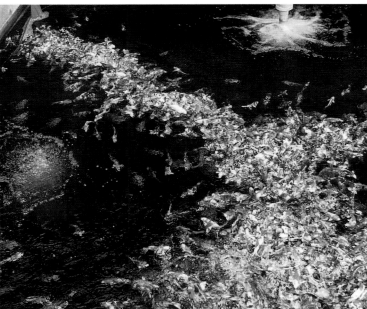

Left: *Yamabuki Ogons in a typical overwintering pond. The ponds are filled to capacity for the winter and many of the koi are sold off during the spring harvest. The Tategoi are retained before being returned to the mud ponds to improve in color and size.*

Above: *Thousands of Kohaku in an indoor holding pond. The koi literally climb over one another the moment they sense someone close by, hoping for a feed. Note the paddle machine at the top of the picture; it agitates the water, forcing in much-needed oxygen.*

Japan and koi breeding are synonymous with the famous "mud ponds" in which young fry and Tategoi are grown on. These man-made ponds are sited on hillsides close to the paddy fields that they once served. These days, far more money is made selling Nishikigoi around the globe than from a kilo of rice! New ponds are dug with excavators, the clay is tamped down by machine to make them impregnable to water and smoothed off for the benefit of the koi and the ease of netting them later. The ponds vary in size, but range from 60 m^2 (646 ft^2) to many hectares, while the depth usually depends on the size of fish being grown on; up to 1 m (39 in) for fry, to over 3 m (10 ft) for the larger fish. Stocking levels for these ponds range from 8,000 to 15,000 fry/100 kiloliters (22,000 gallons) of pond water. This level of stocking allows for up to four culls throughout the summer growing season.

The summers in Japan are extremely warm (above 30°C/86°F), which means that the ponds need heavy aeration. This is achieved using large compressors or paddle-type machines that agitate the water surface. Both methods force air, or dissolved oxygen — the best aeration possible — into the water.

There is only one predator of koi (other than man) that causes problems for the breeder. The indomitable heron is a problem in Japan, just as it is in the rest of the world. Both the tried and tested nylon line and elevated moving scarecrows are used to deter herons from the moment the mud ponds are stocked.

Preparing the mud ponds

In early spring the mud ponds are drained off and allowed to dry out. The ponds are then rotavated and pure lime is added to the mud. The lime not only kills off any parasites that may

THE KOI HARVEST

Left: *A very large natural mud pond being filled with water before the new season's koi are added. The mud allows the koi to root around on the bottom in search of food. This is a natural tendency in the whole of the carp family.*

Right: *When it is time to harvest the large koi, the mud pond is netted and the koi are drawn toward the bankside. Helpers enter the water in giant waders to help catch the prize fish by hand. The fish are then placed into floating baskets to await transport.*

Above: *Having been removed from the floating baskets, the large koi are transferred into containers that are lifted onto trucks. The koi are then transported to nearby indoor holding ponds for sale or overwintering.*

be lurking in the mud, but also helps to increase the pH of the very acid, natural spring water from the mountains that is used to refill the pond. The breeder then adds phosphates and minerals to the pond base before it is tamped down again, ready for refilling. As well as being very acid, the spring water also has a high mineral content, so the water in the pond tends to turn green very quickly.

A few days before spawning, chicken manure is added to the mud ponds and this produces millions of natural infusoria (a class of protozoa — a minute, waterborne life form) and an essential food for young fry. The newly hatched fry require vast amounts of infusoria to sustain their growth rate from day one. Tategoi also enjoy this diet when they are returned to the new season's refreshed mud ponds, having been overwintered in the indoor ponds.

Meanwhile, the indoor spawning pools are also made ready. They are drained down and cleaned thoroughly, and the filters replenished with new oyster shells that help to raise the pH of the water. The pools are then refilled with exactly the same

fresh spring water as the mud ponds. The broodstock, known as Oyagoi, are selected and placed in separate pools, one for males, the other for females.

Preparing for spawning

During May, the pools are prepared for the actual spawning. A large rectangular spawning net about 1 m (39 in) deep is suspended within the pool to prevent the mating koi from damaging themselves on the sides of the pool. Soft, artificial spawning grass (kin-ran) is then attached to the bottom of the net to induce spawning. In June, the brood koi are introduced to the spawning pool. Mature females (over 5 years old) and males (over 4 years old) are normally used for breeding. Experience has shown that younger females do not produce sufficient eggs, while males do not produce sufficient milt (sperm) to fertilize all the eggs, making a spawning commercially uneconomical.

For a natural spawning, one female is introduced to three males. In general, spawning takes place within two days of the fish being placed in the pool. With the help of the net and artificial grass to improve the breeding environment, the female drops her eggs, which are immediately fertilized by the male. The ambient water temperature should be about 17°C (62°F). Spawning nearly always occurs very early in the morning and takes between 5 and 9 hours to complete. A mature female can shed up to 400,000 eggs at one spawning. A member of the breeding team is always available during the mating process to oversee "fair play" and check on the female's condition. The parents are quickly removed from the pool to an outside mud pond to recuperate and to prevent them devouring their offspring.

The pool with the newly hatched eggs is then treated with a mild solution of malachite green to prevent fungal infection *(Saprolegnia)* affecting the eggs. After spawning, the water quality of the pool is constantly checked for ammonia, nitrite and oxygen levels, and, where necessary, spring water is continuously trickled into the pool, creating a gentle but constant water change. Heavy aeration is maintained at all times to produce the high dissolved oxygen levels required. Depending on the water temperature, the eggs hatch in 3 to 5 days.

The fry

After hatching, the fry resemble tiny transparent slivers with eyes and a yolk sac. At first, they live off the yolk sac, and their swimbladder gradually inflates, but within a day they become horizontal in the water and free-swimming. Now the fry are about 7 mm (0.28 in) long and appear pale yellow. They are soon darting around in short bursts, hunting for food. At this stage, they are carefully transported to the enriched waters of the mud ponds to grow on during the summer season.

The first cull takes place a few weeks later. The mud pond is carefully harvested, using huge, fine nets to avoid damaging the stock. About 80 percent of the stock — fish with deformities, or specimens showing poor color, size and shape — are culled. The rest — those already showing signs of good color or pattern — are retained. By this time, they are about 1.25 cm (0.5 in) long.

In late July, when the fry are about 2.5 cm (1 in) long, a further cull takes place. This time, about 50 percent of the fry are retained and their food is supplemented with powdered fry food, suspended in baskets in and around the ponds. The third cull takes place toward the end of August, when about 60 percent of the fry are retained for growing on and the rest are destroyed. The baby koi, now approximately 5 cm (2 in) long, are fed mainly on pelleted food. During late October, when the fish reach about 10 cm (4 in), the mud ponds are completely harvested. Now only the best Tosai koi (less than 1 year old) are finally selected for growing on in the indoor winter ponds, some of which are heated. A further 30 percent are destroyed and the rest are sold off very cheaply, mainly at auction. These are the koi that are sometimes grown on in countries such as Thailand and Taiwan and sold cheaply around the world as Japanese-bred koi. You can now appreciate why the quality of koi to come out of Japan is so high; every fish will have survived as many as four separate culls, purely on merit.

Above: *Hand-selecting Tosai (1-year-old) koi for a prospective customer. Each transaction involves a certain amount of bartering, adding or removing a certain Tategoi from a consignment to achieve the right price.*

Artificial spawning methods

Some countries outside Japan spawn koi to order, using hormone injections of gonadotropin (removed from the pituitary gland of donor wild carp) to induce an almost instant spawning. The method is widely used throughout the world for the mass production of fish destined for the food market, such as trout and salmon. However, Japanese Nishikigoi breeders frown on this process, which they consider poses a risk to their valuable broodstock, and because the natural method still produces more fry than they can economically handle.

Other spawning methods employed in modern koi breeding include "chipping." Here, the parent male and female are tagged with a microchip placed just beneath their scales. The fish can then be readily identified within a breeding program to ensure it "throws true" when attempting to breed a specific variety. This is a term used in breeding programs to describe the offspring from a particular spawning. If the subsequent progeny are identical to the parent (even in the case of cross-breeding — a planned new variety) and have not produced any "throw-backs" (fish varieties of unknown origin and parentage), then the offspring are said to have "thrown true." The information is collated and used for subsequent spawning to achieve the perfect progeny.

Above: *Flock spawning in progress. The males coerce the female into a corner and encourage her to spawn in the blanketweed. The eggs are transferred from the algae (left) to a holding facility before the parents eat them.*

Breeding your own koi

Breeding your own koi can be the culmination of a dream. There is nothing quite like the achievement of bringing a living creature into the world and being involved in its development; in the case of koi, this means from the moment the egg hatches until it grows to full maturity. The following will enable you to tread in the steps of the revered Japanese breeders and perhaps even produce a winner in your local Open Koi Show. However, you should not take the breeding process too seriously. Expense dictates that you will not be able to match the "big boys" from Japan. Even on a very small scale, koi breeding is not cheap, either in terms of money or time, but it is still a very worthwhile experience.

Natural spawning

Koi are oviparous breeders, which means they lay eggs. Once shed, the eggs fall to the bottom or surrounds of the pond and stick to any plant matter or other object in the pond, thanks to a sticky secretion on the outer surface. The survival of the fittest begins right away; remember, only the strongest, but not necessarily the best, will survive.

Koi will spawn naturally, given the ideal water conditions and a temperature of 17°C (62°F) or higher. As the water temperature rises in spring, be prepared for the fish to spawn "en masse." This is known as a flock spawning and can produce many koi, but their quality will leave much to be desired. The size, color and patterns of these koi will be generally poor, although they may be perfectly healthy.

Sexing koi

Koi-keepers often ask, "How do I tell the sex of my koi?" The answer is that even a professional breeder finds it very difficult to sex small koi. As a general rule, koi measuring less than 25 cm (10 in) are presumed to be sexually immature,

Basic genetics

A koi will receive one gene from each parent for each characteristic. It cannot receive two genes from one and none from the other. If you mate a scaled koi with a scaleless (Doitsu) koi, you might expect to produce some of each type, but this is not always the case. One gene can mask the other completely — known as a *dominant* gene masking a *recessive* one. When breeding a particular variety of koi, you must first select suitable broodstock

(parent fish). Like the breeders in Japan, select one suitable female to at least three males to ensure a successful spawning. The chosen parents, both male and female, need not be perfect in every respect (variety, color, shape, deportment, etc.). If you require good color, then select a koi for that feature alone; the fish's other attributes can be secondary. Over several seasons, you will be able to introduce all the prime features into the offspring.

but once past this stage, the sexual organs begin to develop. Mature females are generally plumper in the belly region, whereas mature males tend to be more sylph-like and narrow-bodied when viewed from above. In male koi, the pectoral fins are usually longer, and the ventral fins are longer and more pointed than in females.

When males are ready to spawn, fine, white, raised spots called tubercles appear on the head, gill plates and the leading edges of the pectoral fins. They resemble grains of salt and are often mistaken for — and treated as — white spot (Ichthyophthirius) by the inexperienced koi-keeper, so it is vital to appreciate the difference. The tubercles are most prolific on the pectoral fins, where they occur in fairly regular rows and feel slightly rough. The male uses them during breeding, when he constantly nudges and chases the female to induce spawning.

Having sexed suitable koi, it is best to separate the males from the females in early spring, before any spawning activity takes place. (See also page 127.)

Planning for spawning

There is obviously an advantage to planning a spawning, so that you can control when your fish will mate. By having everything ready for a planned spawning you can start to develop your own strain of koi in your own breeding facility.

If you can divide your pond into sections using floating net cages, so much the better. If this is not feasible, you will need a separate breeding tank. Use either system before the actual spawning to keep the males and females totally separate.

You can make temporary net cages from very fine net curtain material draped over and tied to solid 40 mm (1.5 in) or 50 mm (2 in) pipework. Form the pipework into a large rectangular shape, using 90° bends so that the net can float in the pond, while the bottom is weighted to create a "pool within a pool." The breeding area will now be completely enclosed within the net, which protects the fish and retains all the eggs.

Now follow the professional breeders' regime and tie spawning ropes to the bottom of the netting to replicate the fishes' natural spawning grounds. This method is perfect, as the mating is really quite physical. Most fish, particularly the female, usually end up with scale damage after all the buffeting and bumping involved. Place the parent fish (one female to three males) within the breeding net a few days before the anticipated spawning.

Alternatively, use the excellent spawning ropes or floating spawning cages now available. Spawning ropes are made of fine nylon bristles twisted around a central wire, similar to the brushes used for filtration purposes, but much longer. They are suspended within the pool and imitate underwater plant fronds. When spawning is complete and the ropes are covered in eggs, remove them to a separate facility for hatching.

Floating cages resemble breeding nets, but are much smaller and generally round. The eggs adhere to the soft nylon fronds on the outside of the netting. When spawning has occurred, turn the cage inside out, which protects the eggs and subsequent fry from their parents, although both can remain in the same environment. This method is good for both fry and broodstock and causes them the least amount of stress.

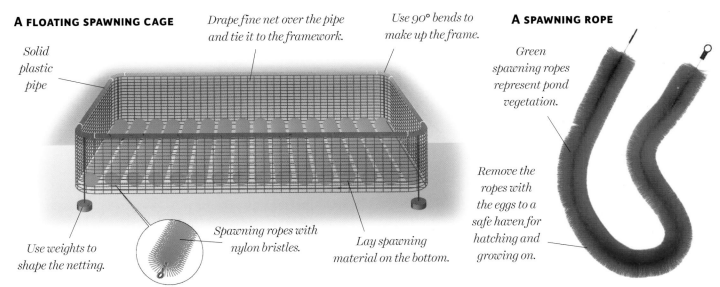

A FLOATING SPAWNING CAGE

Drape fine net over the pipe and tie it to the framework.

Use 90° bends to make up the frame.

Solid plastic pipe

Use weights to shape the netting.

Spawning ropes with nylon bristles.

Lay spawning material on the bottom.

A SPAWNING ROPE

Green spawning ropes represent pond vegetation.

Remove the ropes with the eggs to a safe haven for hatching and growing on.

DRIED FOODS FOR NEWBORN AND SMALL FRY

03-size crumb for small fry contains all the ingredients required for rapid growth.

00-size crumb is a fine powder that supplies week-old fry with nutrients that they can take in easily.

You can make a breeding tank from any large container with an adequate surface area that can sustain some form of filtration and aeration. Always check where containers have come from and what may have been in them; certain materials or liquids could prove highly toxic to fish. A purpose-built quarantine tank can "double up" satisfactorily as a breeding unit. When required, top up the secondary tank with identical pond water, so that there is no difference in water quality. This will ease the stress on the broodstock when they are moved.

The spawning

Now you can apply the same principles to breeding as the professional fish farmer. Clean the breeding tank (if you are using one) and make sure that the water quality and aeration are perfect. Use the same ratio of parent fish for breeding, namely one mature female to at least two or three mature males. This should result in a near-perfect spawning, with all eggs fertilized. Put the brood koi together and if they are ready to mate, the males will soon be chasing the female vigorously, nudging into her rear end, trying to induce her to release her eggs. This mating ritual is known as the "spawning dance."

This magical moment usually happens in the early hours of the morning after a warm night. If you wish to play the expectant parent, it really is an amazing sight. The early morning quiet is broken by the sound of violent thrashing in the water and the surface of the pond becomes a bubbling mass. The mating procedure will last most of the morning and then the pond becomes motionless; in fact, an eerie stillness descends. When everything has settled down, the first thing is to remove the parents from the breeding area. This entails lifting your koi from the floating breeding net or separate breeding tank and returning them to the pond or, if you are using a floating spawning cage, turning it inside out. This is to save the eggs from the predatory instincts of the parent fish, which look upon their newly laid spawn as first-class beluga caviar!

The eggs can either be left in-situ or taken to another hatchery tank containing similar water. In both cases, treat the spawning media containing the eggs with a mild solution of malachite green (3 parts per million) to sterilize the eggs for 10–15 minutes. It is true that some breeders do not do this; they believe that the eggs absorb the chemical, which has a toxic effect and causes congenital defects.

Caring for the fry

Depending on water temperature, the eggs take 4 to 7 days to hatch, although they do not all hatch out together. Once hatched, the fry live off their yolk sac for 2 or 3 days and then require a constant supply of liquid or powdered fry food. Provide a high-protein diet, but take care not to pollute the water. The best advice is to feed little and often, and test the water constantly for ammonia, nitrite and oxygen content. Aerate the water well, but not so severely that it damages the small fry. Strong water currents built up by the airstones can easily lead to the fry being buffeted against the sides of the pond. If the young are held in a separate tank, keep the filtration at a low flow rate so they are not dragged into the filter media. To avoid a buildup of toxic levels of ammonia and nitrite within the hatchery tank, consider installing a constant water change facility, whereby a trickle flow of fresh water is in constant operation, thus avoiding major water changes later on.

Liquid or dry fry food is readily available from koi dealers and aquatic outlets. Choose a liquid fry food specifically for egglayers. It contains extracts that help form instant infusoria on which the minute fry can survive. Add the liquid to the water via a droplet bottle two to four times each day. The dried alternative is supplied in a dust-like powder, but performs in exactly the same way as liquid food.

After a few weeks under ideal conditions, the fry will readily accept broken-up flaked fish food or good-quality, powdered koi pellets. You can even add montmorillionite clay to the water on a regular basis to supply valuable trace elements in readily absorbed quantities, providing the fry with a really healthy start. Because koi do not have a stomach, continue feeding little, but often. Good-quality, dried, tropical fish food is a useful addition to the diet of small koi as it contains many trace elements, plus animal and vegetable extracts. Your local aquarist center may also stock frozen fry food, such as *Daphnia* and bloodworm, which will all be readily accepted. This is a much safer method of feeding "whole" food than catching your own; there is always the risk that you might introduce a waterborne parasite from a natural pond.

From an early stage, check for larger than average fry; these may be eating the smaller fry. Remove the young "predators" to a separate holding facility or cull them if they show any deformity. Once the fry reach 5 cm (2 in), they should be feeding on good-quality dry food, either flake or mini-pellets. From then on, maintain your regular feeding program.

Pay attention to the water conditions to avoid any problems resulting from poor water quality. One of the problems of breeding koi outside Japan is that countries with a temperate climate do not enjoy the same long and very hot summers. Those extra few weeks feeding enable the fry to grow stronger before the onset of winter. In early autumn, consider heating the breeding facility to extend the summer or bring the young fish in from the cold. A large aquarium in a shed, garage, greenhouse or outhouse is the most successful location for overwintering them. When spring comes, you can return them to the garden pond, healthy and well-fed.

Culling

In common with all the professional breeders, you will have to face the fact that culling is necessary. From your initial hatching, many fish will inevitably die of natural causes. Some will suffer from strange deformities or be a poor size, color or shape, and they will all have to be culled. A fish anesthetic obtained from your koi dealer is the most humane method of disposal. Make up a stronger-than-usual dose and leave your culled fry in the anesthetic to pass away without stress. Further culling may become necessary as the fish grow.

Above: *This Taisho Sanke was chosen for its potential at one year old and is described as Tategoi. Koi breeders make these choices all the time.*

Right: *The same koi some years later. Note how the black has come out in just the right proportions over an excellent Kohaku pattern. The breeder probably had a good idea of what to expect, but the exact quality is the mystery and well worth the wait.*

Keep records

Remember to keep a record of your successes and failures. The log should show all the details of your brood koi, both male and female. A diary of the breeding program and relevant information, such as the prevailing weather conditions, etc., will help you when you start breeding your own fish and may even contribute to improving the quality of future generations. Record all deaths due to illness or damage. The accumulated information will help you in future breeding seasons.

Part Two

Introduction

Beginners will frequently ask of a particular koi: "What species is that?" The question merits only one valid reply — Cyprinus carpio — because that is the scientific name carried by all koi, however diverse they appear to be. So, is the word "breed" more appropriate? It works for pedigree dogs, in the sense that if you cross a corgi with another corgi, more corgis result. But, with koi, the outcome is nowhere near as certain. Put a male and a female Sanke together and the resulting fry will certainly contain a percentage of Sanke — plus Bekko, Kohaku and many nondescripts.

The terms used to describe koi are "class" and "variety." These are purely arbitrary, as the fish have all been developed by man, but they do at least give us a yardstick by which koi can be bought and judged. Each class may contain one or many varieties. For example, Kohaku, Sanke and Showa are single-variety classes, whereas the Kawarimono class is home to dozens of nonmetallic koi that do not readily slot elsewhere into the hierarchy. To confuse the issue further, there are subvarieties, with a Japanese terminology that distinguishes them from other, broadly similar, fish. To take the example of Kohaku, there are terms for two-, three- and four-step pattern koi; words to describe their scalation; and others that relate to markings. So a Doitsu Sandan Maruten Kuchibeni Kohaku would be a white and red nonmetallic koi (Kohaku) with mirror scales (Doitsu), three-step pattern (Sandan), including a separate patch of red on the head (Maruten), and red lips (Kuchibeni).

Recognizing all the varieties takes time, and there will always be some koi that spark disputes, even among so-called "experts." More important is to recognize a healthy, well-shaped koi with good skin — the rest will come with practice.

Kohaku

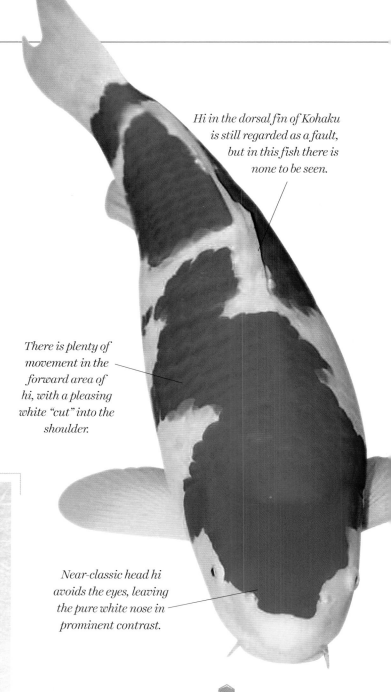

The modern Kohaku reflects rapid cultural changes in the homeland of koi. As Japan broke from its inward-looking feudal traditions to become a living metaphor for the 20th-century technological revolution, the Japanese began to revise their appreciation of this, their "flagship" koi variety. The result is that fish no longer need to conform rigidly to laid-down pattern guidelines to compete at the top level in shows. Today's Kohaku break the rules to challenge once-fixed ideals of beauty. This relaxation in attitude to pattern, but not overall quality, has fed through to the rest of the world, to the extent that koi-keeping can never again "end with Kohaku"; this deceptively simplistic red-and-white fish presents breeders and hobbyists with endless opportunities still waiting to be explored. However, pattern is only one element of a good Kohaku; body shape, intensity of hi and good skin are of equal importance, and the bloodlines favoring these qualities can be traced back more than a century.

Hi in the dorsal fin of Kohaku is still regarded as a fault, but in this fish there is none to be seen.

There is plenty of movement in the forward area of hi, with a pleasing white "cut" into the shoulder.

Near-classic head hi avoids the eyes, leaving the pure white nose in prominent contrast.

The history of Kohaku

Red-and-white mutations of the ancestral black carp (Magoi) first appeared in the early 1800s among fish bred for food by rice farmers in Niigata prefecture. For curiosity's sake, rather than with any thoughts of commercial gain, the farmers kept these back as pets and spawned them together. "Kohaku-like" characteristics emerged in some of these offspring — red heads, gill covers and lips, or small patches of hi on the back and belly, although nothing worthy of being called a pattern. That changed in 1888, when Kunizo Hiroi ran a red-headed female koi with one of his own

KOI DEFINITIONS

Hi ~ Red

Kohaku~ White koi with red markings

Kuchibeni ~ Red lips — literally "lipstick"

Magoi ~ Ancestral black carp

Maruten ~ A self-contained head marking, plus red elsewhere on the body

Tancho~ Circular redspot on head. No other red on the body

Yondan ~ Four-step pattern

PERFECTLY BALANCED PATTERN

"Balance" is not the same as "symmetry." The pattern on the Kohaku above does not favor one side of the fish at the expense of the other, and overall the rather plain hi to the rear of the body is complemented by the interesting zigzag conformation forward of the dorsal fin.

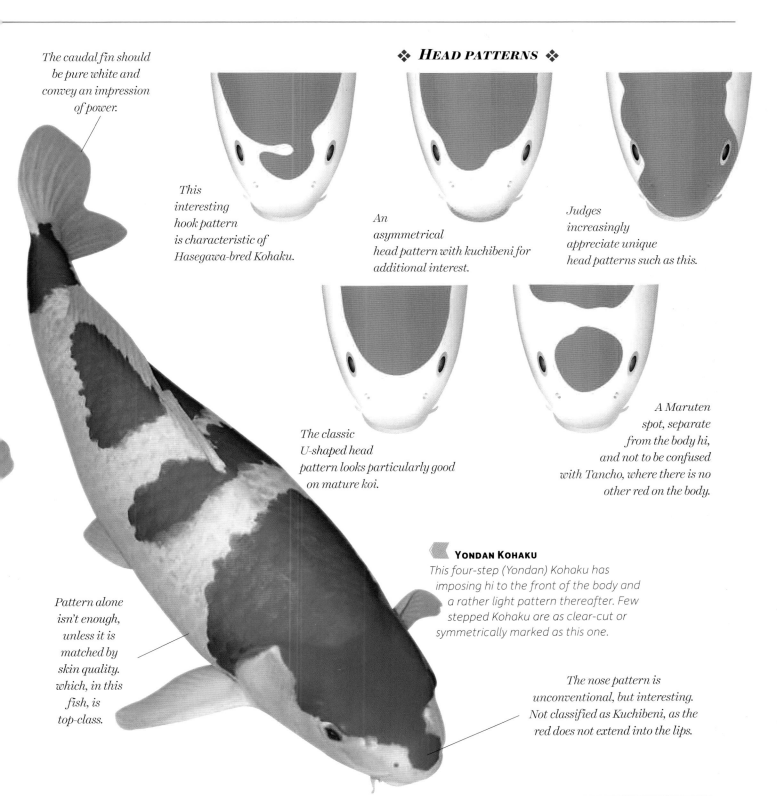

The caudal fin should be pure white and convey an impression of power.

❖ **HEAD PATTERNS** ❖

This interesting hook pattern is characteristic of Hasegawa-bred Kohaku.

An asymmetrical head pattern with kuchibeni for additional interest.

Judges increasingly appreciate unique head patterns such as this.

The classic U-shaped head pattern looks particularly good on mature koi.

A Maruten spot, separate from the body hi, and not to be confused with Tancho, where there is no other red on the body.

YONDAN KOHAKU
This four-step (Yondan) Kohaku has imposing hi to the front of the body and a rather light pattern thereafter. Few stepped Kohaku are as clear-cut or symmetrically marked as this one.

Pattern alone isn't enough, unless it is matched by skin quality. which, in this fish, is top-class.

The nose pattern is unconventional, but interesting. Not classified as Kuchibeni, as the red does not extend into the lips.

male fish, whose markings resembled cherry blossoms. The resulting fry were used by other breeders to establish the now-extinct Gosuke bloodline. All subsequent Kohaku bloodlines (Tomoin, Sensuke, Yagozen, Manzo) arose from fish of Gosuke lineage outcrossed to unrelated fish showing promise. They were named after the breeders who refined their koi over many generations of careful selection. Tomoin and Yagozen are the two major bloodlines today.

This tradition continues. We speak of a "Matsunosuke" bloodline, although the koi of Toshio Sakai and his protégé, Shintaro, draw heavily on their ancestry, even while they forge the future of Nishikigoi. The same can be said of probably the most famous Kohaku breeder of all, Dainichi (Minoru Mano), whose Kohaku have Tomoin blood in their veins.

The Kohaku of almost 100 years ago were recorded by the artist Hikosaburo Hirasawa, who painted the 28 fancy carp sent by the villagers of Niigata prefecture to the 1914 Taisho Exhibition in Tokyo. Looking back at images of these pioneering koi is a revelation — they show just how far Kohaku have progressed in the intervening years.

What makes a good Kohaku?

Kohaku are white koi with hi markings that should be of an even depth. Brownish-red hi is preferred to the purplish type, and can be improved and stabilized over the years by color feeding and constant attention to water quality. The ground color should be snow white, with no yellowing or "shimis," and should exhibit a fine luster The kiwa must be sharp. However, in young, unfinished Kohaku the scales are still kokesuke (semitransparent), which means the pattern definition will not be as good as in mature fish.

Although koi appreciation is no longer laid down in tablets of stone, some of the old terminology remains. Head hi is essential. On "classic" Kohaku, this forms a U-shape ending level with the eyes, but hanatsuki or kuchibeni are now just as acceptable. Hi extending over one or both eyes is not a demerit, but pure white finnage is still preferred. Kohaku whose hi is confined to the head alone are judged in the separate Tancho class, where the ideal marking is a perfect circle mirroring the sun on the Japanese flag and reminiscent of the head of their national bird, the Tancho crane. If a self-contained head marking is accompanied by hi elsewhere on the body of the koi, the term is "Maruten Kohaku."

Japanese names for the "stepped" patterns of body and head hi (nidan, sandan and yondan) are nowadays used

IMPOSING SIMPLICITY

This Nidan (two-step) Kohaku is a very imposing fish. The pattern, with excellent kiwa and sashi, is far from complex, but in a koi with such presence it is entirely appropriate. A white caudal peduncle would improve the appearance, but no matter; koi don't get much better than this in the larger sizes.

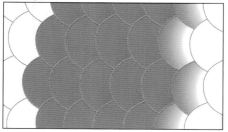

Left: *Sashi (where white scales overlay hi) is never as clearly defined as kiwa (where red scales overlay white).*

A CLASSIC SANDAN KOHAKU
This three-step Kohaku is a fish of the old school, with very clearly delineated blocks of hi. Note how the red on the head is a much deeper color than on the body; this is because there are no scales on the head to tone it down.

The contrast is good between the snow-white dorsal fin and the hi that straddles it.

FLOWERY BUT GOOD
Kohaku with patterns like this are said to be "flowery." This is not a criticism, because in this koi the smaller configurations of hi are well-balanced by the main blocks of color. The overall impression is of light frivolity, helped along by the intriguing head pattern.

Well-shaped, white pectoral fins counterbalance the imposing forward hi.

KOI DEFINITIONS

Hanatsuki ~ A hi pattern that reaches the mouth

Hi ~ Red

Kiwa ~ Border of red and white at the rear edge of hi patterns

Kokesuke ~ Semitranslucent

Kuchibeni ~ Red lips — literally "lipstick"

Nidan ~ Two-step pattern

Sandan ~ Three-step pattern

Sanke ~ White koi with red and black markings

Sashi ~ Overlap of red and white scales at the forward edge of hi patterns

Shimi ~ Undesirable individual dark brown or black scales on areas of ground color

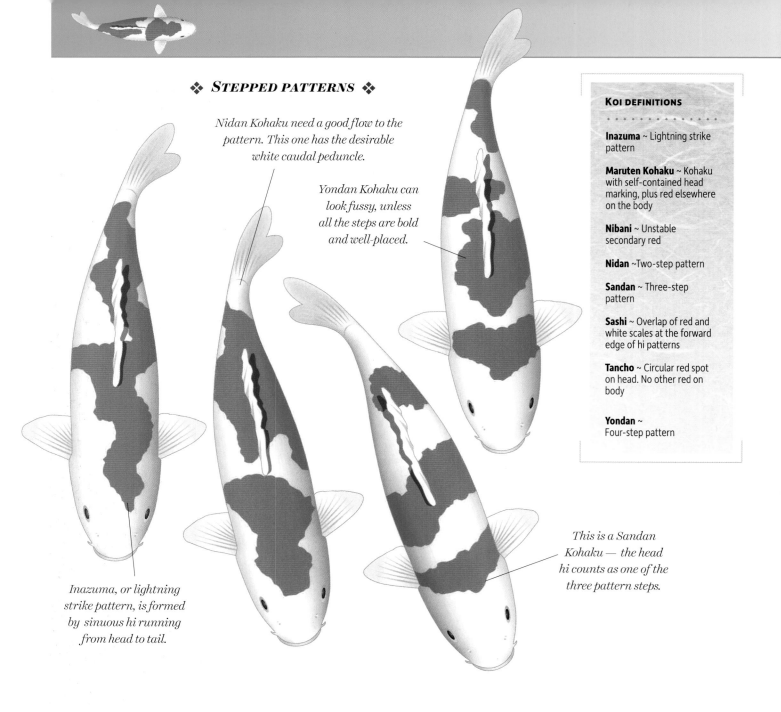

❖ STEPPED PATTERNS ❖

Nidan Kohaku need a good flow to the pattern. This one has the desirable white caudal peduncle.

Yondan Kohaku can look fussy, unless all the steps are bold and well-placed.

Inazuma, or lightning strike pattern, is formed by sinuous hi running from head to tail.

This is a Sandan Kohaku — the head hi counts as one of the three pattern steps.

KOI DEFINITIONS

Inazuma ~ Lightning strike pattern

Maruten Kohaku ~ Kohaku with self-contained head marking, plus red elsewhere on the body

Nibani ~ Unstable secondary red

Nidan ~ Two-step pattern

Sandan ~ Three-step pattern

Sashi ~ Overlap of red and white scales at the forward edge of hi patterns

Tancho ~ Circular red spot on head. No other red on body

Yondan ~ Four-step pattern

---

more for general descriptive purposes than as a measure of how good (or otherwise) a Kohaku is. Modern Kohaku can also exhibit smaller, complementary patches of hi, not to be confused with nibani.

For continuous, head-to-tail hi patterns to be acceptable, they must be interesting. The best example is still the classic inazuma. Today's trend is for Kohaku patterns to be imposing, and this should be taken into account when buying young fish. As the skin stretches, areas of hi move apart from one another, so avoid young koi that appear to be small replicas of finished adults. Conversely, large, apparently dull blocks of hi can "break" later in life to form intriguing patterns. Body hi need not be symmetrical, or even conventionally balanced, as long as it is pleasing to the eye. But hi confined to one side of the koi when viewed from above, or making the fish "head-heavy" or "tail-heavy,"

LIGHTNING STRIKES

This is an Inazuma Maruten Nidan Kohaku. In the naming of koi, all the elements are run together to build up a picture of the fish, but no two individuals are the same.

Not Tancho, but Maruten; Tancho must be stand-alone hi.

FOUR STEPS TO HEAVEN

A Yondan Maruten Kohaku — the hi here is reminiscent of cloud shadows over a snowfield. Kiwa is particularly good on this mature koi, and the skin quality is what one would expect to see on a much younger fish.

is a fault. The Japanese still prefer a break in hi at the base of the tail, although many top-grade Kohaku do not have a white caudal peduncle.

Doitsu, Gin-Rin and metallic Kohaku

Doitsu Kohaku, which lack overall scaling, appear very clean-cut, with razor-sharp kiwa, but are considered rather two-dimensional by the Japanese. In shows without a separate Doitsu judging class, these fish will always lose out to fully scaled fish.

Gin-Rin Kohaku — fish with too many reflective scales to count individually — are judged along with Gin-Rin Sanke and Showa in their own class. The mutant scales, originally known as "dia," appear gold over hi and silver over white areas of skin. Gin-Rin scales are sometimes described as "fukurin," a term that should properly be reserved for the lustrous skin around the scales of metallic koi.

Metallic Kohaku used to be known as "Platinum Kohaku" but are now termed "Sakura Ogon," and are judged in Hikarimoyo. The Doitsu version is called a "Kikusui." All stem from Kohaku x Ogon crosses.

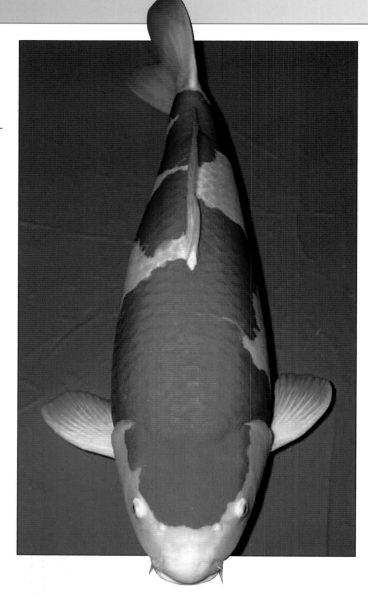

❖ *GIVE IT A BREAK* ❖

Some white on the caudal peduncle is desirable, particularly when hi is heavy.

This is "Ippon hi." Koi like this are normally culled early in life.

A red dorsal fin over unrelieved hi would seriously demerit any Kohaku.

KOI DEFINITIONS

Doitsu ~ Koi with no scales other than enlarged scales along the lateral line and two lines running either side of thedorsal fin

Fukurin ~
Net effect of lustrous skin around the scales of (usually) metallic koi

Gin-Rin ~
Koi with reflective silver scales

Hi ~ Red

Hikarimoyo ~ Class for all multicolored metallic koi except Utsuri and Showa

Ippon hi ~
Where solid red runs from nose to tail without a break

Kikusui ~ Doitsu platinum koi with metallic orange markings

Kiwa ~ Border of red and white at the rear edge of hi patterns

Ogon ~
Single-colored metallic koi

Sakura Ogon ~
Metallic Kohaku

Sanke ~ White koi with red and black markings

Sashi ~ Overlap of red and white scales at the forward edge of hi patterns

Showa ~ Black koi with red and white markings

 SHOW-WINNING KOHAKU
This Kohaku has it all — superb full body shape, an interesting, although unfussy, pattern and the all-important contrasting snow-white skin. Rarely do all these elements come together so well. When they do, you have a show-winner.

 THE SPARKLE OF GIN-RIN
A high-quality Gin-Rin Kohaku. The reflective scales shine silver over white skin and gold over hi. This would still be an impressive koi without the added embellishment, but inferior Gin-Rin fish can make a good first impression that is not borne out by closer scrutiny — "flashy" does not necessarily mean a quality koi. This one passes the test on all counts, however.

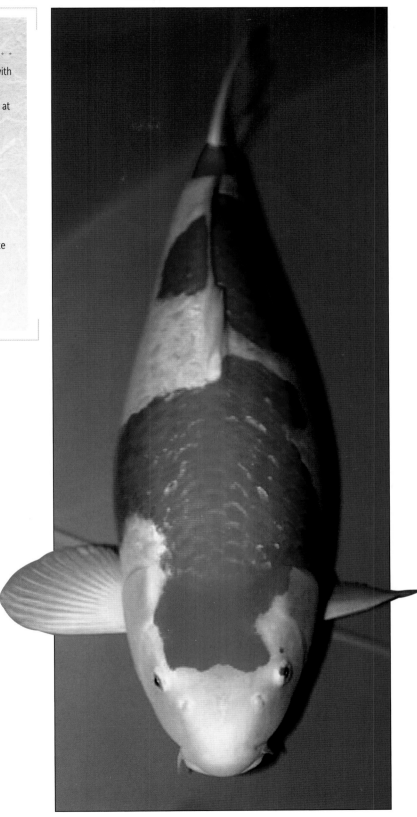

Sanke

Kohaku may be the purists' favorite koi, but the tricolored Sanke is almost as subtle. Its sumi markings set off hi and white skin in almost limitless permutations. The two varieties are closely linked and are the only ones with traceable bloodlines, although exactly when Sanke as we know them first appeared is open to debate. They used to be known as "Taisho Sanke," or "Taisho Sanshuko" (after the era when they were allegedly developed, 1912–26), but plain "Sanke" is now the accepted term.

The history of Sanke

A mature "Sanke" was brought by Gonzo Hiroi to the Tokyo Exhibition in 1914. This suggests that the variety, or at least its forebears, may have been in existence at the end of the 19th-century (which would place it in the Meiji era). Whether there were conscious attempts to line-breed these fish is not known.

In the same year — 1914 — white koi with red and black markings appeared spontaneously in a brood of Kohaku belonging to Niigata rice farmer Heitaro Sato. Attempts to replicate the event were disappointing, and the three parent fish were passed to another breeder before being acquired by Eizaburo Hoshino of Takezawa — the village known as the birthplace of Nishikigoi. In 1917, Mr. Hoshino crossed one of these female Kohaku from Sato with a Shiro Bekko. The resulting fry showed the three characteristic Sanke colors in more or less equal proportions, with added sumi stripes on their pectoral fins.

However, the breeder who "fixed" the strain was Torakichi Kawikame. He spawned a female Hoshino Sanke with a Yagozen Kohaku and the bloodline became known as Torazo, the name of Kawikame's father and the family business.

All modern Sanke are the product of Torazo and the unrelated Sanba strain, which has since died out. The most famous current bloodlines are Matsunosuke, Jinbei, Sadazo and Kichinai.

Matsunosuke Sanke are the joint triumph of Toshio Sakai, who runs the Isawa Nishikigoi center, and his elder brother Toshiyuki, based in Niigata. The bloodline has been reinvigorated with Magoi genes to maximize growth, while retaining quality hi and sumi pigmentation. These koi, slimly built when young, are increasingly showing "Fukurin" scalation, which imparts a unique sheen.

Sanke colors

A Sanke is essentially a Kohaku with Bekko-type sumi, which should not extend below the lateral line. As with Kohaku, the ideal skin is snow-white and lustrous and the

This scarlet hi is accented by small areas of sumi. Where black overlays red, it is known as Kasane sumi.

WHEN LESS IS MORE

A good Sanke is a Kohaku with added sumi, which may or may not extend into the fins. Today's fashion is for fewer sumi than ever before, and some Tategoi Sanke are easily confused with Kohaku until the black comes fully through.

GONE BUT NOT FORGOTTEN

"Doris," arguably the finest Sanke ever to enter the UK, is sadly no longer with us. She was bred by Sakai Matsunosuke, the best breeder of this variety in the world, and was still improving at the time of her death in summer 2001. She won two consecutive BKKS Nationals.

Most of Doris's hi stood alone, with sumi confined to the white ground. This is called Tsubo sumi.

HOW SUMI DEVELOPS

The way sumi develops on Sanke is very much down to bloodline. This fish displays areas of finished sumi towards the tail, and emergent sumi forward of the dorsal fin. This will eventually deepen to jet-black, but the process could take years before the pattern is completely stabilized and the koi is said to be "finished."

This is emerging sumi and not a shimi, or blemish.

A charming, if unconventional, head pattern.

KOI DEFINITIONS

Bekko ~ Black sanke-type markings on red, white or yellow base

Fukurin ~ Net effect of lustrous skin around the scales of (usually) metallic koi

Kohaku ~ White koi with red markings

Magoi ~ Ancestral black carp

Shimi ~ Undesirable individual dark brown or black scales on areas of ground color

Shiro Bekko ~ White koi with black sanke-type markings

Sumi ~ Black

Tategoi ~ "Unfinished" koi of any age that should continue to improve

Beautiful white skin and a regular head pattern make this Sanke very special.

overlaying hi deep and even, with no "windows" (a solid area of red with areas of white inside the pigment) — an early sign that the pattern may be breaking up and disappearing.

Young high-grade Sanke are easily confused with Kohaku, as in some bloodlines no sumi is discernible until the age of 2. Nor is there a guarantee that once the sumi is there it will be stable; it may fade again, only to reemerge later.

Young Matsunosuke Sanke show faint blue-gray sumi that gradually deepens; however, Sanke of the Kichinai bloodline exhibit stable sumi at a very early age, and the only real change in their pattern results from the skin stretching as the koi grow. Early sumi that stays is known as "moto sumi," whereas black markings that appear later are termed "ato sumi."

Sumi is also named for where it appears on the koi. If it overlays the hi, it is "kasane sumi," whereas if it is on white skin it is known as "tsubo sumi." The latter is highly prized, but most examples of Sanke combine the two. Ultimately it is the overall effect that matters.

Sanke patterns

Changing fashions have influenced Sanke patterns, so that fish with heavy sumi are no longer as popular as those with small, accent areas of black — now very much the supporting color. Large areas of red unrelieved by cuts in the pattern are equally frowned upon — fish showing these are known as Aka Sanke.

Sanke are not supposed to have any sumi on the head, just hi on white. When sumi does appear forward of the shoulders,

---

❖ HEAD PATTERNS ❖

Sanke very rarely display any sumi on the head, only hi.

Head sumi points to Showa — but it is not a foolproof way to tell the varieties apart.

A FLOWERY SANKE
This rather flowery Sanke has a fascinating triple hi marking on the face and shoulders. It shows well the difference between Tsubo and Kasane sumi, and how the black is configured Bekko-style, above the lateral line. Note the pectoral fin stripes.

❖ **BODY MARKINGS** ❖

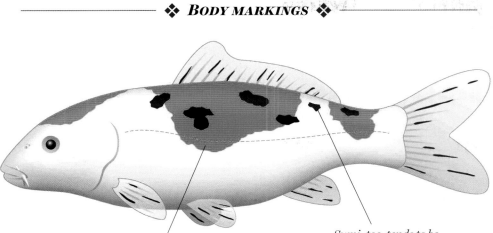

*Viewed sideways, the hi on Sanke
does not usually extend far
below the lateral line.*

*Sumi, too, tends to be
confined to the upper
part of the body.*

*Kasane sumi
(black on red).*

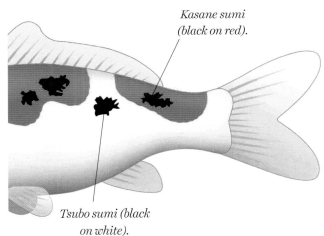

*Tsubo sumi (black
on white).*

BEST OF BOTH WORLDS
*The secret with champion
koi is
to achieve size and
volume in a fish
retaining all the
youthful plus points
relating to skin quality
and pattern. This 70 cm
(28 in) Sanke shows it can
be done.*

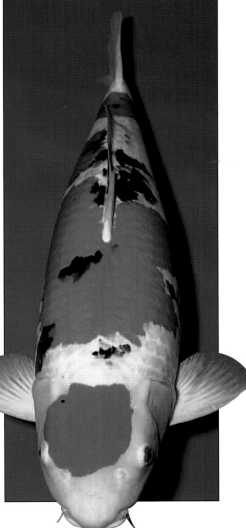

*This hi is already
fragmenting.*

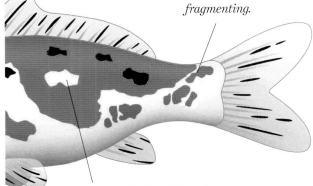

*"Windows" in blocks of hi, or dappled
hi, suggest that the koi may later lose
its red patterning entirely.*

KOI DEFINITIONS

Aka Bekko ~ Red koi with black
Sanke-type markings

Aka Sanke ~ Koi with large areas
of red, unrelieved by cuts
in the pattern

Ato sumi ~ Black markings that
appear later in a koi's life

Bekko ~ Black Sanke-type
markings on a white, red or yellow
base

Hi ~ Red

Kasane sumi ~
Black that overlays red

Kohaku ~
White koi with red markings

Moto sumi ~ Early sumi that
remains on the body

Sanke ~ White koi with
red and black markings

Sumi ~ Black

Tsubo sumi ~ Black on white skin

depending on its position, it can look charming or else detract from the dignity of the fish. The same is true of kuchibeni; neither will make a dull koi more interesting, but if the rest of the pattern is good, it is not seen as a fault.

Hi on any of the fins is less well-tolerated, but sumi on the pectoral, dorsal or caudal fins is a desirable characteristic. The way this black is configured is one sure way of identifying Sanke — stripes on the pectoral fins are quite distinct from the motoguro found in the balljoint of Showa pectorals. Some Sanke, however, have pure white fins becoming translucent toward the leading edges. These are quite acceptable.

Symmetry of markings is never achieved on Sanke, nor should too much store be placed on "balance." It is the total impact of the tricolored pattern that matters, although if all the sumi or hi runs down one flank of the koi this will not be pleasing to the eye. Similarly, not enough hi or too much sumi toward the caudal peduncle (where the body tapers) will make the fish appear head- or tail-heavy.

Sanke with a separate head hi marking and more on the body are known as Maruten Sanke; if the only hi is on the head, the fish is a Tancho Sanke and judged in that class. The term "Menkaburi Sanke" is reserved for fish whose head hi extends down the nose and over the jaws in a hood-like pattern. In Budo Sanke all the sumi overlays the hi. There is no sumi on the white skin and the fish is benched in Kawarimono or Koromo (see also page 166).

❖ *FIN MARKINGS* ❖

Sanke pectoral fins can be clear, or striped, as here. Sometimes the striping is confined to just one fin.

A block of sumi in the pectoral fin joint — motoguro– points to Showa or Utsurimono.

A PROMISING YOUNGSTER

This young Sanke could do with more volume, which will come with age. Its large, symmetrically striped pectoral fins are a strong point, as is the cluster of shoulder sumi. Separate head hi makes the fish a Maruten Sanke.

A CLEAR-CUT DOITSU SANKE
This Doitsu Sanke has many apparently Showa traits — but is still 100 percent Sanke, despite the small patches of sumi on the head and the heavy black body markings. Note the single sumi stripe, too, in the left pectoral fin.

A very striking, though by no means classic, head pattern sets one color off against another.

KOI DEFINITIONS

Doitsu ~ Koi with no scales other than enlarged scales along the lateral line and two lines running either side of the dorsal fin

Hi ~ Red

Hikarimoyo ~ Class for all multicolored metallic koi except Utsuri and Showa

Kawarimono ~ Class for all nonmetallic koi not included in any other group

Kindai ~ White skin predominates

Kuchibeni ~ Red lips — literally "lipstick"

Maruten Sanke ~ Sanke with self-contained head marking, plus red elsewhere on the body

Menkaburi ~ Red head

Motoguro ~ Solid black coloration in the base of pectoral fins on Showa and related varieties

Sanke ~ White koi with red and black markings

Showa ~ Black koi with red and white markings

Sumi ~ Black

Tancho ~ Circular red spot on head. No other red on body

Yamatonishiki ~ Metallic Sanke

Doitsu and other Sanke

Doitsu Sanke look clean-cut, as there is no blurring of the hi and sumi fore and aft. Good examples appear almost synthetic, as though the colors had been applied with a brush.

Although the Japanese do not rate these fish as highly as other Sanke, they do at least give them a separate Doitsu judging class, but in most other countries all Sanke are entered together — when the fully scaled fish almost always tend to win.

All hybrids between Sanke and other, nonmetallic, varieties are judged in the Kawarimono class, whereas Yamatonishiki are grouped in Hikarimoyo, meaning metallic koi of more than one color.

Showa

The Showa is the last of the "Big Three" varieties collectively known as Go Sanke, and historically by far the youngest. It was developed in 1927, in Niigata, by Jukichi Hoshino, who crossed a Ki Utsuri with a Kohaku. These early fish displayed very poor, yellowish hi and indifferent sumi, and it was not until 1965 that Tomiji Kobayashi improved the strain by crossing female Showa with male Sanke and Yagozen Kohaku (see page 176), resulting in the deep scarlet hi, glossy black and snow-white skin we appreciate today.

Outcrosses with Sanke and Kohaku continue to be made, not only to maintain brilliant color, but also to produce fish that satisfy the modern taste. As we shall see, where some Showa closely resemble their forebears, others could be mistaken, at first glance, for Sanke. This is a common error for beginners to make, and not surprising, as both varieties are red, black and white koi. However, Showa are black fish with red and white markings and the distribution and positioning of the sumi is (or at least used to be) very distinctive. Sanke sumi is a subsidiary color, appearing only above the lateral line and rarely on the head, in typical Bekko "tortoiseshell" configuration, whereas the glossy black of Showa is better described as "wrapping"; in some examples it appears to extend from the belly up around the body. Large areas of sumi can blend together to produce a pattern like a lightning bolt (inazuma). This is especially noticeable on the head, where the black cutting across an area of hi can generate bold and striking effects.

The traditional Showa usually has red as the dominant color, with sumi and white in roughly equal proportions. If more than half the body is red, viewed from above, the fish is referred to as a Hi Showa. But whereas an Aka Sanke is not a

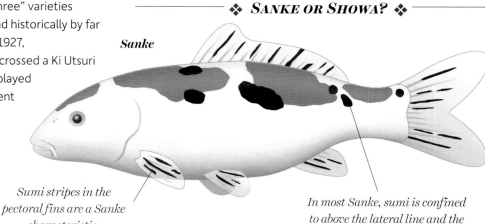

❖ **SANKE OR SHOWA?** ❖

Sanke

Sumi stripes in the pectoral fins are a Sanke characteristic.

In most Sanke, sumi is confined to above the lateral line and the hi pattern is Kohaku-like.

Showa

Motoguro in the pectorals is typical of Showa and Utsurimono.

Showa sumi can extend up from the belly in bold wrappings.

KOI DEFINITIONS

Bekko ~ Black Sanke-type markings on a white, red or yellow base

Go Sanke ~ Koi from the Kohaku, Sanke and Showa classes

Hi Showa ~ More than half the body viewed from above is red

Ki Utsuri ~ Black koi with yellow markings

Kohaku ~ White koi with red markings

Motoguro ~ Solid black coloration in the base of pectoral fins on Showa and related varieties

Sanke ~ "Three color." White koi with red and black markings

Shimi ~ Undesirable individual dark brown or black scales on areas of ground cover

Utsurimono ~ Black koi with white, red or yellow markings

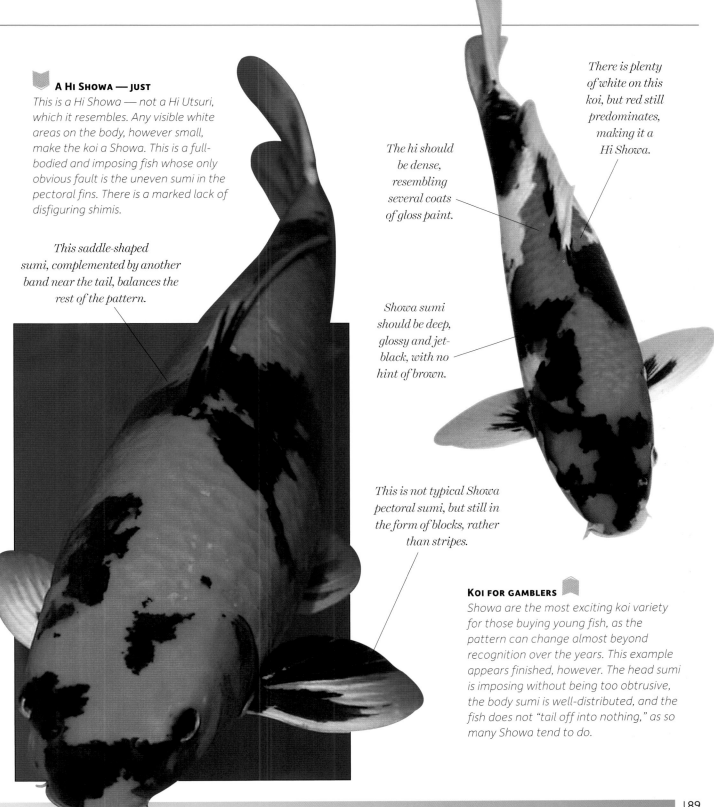

A HI SHOWA — JUST

This is a Hi Showa — not a Hi Utsuri, which it resembles. Any visible white areas on the body, however small, make the koi a Showa. This is a full-bodied and imposing fish whose only obvious fault is the uneven sumi in the pectoral fins. There is a marked lack of disfiguring shimis.

This saddle-shaped sumi, complemented by another band near the tail, balances the rest of the pattern.

The hi should be dense, resembling several coats of gloss paint.

There is plenty of white on this koi, but red still predominates, making it a Hi Showa.

Showa sumi should be deep, glossy and jet-black, with no hint of brown.

This is not typical Showa pectoral sumi, but still in the form of blocks, rather than stripes.

KOI FOR GAMBLERS

Showa are the most exciting koi variety for those buying young fish, as the pattern can change almost beyond recognition over the years. This example appears finished, however. The head sumi is imposing without being too obtrusive, the body sumi is well-distributed, and the fish does not "tail off into nothing," as so many Showa tend to do.

❖ KINDAI SHOWA AND OTHERS ❖

This is a lovely Kindai Showa — until you look at the tail region, where the pattern is not as strong.

White is the dominant color, making this a Kindai Showa.

A traditional Showa pattern, red and black in equal measure, with relatively little white.

A MODERN SHOWA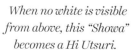

This is a bright, modern Showa, with plenty of sumi still to come through. The black nose, though unusual, imparts charm to an accomplished fish.

When no white is visible from above, this "Showa" becomes a Hi Utsuri.

KOI DEFINITIONS

Aka Sanke ~ Koi with large red areas unrelieved by cuts in the pattern

Hi ~ Red

Hi Utsuri ~ Black koi with red or orange markings

Kage ~ Shadowy black reticulated marking over white (or red on Hi Utsuri)

Kawarimono ~ Class for all nonmetallic koi not included in any other group

Kindai ~ Where white skin predominates

Kiwa ~ Border of red and white scales at the rear edge of hi patterns

Motoguro ~ Solid black coloration in the base of pectoral fins on Showa and related varieties

Sanke ~ "Three color." White koi with red and black markings

Sashi ~ Overlap of red and white scales at the forward edge of hi patterns

Sumi ~ Black

Tategoi ~ "Unfinished" koi of any age that should continue to improve

very subtle fish, its Showa equivalent can look stunning. This is because the sumi takes a more active role in the pattern, which needs very little white to accent it. The effect is helped along by the pectoral fins and their motoguro although, again, perfectly acceptable modern Showa may have clear white fins.

Hi Showa are sometimes difficult to distinguish from Hi Utsuri, but if any white skin is visible when the koi is viewed from above it is a Showa — in name if not in spirit.

Kindai Showa are becoming more popular than ever, and very real classification difficulties present themselves in fish that lack two or more of the traditional Showa identification points, such as head sumi, motoguro or wrap-around markings. At first glance, koi like these can easily be mistaken for Sanke, but experienced hobbyists can get the variety right by a process of elimination in virtually every case. The difficulty is compounded in young Showa because very often the nature and distribution of

the sumi alters dramatically as the fish grow. Tategoi Showa represent not just a challenge, but a substantial gamble. Only by studying many other fish from the same breeder is it possible to make even an educated guess as to how the sumi will look when the koi matures. Areas of red, too, will come and go; it is a myth that hi is always stable and sumi transient, something you can confirm by keeping a photographic record of Showa as they grow.

Emerging Showa sumi can appear blue-gray or brownish-black, and rather than having clearly defined kiwa and sashi, it may cover an area of skin in a reticulated pattern that allows individual scales to show through. Koi that retain a predominance of this shadowy sumi into adulthood are known as Kage Showa, but for every true example there are many more in which the sumi will ultimately develop fully to a deep, lacquer-like gloss.

Shadowy finished sumi, should not be confused with sumi still to emerge fully.

Not Sanke sumi, although it can look similar when not fully developed.

▷ **OUT OF THE SHADOWS**
True Kage Showa are rare, but this is a good example. There are two distinct types of sumi here: the deep, glossy bands and the dappled, shadowy markings. Kage Showa are now benched Showa, rather than Kawarimono, because who is to say when a koi is finished?

MORE BLACK TO COME ◁
This Tategoi modern Showa could easily be mistaken for a Sanke, but for the shoulder sumi, which will probably extend into the head as the fish grows. There is certainly some Sanke influence at work here, though.

To avoid any judging anomalies, Kage Showa in the West are automatically grouped in the main Showa variety, but in Japan they go into Kawarimono. "Boke Showa" is only used today as a descriptive term for fish that do not conform to the standard view of what a Showa ought to look like.

Pattern configuration in Showa is not set in stone; rather, each fish should be judged on the overall impression it makes. It is true to say that really good examples of mature Showa are harder to come by than their Sanke or Kohaku equivalents. A common defect is seen in fish that look wonderful from the head to a point along the dorsal fin, with well-proportioned hi, sumi and white skin, but lack any bold areas of hi from that point back to the caudal fin. The initial impression may still be good, as Showa rely on color contrast for their impact, but for a koi to win shows it must display uniform excellence from nose to tail.

The pectoral fins can let down an otherwise good Showa. Motoguro can be present on one and not on the other or, more commonly, both fins are a uniform black. Depending on the parentage, the sumi may or may not recede later. There are even cases of koi with one pectoral fin showing motoguro and the other the typical striping of a Sanke — the result of outcrossing to a Sanke parent.

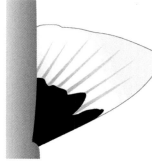

In the classic motoguro, the sumi in the pectorals forms an even block spreading up from the ball joint of the fin.

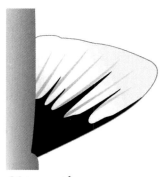

Motoguro plus radiating stripes is still the mark of a Showa, rather than a Sanke.

Showa do not have bloodlines in the same sense as the other Go Sanke, and a relatively small percentage of any spawning will be true to type. The first culling retains only all-black fish, which may represent as little as 30 percent of the total, while subsequent thinnings need to be severe. Inbreeding in this variety leads to a higher than normal number of fish with congenital defects, which may be as obvious as a deformed mouth or spine, or as subtle as a slight misalignment of the tail when viewed from above.

The Showa variety lends itself to some interesting crosses, notably Koromo Showa (judged in Showa) and Showa Shusui (judged in Kawarimono). Tancho Showa are effectively Shiro Utsuri with a patch of hi confined to the head. This is usually struck through with sumi in the same way as the head marking of conventional Showa. A word of warning here: if a Shiro Utsuri displays any hi at all, even a tiny marking barely noticeable on the lip, it is technically a Showa.

HEADING FOR PERFECTION
A head study of a classy Hi Showa, showing the three primary colors — black, red and white — setting one another off to perfection. The white element in the fins relieves any impression of pigment overkill.

KOI DEFINITIONS

Boke Showa ~ Showa with indistinct grayish black pattern

Chagoi ~ Nonmetallic brown koi

Doitsu ~ Koi with no scales other than enlarged scales along the lateral line and two lines running either side of the dorsal fin

Go Sanke ~ Koi from the Kohaku, Sanke and Showa classes

Hi ~ Red

Hi Showa ~ More than half the body viewed from above is red

Kawarimono ~ Class for all nonmetallic koi not included in any other group

Kin-Gin-Rin/Gin-Rin ~ Koi with highly reflective gold and/or silver

scales

Koromo Showa ~ Solid black joins black reticulation over the red

Motoguro ~ Solid black coloration in the base of pectoral fins on Showa and related varieties

Sanke ~ "Three color." White koi with red and black markings

Showa Shusui ~ A Doitsu koi with intermediate markings showing elements of both varieties

Sumi ~ Black

Tancho ~ Circular red spot on head. No other red on body

Shiro Utsuri ~ Black koi with white markings

Gin-Rin Showa, with the other two Go Sanke classifications, are the only ones judged in Kin-Gin-Rin in the West. In all other varieties, these reflective scales do not affect how it is benched, so a Gin-Rin Chagoi is still a Chagoi and grouped in Kawarimono.

Doitsu Showa, although regarded as unrefined by the Japanese, are striking koi that carry the interaction of the three colors on the head right along the body, with no scales to blur the pattern edges. Good examples must also have impeccable white skin and a high luster. Doitsu Go Sanke do have their own judging class in Japan, which would seem a fair and logical way of evaluating their clear-cut charms.

CLEAN AND STRIKING PATTERN

This Doitsu Showa has an imposing and strong body shape, excellent skin and clean finnage. Note the extent of the hi, which is consistent over most of the body length (in many Showa, hi pattern stops at the dorsal line). The white skin offers an ideal contrast to the bright, consistent hi and excellent sumi.

Utsurimono

Although a trio of koi reside in this variety, only one is truly popular — the Shiro Utsuri. Another is relatively rare, while a third is almost never seen. Despite their monochrome black-and- white patterning, Shiro Utsuri have achieved a status only a little below that of Kohaku, Sanke and Showa, to the point where they are sometimes referred to as "honorary Go Sanke."

The history of Utsurimono

The origin of Utsurimono is unclear. Some authorities claim that the fish are of Magoi lineage, first produced in 1925 by Kazuo Minemura. Others maintain that they are of much more recent Showa descent. Both theories are hard to disprove; all koi originate from Magoi, and a Shiro Utsuri could be viewed, unkindly, as a defective Showa without the hi, just as a Shiro Bekko is basically a Sanke lacking a third color. Nowadays, however, Shiro Utsuri parent koi are spawned together to produce this specific variety, and only a few arise unwanted from Showa spawnings.

Shiro Utsuri are most often confused with Bekko, but by applying the same criteria that differentiate Showa from Sanke, the difference becomes clear. A Shiro Utsuri is a black fish with white markings, a Shiro Bekko the reverse, and all Utsuri sumi is of the typical Showa wraparound type.

Hi Utsuri are best visualized as Showa without the white. Until recent years, the hi was rarely scarlet, but outcrossings with Kohaku have greatly improved it. Some breeders have also reintroduced Magoi genes into their strain of Hi Utsuri, which allows the koi to attain a greater size without any fall-off in pattern or skin quality. The pectorals rarely show true motoguro: more often they are candy-striped black and red, with a red leading edge.

Ki Utsuri is a very old variety traceable back to 1875, at the beginning of the Meiji Era. Eizaburo Hoshino, who was also responsible for improving Sanke bloodlines in the early 20th century, coined the term "Ki Utsuri" for the fish that were earlier known as Kuro-Ki-Han. The yellow of this variety tends to be pale and washed out, and both Hi Utsuri and Ki Utsuri are prone to developing "shimis."

A CLASSIC SHIRO UTSURI
This Shiro Utsuri shows the wraparound pattern typical of an old-style Showa minus the hi. The sumi sets off the clear white skin beautifully and the small patch on the caudal peduncle holds up the rear end. Head pattern is heavy, but not overwhelming. The left pectoral fin shows classic motoguro.

Sumi must be jet-black, with no hint of a brownish tinge.

❖ HEAD PATTERNS ❖

"Lightning strike" or "Menware" head pattern is a showstopper.

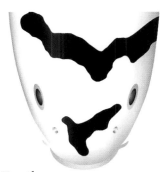

Here the head sumi is in two parts — clean and balanced.

This interesting, but rather heavy and fussy head sumi may fuse together later.

In modern-style Shiro Utsuri the head sumi is uncluttered to show off the white skin.

> **GOOD POTENTIAL**
> *This Tategoi Shiro Utsuri has more sumi still to come through, but already the pattern, though sparse, is pleasing. The skin quality is breathtaking and body shape potential is promising for what is presently a slim, young fish.*

❖ MOTOGURO ❖

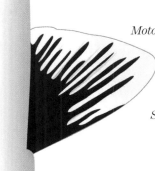

Motoguro may take the form of a solid patch of sumi at the pectoral fin ball joint or a radiating style, as here. Both are quite distinct from Sanke pectoral fin patterns.

KOI DEFINITIONS

Bekko ~ Black Sanke-type markings on a white, red or yellow base

Go Sanke ~ Koi from the Kohaku, Sanke and Showa classes

Hi ~ Red

Hi Utsuri ~ Black koi with red or orange markings

Kohaku ~ White koi with red markings

Magoi ~ Ancestral black carp

Menware ~ Showa head pattern

Motoguro ~ Solid black coloration in the base of pectoral fins on Showa and related varieties

Sanke ~ White koi with red and black markings

Shiro Bekko ~ White koi with black, Sanke-type markings

Showa ~ Black koi with red and white markings

Sumi ~ Black

Tategoi ~ "Unfinished" koi of any age that should continue to improve

Utsurimono ~ Black koi with white, red or yellow markings

Curiously, Kin Ki Utsuri are quite common, whereas the nonmetallic equivalent has almost vanished from the hobby.

Shiro Utsuri share more than just body pattern with Showa; ideally, the pectoral fins display the classic motoguro, and the taste for fish with a preponderance of white is now common to both varieties.

Because a Shiro Utsuri, like a Kohaku, is a classically simple two-colored fish, great store is placed on the quality of the white skin. This should be the color of a snowfield, with a subtle sheen, but the skin of young examples often gives few clues as to how the finished koi will look. The commonest "fault" in yearling Shiro Utsuri is a yellowish head. This is variously interpreted as a sign that the fish is male, or that it will grow into a quality koi — and to confuse the issue further, some examples never quite lose this tinge. Similarly, the white on the body can appear rather dingy, as areas of sumi still to come out give the skin a bluish-gray tinge. It is said that the best guide to how the finished koi will look is to examine the white base of the tail, which clears sooner than the rest of the body.

When choosing young Shiro Utsuri, steer clear of fish that look like miniature versions of the ideal adult. More sumi will almost certainly come later, making the koi "black heavy."

SURPRISE, SURPRISE

A fine, mature modern Shiro Utsuri. The absence of more than a suggestion of sumi on the head is unusual, but compensated for by the eyebrow-shaped shoulder markings, which give this koi a somewhat surprised expression!

KOI DEFINITIONS

Gin-Rin ~ Koi with reflective silver scales

Hi ~ Red

Hikariutsuri ~ Class for metallic Utsuri and Showa

Hi Utsuri ~ Black koi with red or orange markings

Kage ~ Shadowy black reticulated marking over white (or red on Hi Utsuri)

Ki ~ Yellow

Kin Ki Utsuri ~ Metallic yellow koi with Showa-type sumi

Ki Utsuri ~ Black koi with yellow markings

Kohaku ~ White koi with red markings

Menware ~ Showa head pattern

Motoguro ~ Solid black coloration in the base of pectoral fins on Showa and related varieties

Sanke ~ White koi with red and black markings

Shimi ~ Undesirable individual dark brown or black scales on areas of ground color

Shiro Utsuri ~ Black koi with white markings

Showa ~ Black koi with red and white markings

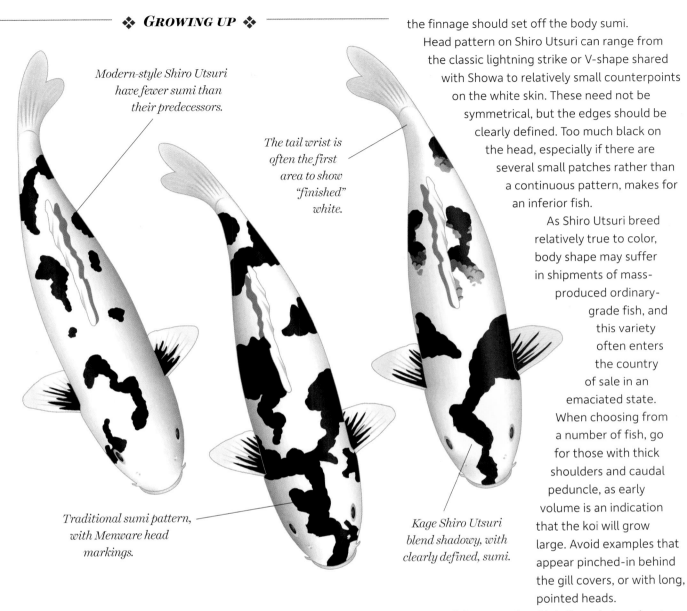

❖ *GROWING UP* ❖

Modern-style Shiro Utsuri have fewer sumi than their predecessors.

The tail wrist is often the first area to show "finished" white.

Traditional sumi pattern, with Menware head markings.

Kage Shiro Utsuri blend shadowy, with clearly defined, sumi.

the finnage should set off the body sumi.

Head pattern on Shiro Utsuri can range from the classic lightning strike or V-shape shared with Showa to relatively small counterpoints on the white skin. These need not be symmetrical, but the edges should be clearly defined. Too much black on the head, especially if there are several small patches rather than a continuous pattern, makes for an inferior fish.

As Shiro Utsuri breed relatively true to color, body shape may suffer in shipments of mass-produced ordinary-grade fish, and this variety often enters the country of sale in an emaciated state. When choosing from a number of fish, go for those with thick shoulders and caudal peduncle, as early volume is an indication that the koi will grow large. Avoid examples that appear pinched-in behind the gill covers, or with long, pointed heads.

The sumi should ideally be jet-black and glossy, as in Showa. The Japanese recognize several "shades of black," and although this sounds strange to Western hobbyists, they have a point: on close inspection in good daylight, some Shiro Utsuri have very dark, chocolate-brown markings. Another fault is too much black in the finnage. Rather than neat motoguro on the pectorals, low-grade Shiro Utsuri, exhibit solid sumi at the balljoint, which radiates outward. If this spread is excessive, the whole fin will appear black. Dorsal and caudal fins are allowed some sumi, but, again, if there is too much, the koi will appear unbalanced. Ideally, the white on

The chemistry of the water in which these koi are kept can influence how they look. Sumi develops best in hard, alkaline water, but in softer, more acidic ponds it takes on a grayish tinge.

A Gin-Rin Shiro Utsuri can be an impressive fish. The reflective scales show silver over both white skin and sumi. Such koi will be benched Kin-Gin-Rin in Western-style shows, but they have to be good Shiro Utsuri first and good Gin-Rin second.

In Kage Shiro Utsuri and Kage Hi Utsuri, like Showa, the shadowy sumi may or may not stabilize.

Doitsu Shiro Utsuri are unlikely to be confused with any other variety except, perhaps, Kumonryu (see page 218). Both are black, German-scaled fish with white markings, but the overall impression of the latter is of cloud-like patterns on a black ground, rather than an asymmetrical checkerboard. The head of a Kumonryu also lacks the traditional Utsurimono markings, and its white skin often carries a bluish tinge — sea ice, rather than snow.

 **BLACK, WHITE AND BEAUTIFUL**
For that 1960s look, this "designer" Doitsu Shiro Utsuri is hard to beat. More sumi may yet emerge, as the shoulder patch is not as clear-cut as it might be. The body could do with more volume, but that will come. Pectoral sumi is beautifully balanced.

❖ *MAKE-OR-BREAK FINS* ❖

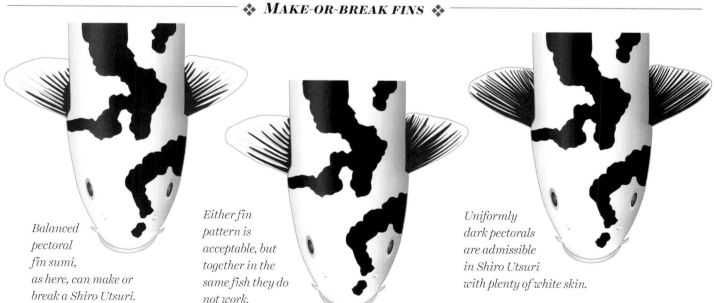

Balanced pectoral fin sumi, as here, can make or break a Shiro Utsuri.

Either fin pattern is acceptable, but together in the same fish they do not work.

Uniformly dark pectorals are admissible in Shiro Utsuri with plenty of white skin.

KOI DEFINITIONS

Doitsu ~ Koi with no scales other than enlarged scales along the lateral line and two lines running either side of the dorsal fin

Gin-Rin ~ Koi with reflective silver scales

Hi Showa ~ More than half the body viewed from above is red

Hi Utsuri ~ Black koi with red or orange markings

Kage ~ Shadowy black reticulated marking over white (or red on Hi Utsuri)

Kumonryu ~ Black doitsu koi with some white on head, fins, and body

Shimi ~ Undesirable individual dark brown or black scales on areas of ground color

Shiro Utsuri ~ Black koi with white markings

Showa ~ Black koi with red and white markings

Sumi ~ Black

Utsurimono ~ Black koi with white, red or yellow markings

RED MEETS BLACK

Hi Utsuri are Utsurimono with red as the secondary color. Often confused with Hi Showa, the way to tell them apart is to look at them from an angle of 45 degrees; if any white is evident, the fish is a Showa. This Hi Utsuri's pectoral fins spoil an otherwise nice, although rather slim, koi.

Skin on a Hi Utsuri should be bright red, contrasting with deep, lacquered sumi.

RARE AND WELL DONE

You could spend a lifetime in koi and not see a Ki Utsuri, let alone one as accomplished as this. It is a nonmetallic black koi with yellow markings. Shimis often plague this variety, but this fish is free of any blemishes.

Bekko

Certain koi varieties are subject to the vagaries of fashion, first enjoying spells of popularity and then fading from favor. Bekko are a case in point. When koi-keeping began to take off outside Japan about 30 years ago, these fish were very much in vogue; indeed, they were given (and still have) their own benching classification. However, Bekko today are underrepresented at most shows. This is a pity, as good specimens are as appealing as ever, in a chic and understated way.

Although three types of koi are recognized as Bekko, only one — the Shiro Bekko — is widely known. This is a Sanke derivative, but lacking any hi — in other words, a white koi with sumi markings. Although they are still produced from parent fish of this variety, they are just as likely to be thrown from spawnings of Sanke, especially Tancho Sanke. Bear in mind that any hi at all on a Shiro Bekko, even on the lips, technically makes it a Sanke, and a fish like this would be valueless for showing.

The sumi on Shiro Bekko has evolved in line with that of Sanke. Ten years ago, examples would have had a fairly heavy complement of tortoiseshell dappling, whereas today the sumi tends to be more sparsely distributed in smaller patches. It should be confined to the area above the lateral line, over the dorsal surface.

The judging standard now permits a little sumi on the head, as in Sanke, but the best examples have a clear white face, with the black markings beginning on the shoulder. A common fault is a yellowish head, which may or may not clear as the koi develops. The eyes are usually blue. The skin should be snow-white with a high luster. Sumi patterning need not be symmetrical, but should balance overall; if confined to one side of the fish, the effect is not pleasing. Avoid Bekko with too much sumi on the caudal peduncle. Ideally, as in Kohaku, there should be an area of white at the junction of body and tail fin.

Shiro Bekko finnage can either be white or striped with sumi, similar to that of Sanke. It is widely accepted that Japanese koi are visibly superior to those from anywhere else in the world, yet Shiro Bekko are a variety at which

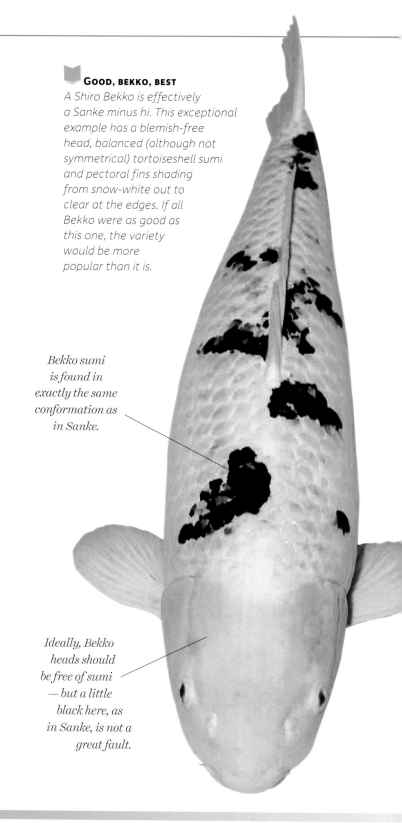

GOOD, BEKKO, BEST
A Shiro Bekko is effectively a Sanke minus hi. This exceptional example has a blemish-free head, balanced (although not symmetrical) tortoiseshell sumi and pectoral fins shading from snow-white out to clear at the edges. If all Bekko were as good as this one, the variety would be more popular than it is.

Bekko sumi is found in exactly the same conformation as in Sanke.

Ideally, Bekko heads should be free of sumi — but a little black here, as in Sanke, is not a great fault.

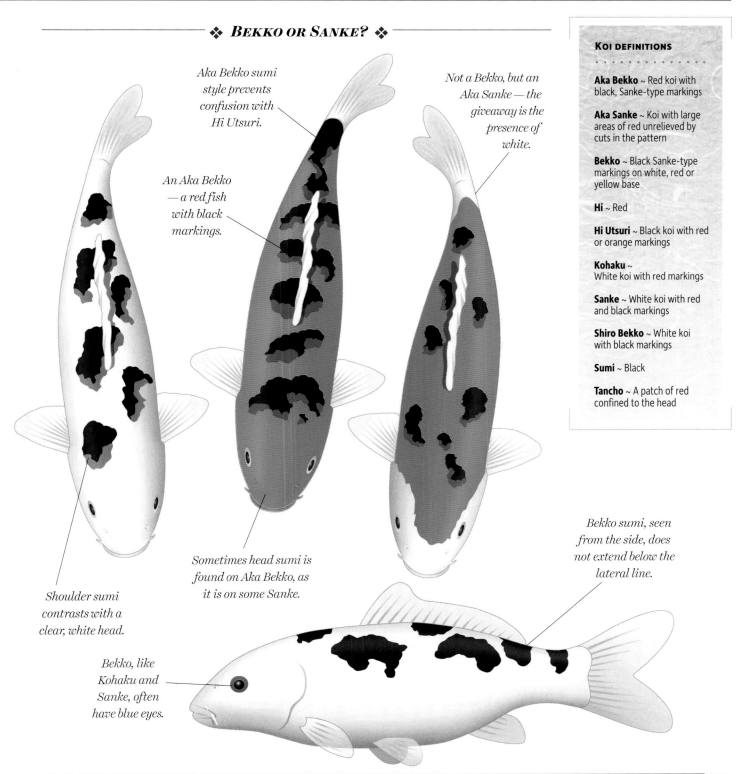

❖ **BEKKO OR SANKE?** ❖

Aka Bekko sumi style prevents confusion with Hi Utsuri.

An Aka Bekko — a red fish with black markings.

Not a Bekko, but an Aka Sanke — the giveaway is the presence of white.

KOI DEFINITIONS

Aka Bekko ~ Red koi with black, Sanke-type markings

Aka Sanke ~ Koi with large areas of red unrelieved by cuts in the pattern

Bekko ~ Black Sanke-type markings on white, red or yellow base

Hi ~ Red

Hi Utsuri ~ Black koi with red or orange markings

Kohaku ~ White koi with red markings

Sanke ~ White koi with red and black markings

Shiro Bekko ~ White koi with black markings

Sumi ~ Black

Tancho ~ A patch of red confined to the head

Shoulder sumi contrasts with a clear, white head.

Bekko, like Kohaku and Sanke, often have blue eyes.

Sometimes head sumi is found on Aka Bekko, as it is on some Sanke.

Bekko sumi, seen from the side, does not extend below the lateral line.

the Israeli fish farmers seem to excel. Their warm climate is conducive to good sumi development.

Aka Bekko (never Hi Bekko) are red koi with sumi markings. Pure red koi are usually thrown from Kohaku spawnings and not highly regarded unless the hi is a deep, even crimson, in which case they are called "Benigoi" (and benched Kawarimono). These fish are rather plain for most tastes, but when the hi is overlain with deep sumi, the effect is striking. The only fish likely to be confused with Aka Bekko are Aka Sanke, which show white areas when viewed from above. Aka Bekko are allowed some hi in the finnage, which tends to appear in blotches rather than stripes, although pure white pectoral fins set off the hi nicely.

Ki Bekko are the rarest koi in the group, and sport a lemon-yellow body overlain with sumi. They are not a variety deliberately spawned, but may arise from Shiro Bekko x Kigoi or Sanke x Kigoi crosses. Curiously, the metallic equivalent of a Ki Bekko (known as a Tora, or Tiger, Ogon) is commonly seen.

ALSO KNOWN AS BEKKO

This Aka Bekko has pectoral fins typical of a Sanke, but with no visible white on the body, it has to be benched Bekko — where, incidentally, this particular example would stand the better chance of winning a "best in variety."

BETWEEN TWO STOOLS

This is a Doitsu Aka Sanke — just! Although a pleasing koi, its chances in a show would be remote, first because it is Doitsu, rather than fully scaled, and secondly because the small area of white means it must be judged in Sanke, rather than in the Bekko classification with which it has more affinity.

This fish does have some white on the body, but is very nearly an Aka Bekko. Note the "tortoiseshell" sumi.

In young fish like this, body shape is bound to be slimmer than in mature koi.

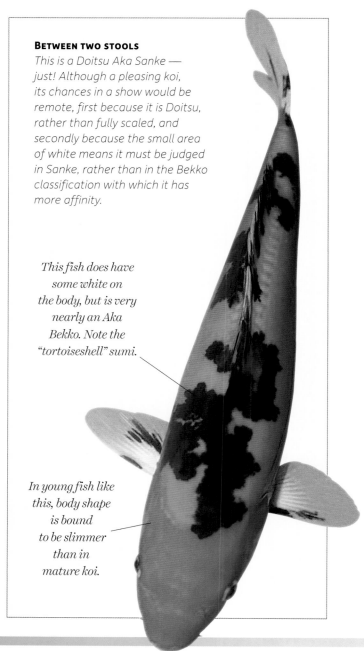

Doitsu and Gin-Rin Shiro Bekko (both benched Bekko in the UK) make striking pond fish. The dorsal mirror scales of the former are silvery white, contrasting beautifully with any sumi they overlay.

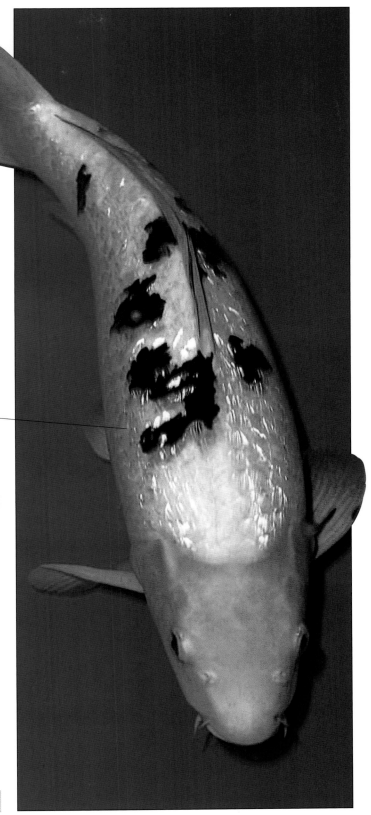

▶ **BEKKO THROUGH FROSTED GLASS**
An accomplished Gin-Rin Shiro Bekko. It stands up well, first as a Bekko, second as a Gin-Rin koi. The sparkling scales over the jet-black sumi give a "frosted glass" effect. A yellow head is a common fault in Shiro Bekko, but this one has beautifully clear skin.

"Tortoiseshell" sumi, typical of Bekko — and the closely allied variety, Sanke.

KOI DEFINITIONS

Aka Bekko ~ Red koi with black Sanke-type markings

Aka Sanke ~ Koi showing large areas of red unrelieved by cuts in the pattern

Bekko ~ Black Sanke-type markings on a white, red or yellow base

Benigoi ~ Nonmetallic, deep crimson koi

Doitsu ~ Koi with no scales other than enlarged scales along the lateral line and two lines running either side of the dorsal fin

Gin-Rin ~ Koi with reflective silver scales

Kawarimono ~ Class for all nonmetallic koi not included in any other group

Ki Bekko ~ Lemon-yellow with black Sanke-type markings

Kigoi ~ Nonmetallic yellow koi

Kohaku ~ White koi with red markings

Sanke ~ White koi with red and black markings

Shiro Bekko ~ White koi with black Sanke-type markings

Sumi ~ Black

Tora, or Tiger, Ogon ~ Metallic equivalent of Ki Bekko

Asagi and Shusui

Asagi are fully scaled, nonmetallic fish with a long history, but because they closely resemble Magoi (the wild black carp), some hobbyists see them as unrefined, dull and not "proper" koi at all. Certainly they are an acquired taste, far removed from the brilliantly tricolored modern Showa or the flashy koi grouped in Hikariutsuri. But their quiet elegance serves as a counterpoint to their more exotic pondmates and they also have the potential to grow very large.

The Japanese recognize three types of Magoi, one of which, the Asagi Magoi, is the forerunner of all modern koi. Its back is bluish, with a reticulated scale pattern, and some hi is present on the cheeks, flanks and pectoral fins. About 160 years ago, two mutants arose from this proto-koi, namely the Konjo and the Narumi Asagi. Although instrumental in the development of Matsuba koi, the dark Konjo Asagi are valueless in their own right except as food fish. However, Narumi Asagi have gone on to become one half of a recognized judging variety — the other being their Doitsu counterparts, Shusui.

The history of Asagi

The prefix "Narumi" is derived from the town of the same name in Ichi Prefecture, where a locally made fabric was said to resemble the pattern on the backs of these koi. Asagi seem to have appeared all over Japan, not just in Niigata — this at a time when interest in mutant fish led to their being kept back from the food crop and bred together for curiosity's sake, long before koi were seen as a commercial proposition.

Modern Asagi

Because they breed relatively true, countless ordinary-grade Asagi are produced each year, and newcomers to koi can gain an unfavorable impression of the variety because really good examples are so seldom seen. Ideally, the back should be evenly covered in scales that are pale blue where they enter the skin, but with a darker edging — not the other way around, as is sometimes stated. The sharper the definition between these two shades, the more impressive the koi will

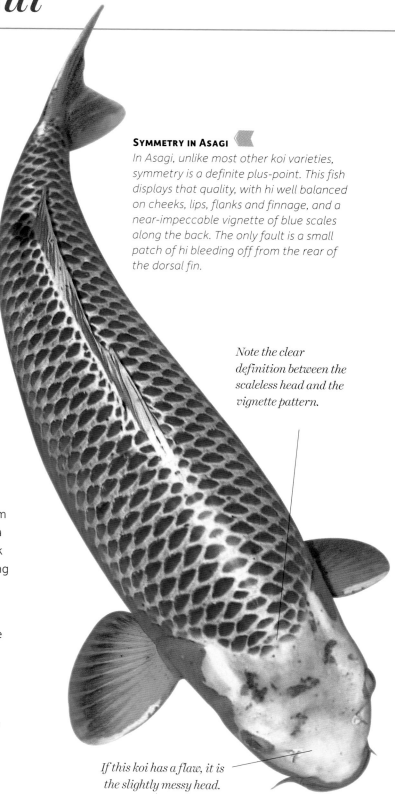

SYMMETRY IN ASAGI

In Asagi, unlike most other koi varieties, symmetry is a definite plus-point. This fish displays that quality, with hi well balanced on cheeks, lips, flanks and finnage, and a near-impeccable vignette of blue scales along the back. The only fault is a small patch of hi bleeding off from the rear of the dorsal fin.

Note the clear definition between the scaleless head and the vignette pattern.

If this koi has a flaw, it is the slightly messy head.

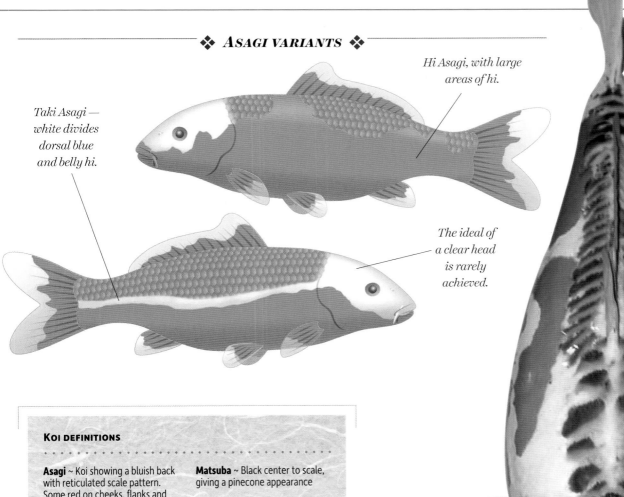

❖ ASAGI VARIANTS ❖

Taki Asagi — white divides dorsal blue and belly hi.

Hi Asagi, with large areas of hi.

The ideal of a clear head is rarely achieved.

KOI DEFINITIONS

Asagi ~ Koi showing a bluish back with reticulated scale pattern. Some red on cheeks, flanks and pectoral fins

Asagi Magoi ~ Forerunner of all modern koi

Doitsu ~ Koi with no scales other than enlarged scales along the lateral line and two lines running either side of the dorsal fin

Fukurin ~ Net effect of lustrous skin around the scales of (usually) metallic koi

Hi Asagi ~ Asagi in which red patterning extends almost up to the dorsal fin

Hikari Utsuri ~ Class for metallic Utsuri and Showa

Matsuba ~ Black center to scale, giving a pinecone appearance

Menkaburi ~ Red head

Motoguro ~ Solid black coloration in the base of pectoral fins on Showa and related varieties

Narumi Asagi ~ Asagi with light blue pattern

Showa ~ Black koi with red and white markings

Shusui ~ Doitsu Asagi

Taki Asagi ~ Asagi koi with white line dividing areas of red and blue on the flanks

▶ KEEPING A CLEAR HEAD

On the plus side, this Shusui has a clear head, pleasing hi and sky-blue dorsal scales; in many examples, these scales turn gray or black. However, scalation forward of the dorsal fin is rather uneven. Rarely do all elements come together in this variety.

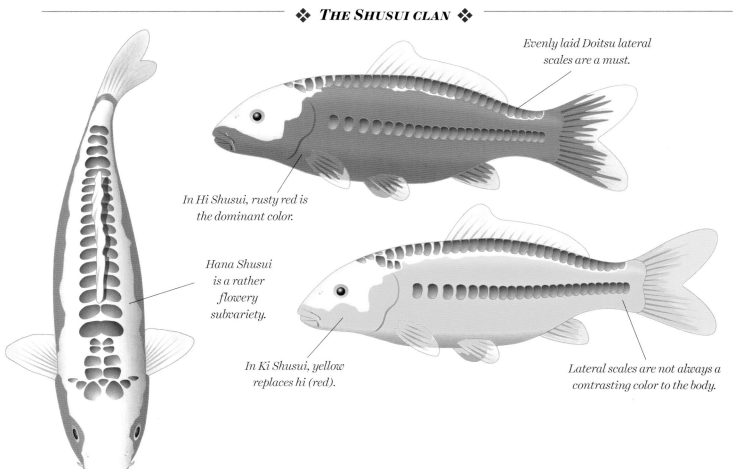

Evenly laid Doitsu lateral scales are a must.

In Hi Shusui, rusty red is the dominant color.

Hana Shusui is a rather flowery subvariety.

In Ki Shusui, yellow replaces hi (red).

Lateral scales are not always a contrasting color to the body.

look. As the fish grow, the skin stretches and this reticulation becomes even more apparent — this is true Fukurin. Because they are so obvious in this variety, missing or damaged scales will seriously devalue an otherwise good koi. The head is often a disappointing feature in Asagi. Ideally, it should be a uniform clear white, but more often takes on a blue or grayish tint. In young examples, the bones of the skull show through, but this effect disappears as the translucent skin thickens. If there is a lot of head hi forming a hood pattern, the fish is known as a Menkaburi Asagi.

Asagi hi is more of a rusty red than the bright scarlet associated with the Kohaku. Typically, it runs up from the belly to the lateral line or beyond, also covering the jaw, cheeks and some or all of the fins. On the pectorals it can be configured like the motoguro of Showa, or else spread out over the entire area of the fins. Wherever hi appears in this variety it should be symmetrical. Some Asagi have a greater than usual percentage

of red patterning, which can extend almost up to the dorsal fin. These are known as Hi Asagi. Others — Taki Asagi — have a white line dividing the areas of red and blue on the flanks. Both these subvarieties are still grouped in Asagi.

Shusui

The second element of an odd variety partnership is the Shusui, which means "autumn water" in Japanese. At first sight, these mirror-scaled koi seem to have little in common with Asagi, but that variety was first crossed with a German table carp in 1910 by Yoshigoro Akiyama, resulting in the first Shusui.

The color distribution is essentially the same as in the Asagi, but because there are no normal scales to give an overall reticulated effect, the smooth, sky-blue back is instead highlighted by the Doitsu scalation. In good examples, these armored scales form a regular pattern on the shoulders of the koi and then run in two lines on either side of the dorsal fin, returning to a single line on the caudal peduncle. A further line is usually present along each flank, roughly following the lateral line.

The most common fault on Shusui is a messy shoulder scale pattern that lacks symmetry. Rogue scales can appear elsewhere on the body, further devaluing the fish. In hard water, the mirror scales can turn grayish or black, and once this happens they never revert back to blue. A clear head is essential on Shusui, as it is on Asagi. The skin is never snow-white, more of an ice blue, but should be blemish-free.

The distribution of the red and blue on a Shusui determines its subclassification. On Hi Shusui the hi extends up over the back, so that the two contrasting colors are red and dark blue. These are unsubtle,

KOI DEFINITIONS

Ginsui ~ Metallic Shusui with a silver luster

Goshiki Shusui ~ Doitsu, nonmetallic blue Goshiki

Hana Shusui ~ Red in a wavy pattern to give a flowery effect

Hikarimoyo ~ Class for all multicolored metallic koi except Utsuri and Showa

Hikarimuji ~ Class for single-colored metallic koi

Hi Shusui ~ Red extends up over the back contrasting with the dark blue

Kawarimono ~ Class for all nonmetallic koi not included in any other group

Ki Matsuba ~ Metallic gold koi

with pinecone scalation

Kinsui ~ Metallic Shusui with a gold luster

Ki Shusui ~ Shusui with yellow instead of red coloration

Midorigoi ~ Greenish-yellow with mirror scales

Ogon ~ Single-colored metallic koi

Sanke Shusui ~ Doitsu Sanke whose pattern is underlaid with the blue back of the Shusui

Showa Shusui ~ Doitsu koi with intermediate markings showing elements of both varieties.

Taki Asagi ~ Asagi koi with white line dividing areas of red and blue on the flanks

quite striking, koi. Hana Shusui also have more red than normal, but here it is in the form of an extra band between the lateral line and dorsal fin, with a break in between. In the best examples, the hi is laid on in a wavy pattern to give a flowery effect.

In Ki Shusui, yellow replaces the red. This is a confusing subvariety, because if the blue dorsal scales turn black it is easy to confuse with a Doitsu Ki Matsuba. Another rare, Shusui-like koi is the Midorigoi, which is greenish-yellow with mirror scales. This one is benched in Kawarimono.

Shusui have been crossed with several normally scaled koi varieties to produce interesting variations on a theme. The commonest in the hobby are Showa Shusui, Sanke Shusui and Goshiki Shusui. Crosses with the Ogons (in the Hikarimuji classification) resulted in Ginsui and Kinsui, which used to be quite popular, but have now been superseded by more refined Doitsu fish in the Hikarimoyo class.

THE FACE OF QUALITY
A lovely Hi Shusui with an unusual head pattern and impressive blue dorsal scales. The intrusion of hi into the fins merely adds to the interest of this beautiful fish.

Koromo

Koromo means "robed" in Japanese and describes a group of koi whose quiet elegance finds favor with connoisseurs, even though the fish did not become available until the early 1950s. Strictly speaking, Koromo are crossbred fish; the first example resulted from a spawning between a male Kohaku and a female Narumi Asagi.

Ai Goromo

The collective name "Koromo" covers several varieties, the best known being Ai Goromo. This is a white koi with the hi pattern of a Kohaku, but each red scale is reticulated in black or dark blue — an indication of Asagi ancestry. To obtain a good Ai Goromo you must first have a good Kohaku, with all the qualities expected of that variety: snow-white skin, deep crimson hi and an interesting traditional or modern pattern. The dark edging to the scales appears only faintly to begin with and may take years to come out fully. Too much sumi early in life is an indication that this color will eventually overwhelm the koi. But in mature fish, the sumi should be evenly distributed over all patches of hi, with the exception of the head.

From a classification point of view, it is important that the black/dark blue color does not intrude into the white areas. If it does, the fish is no longer an Ai Goromo, but becomes a Goshiki. This extremely variable variety is now grouped in Koromo in the West, but still judged in Kawarimono in Japan. Many apparently good-quality baby Ai Goromo develop into Goshiki, which are in no way inferior koi; it was purely to avoid benching disputes in borderline cases that Goshiki went into Koromo.

Sumi Goromo

There is much confusion between Ai Goromo and Sumi Goromo. The latter are white koi with black patterns, the edge of each scale reticulated in red — a mirror image of what happens in Ai Goromo. An alternative definition of a Sumi Goromo is a red-and-white koi in which the areas of hi are lightly overlaid with black. This ties in with the dusky red head of these fish, but does not explain the distinct scale reticulation still apparent. The

▶ **MODERN GOSHIKI FINERY**
A modern Goshiki of some accomplishment. The scale vignette extends over the white, as well as the hi, but clear pectorals and the white shoulder patch open up the pattern. The sumi on the head lends the koi a somewhat quizzical look. Volume and skin quality are both excellent.

The dark scale edging should improve further as the koi grows.

Hi, sumi and clear white combine in an interesting head pattern.

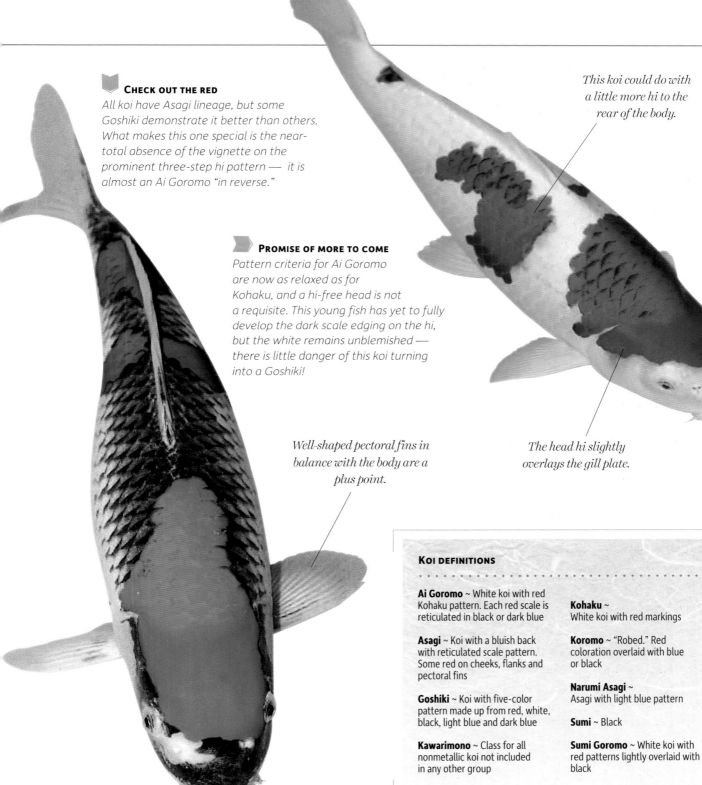

CHECK OUT THE RED

All koi have Asagi lineage, but some Goshiki demonstrate it better than others. What makes this one special is the near-total absence of the vignette on the prominent three-step hi pattern — it is almost an Ai Goromo "in reverse."

PROMISE OF MORE TO COME

Pattern criteria for Ai Goromo are now as relaxed as for Kohaku, and a hi-free head is not a requisite. This young fish has yet to fully develop the dark scale edging on the hi, but the white remains unblemished — there is little danger of this koi turning into a Goshiki!

This koi could do with a little more hi to the rear of the body.

Well-shaped pectoral fins in balance with the body are a plus point.

The head hi slightly overlays the gill plate.

KOI DEFINITIONS

Ai Goromo ~ White koi with red Kohaku pattern. Each red scale is reticulated in black or dark blue

Asagi ~ Koi with a bluish back with reticulated scale pattern. Some red on cheeks, flanks and pectoral fins

Goshiki ~ Koi with five-color pattern made up from red, white, black, light blue and dark blue

Kawarimono ~ Class for all nonmetallic koi not included in any other group

Kohaku ~ White koi with red markings

Koromo ~ "Robed." Red coloration overlaid with blue or black

Narumi Asagi ~ Asagi with light blue pattern

Sumi ~ Black

Sumi Goromo ~ White koi with red patterns lightly overlaid with black

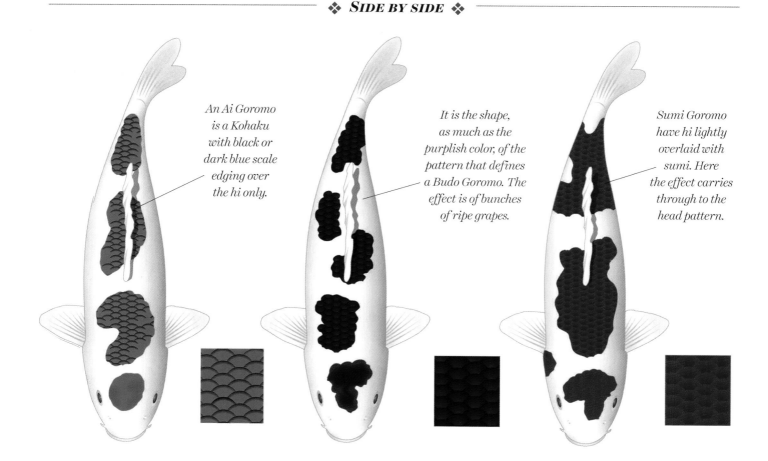

An Ai Goromo is a Kohaku with black or dark blue scale edging over the hi only.

It is the shape, as much as the purplish color, of the pattern that defines a Budo Goromo. The effect is of bunches of ripe grapes.

Sumi Goromo have hi lightly overlaid with sumi. Here the effect carries through to the head pattern.

truth is, dark Ai Goromo and light Sumi Goromo can look very similar. However, once again, if sumi migrates on to the white areas of skin, a Sumi Goromo becomes a Goshiki.

Budo Goromo
Budo Goromo is a variant of the Sumi Goromo, the overall effect being of a white fish with purplish patches of overlaid hi. The leading edges (kiwa) show individual scales picked out against white, reminiscent in both shape and color of bunches of grapes.

Budo Sanke
This fish is simply a Budo Goromo with additional Hon sumi. For judging purposes, it goes in Kawarimono, although obviously of Koromo lineage.

Koromo Sanke
This is a Taisho Sanke x Ai Goromo cross, similar to the above but with more distinct reticulation. It is essentially an Ai Goromo with Sanke Hon sumi, in addition to the black edging to each red scale.

Koromo Showa
This Showa x Koromo cross can be a very striking koi, even though the hi tends to be more rusty red than crimson. The Hon sumi here is a dominant color, extending over the head in typical Showa fashion.

Doitsu Ai Goromo
This very rare and prized koi is easily confused with a Doitsu Sanke, as both are tricolored German-scaled koi. However,

CLEARLY A BUNCH OF GRAPES

A very light Budo Goromo, proving that clear white skin is essential to set off any pattern. This fish shows the "bunch of grapes" markings characteristic of the variety.

in the Doitsu Ai Goromo the only blue/ black scales are the enlarged ones along the back. In all other respects the fish is a Doitsu Kohaku, with no further intrusion of a third color into the body hi. As all recognized Doitsu koi, with the exception of Go Sanke, are benched under their own variety, the correct classification of this type of fish is Koromo.

Goshiki

This is probably the most diverse koi variety known. Goshiki are said to be five-colored koi, although you need to be very creative to pick out the alleged red, black, white, light blue and dark blue elements. Confusingly, a sixth color — purple — is formed when black and blue overlay one another.

Goshiki have strong Asagi lineage, which lends a reticulation to some or all of the scales. The traditional Goshiki is a rather dark fish, with messy, indistinct patterning, sometimes relieved by clear patches of hi, especially on the face and back. Others look like straight Kohaku x Asagi crosses, with a black, net-like reticulation covering the whole body. However, the best modern Goshiki are simply amazing.

KOI DEFINITIONS

Ai Goromo ~ White koi with red Kohaku pattern. Each red scale is reticulated in black or dark blue

Asagi ~ Koi showing a bluish back with reticulated scale pattern. Some red on cheeks, flanks and pectoral fins

Budo Goromo ~ White koi with purplish patches of black overlaying red in a pattern resembling bunches of grapes

Budo Sanke ~ Budo Goromo with additional solid black markings

Doitsu ~ Koi with no scales other than enlarged scales along the lateral line and two lines running either side of the dorsal fin

Doitsu Ai Goromo ~ Only the enlarged scales running along the back are blue/black.

Go Sanke ~ Koi from the Kohaku, Sanke and Showa classes

Goshiki ~ Koi with five-color pattern made up from red, white, black, light blue and dark blue

Hon sumi ~ Solid Sanke-type black markings

Kawarimono ~ Class for all nonmetallic koi not included in any other group

Kiwa ~ Border of red and white at the rear edge of hi patterns

Kohaku ~ White koi with red markings

Sanke ~ White koi with red and black markings

Showa ~ Black koi with red and white markings

Sumi Goromo ~ White koi with red patterns lightly overlaid with black

Taisho Sanke/Taisho Sanshoku ~ Full names for Sanke

In 1993, a UK koi company based in the Midlands imported a fish called "Polo," whose distinguishing feature is a black-bordered window of white on the large, otherwise clear, forward hi marking. The fish has snow-white skin and nose sumi that would do credit to any Showa. The rear hi pattern is classic Ai Goromo. In fact, this fish was close to being a Koromo Showa; only a little reticulation over the white tipped it over into Goshiki. An even better Goshiki arrived at the same company 4 years later, a female from the breeder Maru. This one has a classic stepped Kohaku pattern touched with gray and black, perfect skin and a fetching nose spot set off by bright blue eyes.

Gin-Rin Goshiki and Doitsu Goshiki add further to the complexity of an already fathomless variety. Because the appearance of the reflective scales is influenced by the skin colors beneath, they can appear gold, silver or bluish-gray in a good Gin-Rin Goshiki. Often these combine in a single fish and the effect is almost unreal.

A WHOLLY EXCEPTIONAL KOI

This male Goshiki named "Polo" for the black-bordered window of white on its back, arrived in the UK in 1993 and laid down new criteria of excellence with its clear-cut and unusual pattern.

GOSHIKI, WHAT A BEAUTY

Arguably the best Goshiki currently in the West. The clear white saddle, deep vignetting on the hi and charming nose spot are teamed with a voluminous body to make this koi a winner all down the line.

GIN-RIN PLUS POINTS

This is a Gin-Rin Goshiki. This variety needs clearly delineated patterning for the sparkling scales to work to the koi's advantage, and this is a good example, with uncluttered hi. The body could do with a little more volume, however.

THE FACE OF THE FUTURE

This is a modern Goshiki — almost an Ai Goromo — in which white predominates. The head hi is particularly interesting, and note the blocks of hi in the joints of the pectoral fins — a nice finishing touch.

KOI DEFINITIONS

Ai Goromo ~ White koi with red Kohaku pattern. Each red scale is reticulated in black or dark blue

Asagi ~ Koi showing a bluish back with reticulated scale pattern. Some red on cheeks, flanks and pectoral fins

Doitsu ~ Koi with no scales other than enlarged scales along the lateral line and two lines running either side of the dorsal fin

Gin-Rin ~ Koi with reflective silver scales

Goshiki ~ Koi with five-color pattern made up from red, white, black, light blue and dark blue

Kohaku ~ White koi with red markings

Koromo ~ "Robed." Red coloration overlaid with blue or black

Showa ~ Black koi with red and white markings

Kawarimono

Kawarimono is the "catch-all" classification for nonmetallic koi not benched elsewhere. Some are varieties in their own right, whereas some are crosses that display characteristics of both parents. Others are true "one-offs," whose origins would be hard to pin down. Finally, there are a few koi that deviate so much from the judging criteria applied to their variety that they are placed in Kawarimono to give them a realistic chance against the opposition. One example is the Kanoko Kohaku, with dappled hi, where individual scales show against the white ground like the markings of a young deer. It could never compete against conventionally marked Kohaku.

However, Kawarimono is by no means a dumping ground for the oddities of the koi world. There is no place in this classification (or anywhere else) for sub-standard fish whose only claim to fame is their uniqueness, because no two koi of any variety are ever exactly alike. The usual criteria of good body shape and skin quality and, where applicable, an interesting pattern, still hold true. Cross-bred koi should display the best, rather than the worst, features of the union, combined in a pleasing manner. That, after all, is how several accepted varieties were developed in the first place.

For convenience, varieties in Kawarimono can be grouped into single-colored koi, black koi (of Karasu lineage) and others. Some are readily available, but others are not bred intentionally — they arise as "sports" from other spawnings.

Single-colored koi

Benigoi, or Aka Muji, are all-red Kohaku derivatives resembling giant goldfish. Their fins can be either red or tipped with white. Koi with the latter feature are sometimes known as Aka Hajiro. For the fish to be of any value, the hi must be uniformly deep crimson, and the body shape voluminous without being fat. The plainer the koi, the more obvious any minor blemishes.

Shiro Muji are also thrown from Kohaku spawnings, but this time the hi is absent. These all-white fish are normally culled out, but occasionally one with exceptional skin quality is kept back and grown on. Albinos, with red eyes, are sought-after rarities, as are those with Gin-Rin scalation.

Kigoi are koi of a uniform lemon yellow, and quite an old variety. When the metallic Ogons first appeared, these koi lost popularity, but are now staging a comeback. Two types are available: leucistic (with black eyes) and true, red-eyed albinos, known as Akame Kigoi. These fish — particularly the males — can grow to 1 m (39 in) or more. Good examples are free from red blemishes or silvery patches above the lateral line. Black-eyed Kigoi are sometimes confused with saffron-colored Chagoi, as the latter vary greatly in color.

In Magoi, the scales are actually deep bronze, but the fish appear black when viewed from above. Magoi are not recognized as true koi by some show organizers, but that does not stop them being kept. Free of the stunting effects that can arise from selective breeding for color or pattern, these

KOI NOT GOLDFISH

All-red koi are known as Benigoi, but when the fish has white-tipped fins — as here — it is known as an Aka Hajiro. The overall impression is similar to that of the Hajiro (hence the name), but the latter is an all-black koi with white on its fins.

A clear, crimson head is an essential attribute of Benigoi.

❖ PLAIN AND DAPPLED ❖

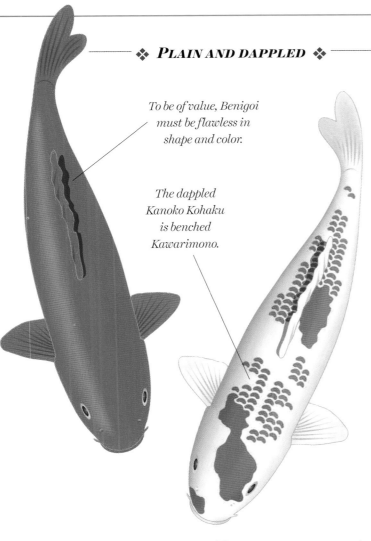

To be of value, Benigoi must be flawless in shape and color.

The dappled Kanoko Kohaku is benched Kawarimono.

KOI DEFINITIONS

Aka Hajiro ~
Red koi with white-tipped fins

Aka Muji ~
Nonmetallic all-red koi

Akame Kigoi ~
Red-eyed albino koi

Benigoi ~
Nonmetallic, deep crimson koi

Chagoi ~
Nonmetallic brown koi

Hajiro ~ Black koi with white nose and white-tipped fins

Kanoko Kohaku ~
Kohaku with dappled red pattern

Kawarimono ~ Class for all nonmetallic koi not included in any other group

Kigoi ~
Nonmetallic lemon-yellow koi

Kohaku ~
White koi with red markings

Ogon ~
Single-colored metallic koi

Shiro Muji ~
All-white, nonmetallic koi

▶ **LEMON FIZZ**
Not a Gin-Rin Ogon, which would be a metallic fish, but a Gin-Rin Kigoi. The clear, lemon-yellow skin is overlaid with even, sparkling scales.

❖ THE EYES HAVE IT ❖

Red-eyed Kigoi (Akame Kigoi) are sought-after fish, now rarely bred.

Black-eyed (leucistic) Kigoi are not true albinos, but still eye-catchers.

215

fish can become huge. For that reason, Magoi blood is being reintroduced into some Go Sanke bloodlines to speed and maximize growth.

Chagoi are uniform brown koi. The word "Cha" derives from the Chinese/Japanese for tea, which describes their color. They are noted for two qualities: their capacity to grow very large and their extreme friendliness. Introducing a Chagoi to a pondful of nervous koi has a calming effect, and soon they will all be feeding from the hand of their owner. The color of Chagoi can vary from saffron through reddish brown to almost black, the paler fish being the most highly valued. Good, blemish-free scale reticulation is a requirement. Some Japanese breeders are introducing metallic blood into this variety to produce fish with matt scalation but Ogon-like pectoral fins. Gin-Rin Chagoi are also finding favor.

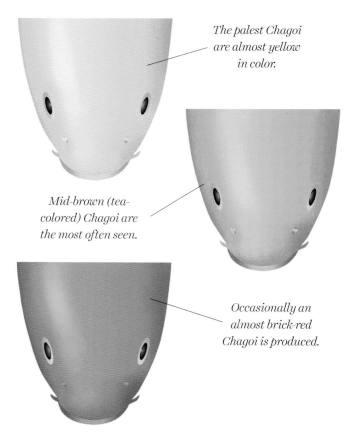

❖ *SHADES OF BROWN* ❖

The palest Chagoi are almost yellow in color.

Mid-brown (tea-colored) Chagoi are the most often seen.

Occasionally an almost brick-red Chagoi is produced.

Soragoi are plain blue-gray koi. They are not a popular variety in their own right, but crossed with Chagoi they become Ochiba Shigure. Here, the gray base color of the Soragoi is patterned with the brown of the Chagoi. The best examples show Kohaku-like markings, but more often the brown is confined to the head or to small patches on the body. Doitsu and Gin-Rin Ochiba are available.

BIG AND FRIENDLY
With mature Chagoi, one could be forgiven for thinking koi were sold by weight and volume. But "battleships" like this big female need to display more than just bulk to be acceptable koi.

KOI DEFINITIONS

Chagoi ~
Nonmetallic brown koi

Doitsu ~ Koi with no scales other than enlarged scales along the lateral line and two lines running either side of the dorsal fin

Gin-Rin ~ Koi with reflective silver scales

Go Sanke ~ Koi from the Kohaku, Sanke and Showa classes

Kohaku ~
White koi with red markings

Magoi ~ Ancestral black carp

Ogon ~
Single-colored metallic koi

Ochiba/Ochiba Shigure ~
Blue-gray koi with a brown pattern

Soragoi ~ Plain blue-gray koi

TEUTONIC ELEGANCE
This Doitsu Ochiba Shigure clearly lacks reticulated scalation, but this clear-headed and evenly German-scaled example would look good in anyone's pond.

LEAVES ON THE WATER
The gray fish marked with brown, known as Ochiba Shigure (meaning "leaves on the water"), is probably a Chagoi/Soragoi cross. This variety has become very popular, but really good examples are still hard to find.

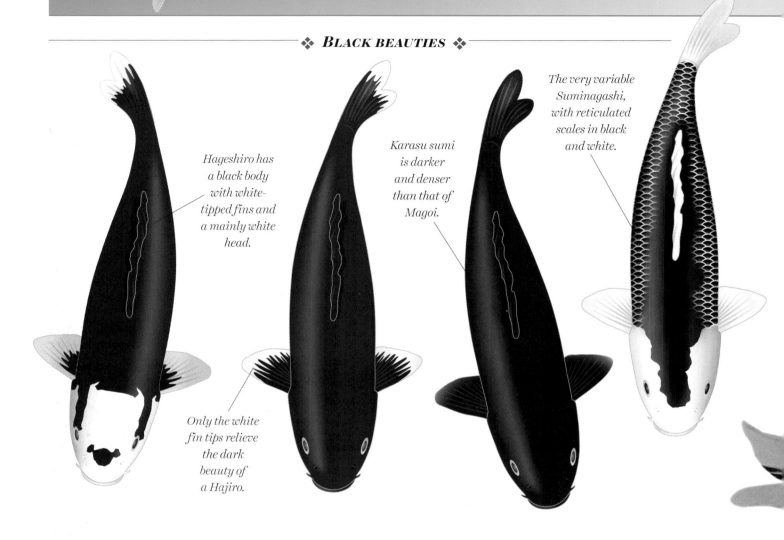

Hageshiro has a black body with white-tipped fins and a mainly white head.

Only the white fin tips relieve the dark beauty of a Hajiro.

Karasu sumi is darker and denser than that of Magoi.

The very variable Suminagashi, with reticulated scales in black and white.

Black koi and their derivatives

The Karasu, or "Crow," is a very old variety, with matt black fins and body and a white or orange belly. The very similar Hajiro is a black koi with a white nose and white-tipped pectoral fins, which make it more visible in the water. The Hageshiro adds a white head to this color combination, whereas the Yotsujiro's fins are completely white. All four koi should display deep and even sumi, darker than that of the Magoi.

Suminagashi are fully scaled koi with black scales picked out in white. In this highly variable variety, the reticulated scales can cover all or part of the body. The similar-looking Matsukawabake is an oddity, in that the distribution of black and white areas changes according to the seasons and the temperature of the water in which it is kept. However, this does not amount to a complete reversal of pattern. Fish can turn completely black or completely white under some

circumstances, but display interesting shadowy sumi in the transition period.

Kumonryu, which first appeared in the 1980s, is the most popular of all black koi derivatives in Kawarimono. The name means "dragon fish" and is applied to these koi because their markings are reminiscent of the coiled bodies of these mythical beasts as depicted in oriental paintings. Kumonryu are always Doitsu, which means the delineation between areas of white and sumi is sharp. Patterning is highly variable; the best examples show large, wavy-edged blocks of white along the flanks and dorsal surface. However, these fish are effectively Doitsu Matsukawabake, so their patterning can change dramatically for better or worse after you have bought them. In extreme cases, the hobbyist ends up with an all-white Doitsugoi, which is valueless.

KOI DEFINITIONS

Doitsu ~ Koi with no scales other than enlarged scales along the lateral line and two lines running either side of the dorsal fin

Hageshiro ~ Black koi with white on the head and white-tipped pectoral fins

Hajiro ~ Black koi with white tail tip and white-tipped pectoral fins

Karasu ~ Koi with matt black fins and body and a white or orange belly

Kawarimono ~ Class for all nonmetallic koi not included in any other group

Kumonryu ~ Black doitsu koi with some white on head, fins and body

Magoi ~ Ancestral black carp

Matsukawabake ~ Nonmetallic black and white koi, whose pattern changes significantly with season/water temperature

Sumi ~ Black

Suminagashi ~ Koi with black scales picked out in white

Yotsujiro ~ Black koi with white head, pectoral, dorsal and caudal fins

▶ KING OF KAWARIMONO
This lovely Kumonryu shows why the Japanese revere the variety. Always Doitsu, note how the sumi runs from head to tail, rather than in patches from flank to flank and over the dorsal surface. The effect is of ink calligraphy.

▶ QUICK CHANGE ARTIST
The distribution of sumi and white on Matsukawabake can change from season to season and according to water temperature and chemistry. Some of these fish will end up all-white, and the black may or may not then return.

Nose sumi sets off an otherwise clear white head.

Other Kawarimono

Matsuba, or Matsubagoi, are most commonly bred as metallic fish, and benched in Hikarimuji. The reticulated scalation is counted as only one color by the Japanese. However, matt-scaled Matsubagoi go into Kawarimono. These are understated koi and quite rare, although Aka Matsuba are sometimes seen entered in the Jumbo class; being a very early variety, they grow large. Aka Matsuba are red koi with dark scale reticulation, and of Asagi lineage. However, the head should be red, rather than white. Any patches of blue and the fish is classed as an Asagi.

Ki Matsuba are most often seen in their Doitsu form, and resemble a Shusui in which the red and blue skin is replaced by yellow. The white equivalent is the rare Shiro Matsuba.

Midorigoi are green Doitsu koi, the only variety to show this color. The actual shade is more of a translucent greenish-yellow, while the mirror scales can be black or silver. These fish originally resulted from a cross between a Shusui and a Yamabuki Ogon. The only variety likely to be confused with them is the Doitsu Ki Matsuba. Crossings between Shusui and Midorigoi occasionally throw up the rare Enyu, a purplish koi with hi markings.

Hybrids

Several koi in Kawarimono have Shusui lineage, but first-generation crosses between these and Sanke or Showa can result in particularly striking Doitsu Kawarimono.

Kage Utsuri and Showa

These koi are benched Kawarimono in Japanese shows, but under their own variety elsewhere. For example, a Kage Hi Utsuri would go into Utsurimono. The shadowy Kage sumi overlays the base red, white or yellow skin in a reticulated pattern, alongside solid black patterning, but may not stay throughout the lifetime of the koi. Likewise, Goshiki in Japan are benched Kawarimono, but in the West they are classed as Koromo.

UP-AND-COMING VARIETIES

Gin-Rin scalation adds an extra dimension to otherwise rather plain koi grouped in Kawarimono. Quick to pick up the trend, Japanese breeders are now producing many Gin-Rin Chagoi, Soragoi and Ochiba Shigure. In single-colored koi, there is nothing to distract the eye from the beauty of even, sparkling scales, while in varieties such as Ochiba Shigure, the Gin-Rin takes on a quality of its own, depending on which skin color the scales overlay.

Left: *Gin-Rin Soragoi. Reflective silver scales add a new dimension to a great blue-gray fish.*

Right: *This Gin-Rin Ochiba is a large and imposing koi with real presence.*

KOI DEFINITIONS

Aka Matsuba ~ Red koi with dark scale reticulation

Asagi ~ Koi with a bluish back with reticulated scale pattern. Some red on cheeks, flanks and pectoral fins

Chagoi ~ Nonmetallic brown koi

Doitsu ~ Koi with no scales other than enlarged scales along the lateral line and two lines running either side of thedorsal fin

Enyu ~ Purplish koi with red markings

Gin ~ Silver

Gin-Rin ~ Koi with reflective silver scales

Goshiki ~ Koi with five-color pattern made up from red, white, black, light blue and dark blue

Hi ~ Red

Hikarimuji ~ Class for single-colored metallic koi

Hi Utsuri ~ Black koi with red or orange markings

Kage ~ Shadowy black reticulated marking over white (or red on Hi Utsuri)

Kawarimono ~ Class for all nonmetallic koi not included in any other group

Ki Matsuba ~ Nonmetallic yellow koi with pinecone scalation

Kin ~ Gold

Koromo ~ "Robed." Red coloration overlaid with blue or black

Matsuba/Matsubagoi ~ Black center to scale, giving a pinecone appearance

Midorigoi ~ Greenish-yellow koi with mirror scales

Ochiba/Ochiba Shigure ~ Blue-gray koi with a brown pattern

Ogon ~ Single-colored metallic koi

Sanke ~ White koi with red and black markings

Shiro Matsuba ~ White koi with black pinecone reticulation

Showa ~ Black koi with red and white markings

Shusui ~ Doitsu Asagi

Soragoi ~ Plain blue-gray koi

Sumi ~ Black

Utsuri ~ Reflections

Utsurimono ~ Black koi with white, red or yellow markings

Yamabuki Ogon ~ Yellow-gold Ogon

RARITY VALUE

Aka Matsuba, unlike Gin and Kin Matsuba, are nonmetallic koi and grouped in Kawarimono. It is rarely seen nowadays, but good examples have crimson scales with the typical "pinecone" dark reticulation. This variety can grow to a huge size.

Midorigoi are greenish-yellow Doitsu koi with rather translucent skin. Good examples, with even dorsal scalation, are rare, and the yellow color tends to fade with age.

Hikarimuji

The Japanese word *Hikari* means "shining," and Hikarimuji are single-colored koi with an overall dull, metallic luster. The fish most commonly associated with this group are Ogon (formerly spelt "Ohgon"), but the classification also takes in metallic Matsuba, even though to Western eyes the scale reticulation of these involves an extra color, namely black.

The history of Ogon

In 1921, a Magoi with a gold-striped back was caught from a river in Takezawa, Yamakoshi prefecture, by Sawata Aoki. Fascinated by this unusual carp, he and his son Hideyoshi embarked on a process of selective breeding, keeping back only those fish that showed some golden scalation. After four or five generations, Aoki succeeded in producing the forerunners of the Ogon — Ginbo and Kinbo, and Kin Kabuto and Gin Kabuto. The latter had silver edges to their dark scales and a characteristic helmet-shaped head marking, rather like that found on today's ghost koi. All four types are still thrown in spawnings today, but are considered valueless.

Aoki spawned the first true Ogon in 1946, the result of a union between a female Shiro Muji and eight males from his 25-year breeding program.

Modern Ogon

Ogon have an immediate appeal to newcomers to the hobby. These koi grow large, are easily visible in the pond and are lively and intelligent. Later, as koi-keepers become more discerning, Ogon tend to be abandoned in favor of the Go Sanke, but few ponds are without at least one of these imposing, shining fish as a reminder of early days in the hobby.

Modern Ogon are produced in huge numbers all around the world, and their overall quality is not good. To succeed in shows they must be exceptional specimens, with fine skin, even, blemish-free scalation and a clear, broad, lustrous head. The metallic sheen should extend into the finnage, especially the pectorals. As the fish grow large and their skin stretches, the scales should take on an almost three-dimensional quality due to their lighter, leading edges.

KOI DEFINITIONS

Ginbo ~ Dark koi with an overall silver sheen

Gin Kabuto ~ Black-helmeted koi with silver edges to scales

Go Sanke ~ Koi from the Kohaku, Sanke and Showa classes

Hikarimuji ~ Class for single-colored metallic koi

Kigoi ~ Nonmetallic lemon-yellow koi

Kinbo ~ Dark metallic koi with an overall golden sheen

Kin Kabuto ~ Black-helmeted koi with gold edges to scales

Magoi ~ Ancestral black carp

Matsuba ~ Black center to scale giving a pinecone appearance

Ogon ~ Single-colored metallic koi

Shiro Muji ~ White, nonmetallic koi

Yamabuki Ogon ~ Yellow-gold Ogon

WHAT'S MATSUBA ABOUT THIS?
This type of koi can cause huge identification problems. It's a Doitsu Kin Matsuba — although, with enlarged scales confined to the flank and dorsal surface, the "pinecone" effect is mainly absent. Because there is no true "pattern," the koi is classed as single colored.

A good metallic shine should be present on the fins, as well as on the body.

The most common faults with Ogon are discoloration on the head, pectoral fins that are too small for the body and, in larger examples, a tendency to grow fat. Champion Ogon should be voluminous but not obese, so provide strong circulating currents in their pond for them to swim against, which gives them the exercise they need. When buying, look out for mouth deformities and even the absence of one or both pelvic fins — these faults arise from inbreeding, and can be easily overlooked at a casual glance.

A desirable characteristic of Ogon is their imposing presence in the pond, so choose fish that have the potential to grow big. You can recognize them by their strong, thick caudal peduncle and wide shoulders, even when young.

Ogon colors

Early Ogon were golden, but with a tendency to turn blackish in warm water. This trait was bred out in 1957 by Masasuke Kataoka when he spawned one of these fish with a Kigoi. Modern yellow Ogon are known as Yamabuki Ogon; watch for orange flecks on the head, which devalue them.

Platinum Ogon, or Purachina, are white koi whose body shines with the same luster as the precious metal. These first appeared in 1963, probably from outcrossing Kigoi with the grayish silver Nezu ("Mouse") Ogon — which remains a variety in its own right. At about the same time, the Cream Ogon became popular. This is an understated

SILVER SUBMARINE
The Platinum Ogon, or Purachina, is available fully scaled or Doitsu. Good examples have a dull but deep metallic shine. The skin quality, known as Fukurin, imparts a 3D effect, which is evident in this particular koi.

CALL IT MELLOW YELLOW
A classic Yamabuki (yellow) Ogon. A clear head, even and blemish-free metallic scales and finnage, a voluminous (but not fat) body and well-proportioned pectoral fins are a must in this variety.

metallic koi, midway between a Purachina and a Yamabuki Ogon. Examples are still obtainable from one or two breeders, but rare.

Orenji Ogon resulted from crossing Higoi with the original yellow metallics, and later with Yamabuki Ogon. These are startlingly bright koi, but rather prone to shimis.

Kin-Gin-Rin Ogon

When the overall sheen of an Ogon is overlaid by sparkling Kin-Rin or Gin-Rin scales, the effect can be stunning. A good, clear head with "Fuji" (where the skin appears to have been sprayed with metallic car paint that has then developed tiny bubbles) is the hallmark of a fine Kin-Rin or Gin-Rin Ogon. This koi will still be benched Hikarimuji in Western shows.

Doitsu Ogon

Doitsu Ogon are grouped with their normally scaled counterparts for judging purposes. The Doitsu scalation should be neat and symmetrical and the same color as the body of the koi. These scales counterpoint what should be a deep luster on the areas of naked skin. There is also a "leather" version of the Doitsu Purachina, which is completely scaleless and very striking.

Matsuba Ogon

Matt-scaled Matsuba are grouped in Kawarimono, but their metallic equivalents are benched Hikarimuji. The most commonly available are Kin Matsuba (metallic gold, first produced in 1960) and the Gin Matsuba, its silver equivalent. Orenji Matsuba and Aka Matsuba Ogon are not often seen. The pinecone scalation must be pronounced; if the black is more of a gray, these koi look washed-out. Beginners are often confused by the Doitsu Matsuba Ogon, as the scale reticulation is not present. Instead, the black, German scales are aligned in the usual position, where they contrast sharply with the metallic body. Orange Doitsu Ogon, although rare, are particularly striking. They are also known as Mizuho ("Rice Ear") Ogon.

Ogon are important fish in their own right, but have also been instrumental in the development of many other metallic koi varieties in Hikari Utsuri and Hikarimoyo.

 CREAM OF THE CROP

This Cream Ogon, the forerunner of the Yamabuki, is a very subtle fish still being bred by a few Japanese enthusiasts. The color is that of rich, full-cream milk.

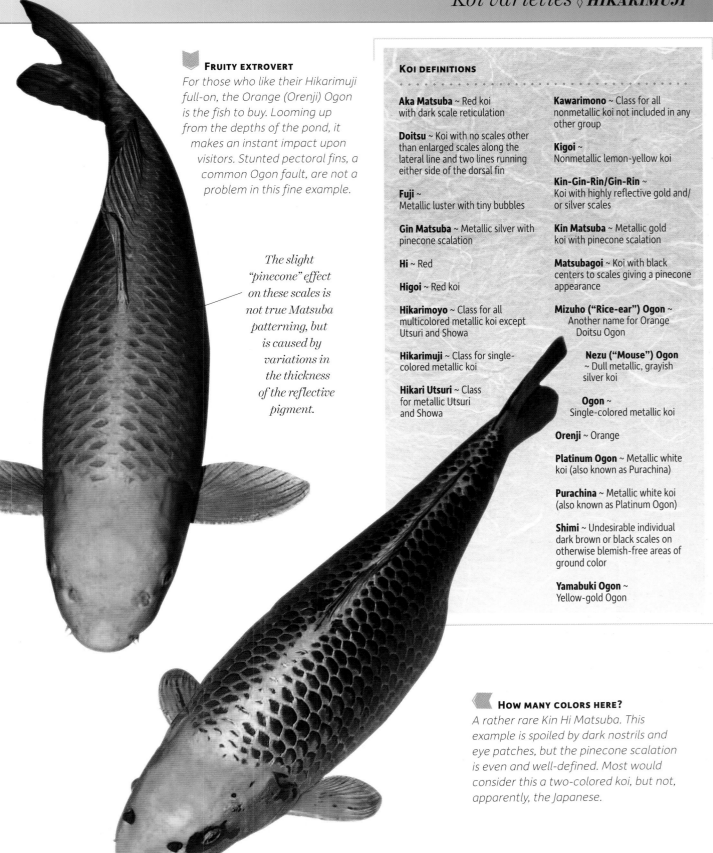

FRUITY EXTROVERT

For those who like their Hikarimuji full-on, the Orange (Orenji) Ogon is the fish to buy. Looming up from the depths of the pond, it makes an instant impact upon visitors. Stunted pectoral fins, a common Ogon fault, are not a problem in this fine example.

The slight "pinecone" effect on these scales is not true Matsuba patterning, but is caused by variations in the thickness of the reflective pigment.

KOI DEFINITIONS

Aka Matsuba ~ Red koi with dark scale reticulation

Doitsu ~ Koi with no scales other than enlarged scales along the lateral line and two lines running either side of the dorsal fin

Fuji ~ Metallic luster with tiny bubbles

Gin Matsuba ~ Metallic silver with pinecone scalation

Hi ~ Red

Higoi ~ Red koi

Hikarimoyo ~ Class for all multicolored metallic koi except Utsuri and Showa

Hikarimuji ~ Class for single-colored metallic koi

Hikari Utsuri ~ Class for metallic Utsuri and Showa

Kawarimono ~ Class for all nonmetallic koi not included in any other group

Kigoi ~ Nonmetallic lemon-yellow koi

Kin-Gin-Rin/Gin-Rin ~ Koi with highly reflective gold and/or silver scales

Kin Matsuba ~ Metallic gold koi with pinecone scalation

Matsubagoi ~ Koi with black centers to scales giving a pinecone appearance

Mizuho ("Rice-ear") Ogon ~ Another name for Orange Doitsu Ogon

Nezu ("Mouse") Ogon ~ Dull metallic, grayish silver koi

Ogon ~ Single-colored metallic koi

Orenji ~ Orange

Platinum Ogon ~ Metallic white koi (also known as Purachina)

Purachina ~ Metallic white koi (also known as Platinum Ogon)

Shimi ~ Undesirable individual dark brown or black scales on otherwise blemish-free areas of ground color

Yamabuki Ogon ~ Yellow-gold Ogon

HOW MANY COLORS HERE?

A rather rare Kin Hi Matsuba. This example is spoiled by dark nostrils and eye patches, but the pinecone scalation is even and well-defined. Most would consider this a two-colored koi, but not, apparently, the Japanese.

Hikarimoyo

Ogon, Kin and Gin Matsuba fall into the Hikarimuji classification. But these fish have all been crossed with other varieties to produce metallic koi of more than one color, known as Hikarimoyo (abbreviated from Hikarimoyo-Mono). The only exceptions are Hikari Utsuri, which are essentially metallic Utsuri or Showa and judged in a separate class.

Hikarimoyo are immediate eye-catchers that appeal both to beginners and more experienced hobbyists. The color permutations are almost limitless and this quality, enhanced by a high luster, makes a strong impact. Even low-grade examples can look stunning when young, but as they grow any defects become more apparent. Chief among these are dark lines running from the eyes down to the nose — a throwback to the Gin and Kin Kabuto forerunners of the Ogon — and discoloration on what should be a clear head.

Hikarimoyo are subdivided, somewhat arbitrarily, into Hariwake and the rest. Hariwake are two-colored koi with a platinum base color overlaid with yellow, and are available in fully scaled or Doitsu form. Hariwake Matsuba have the same coloration, but the scales have Matsuba markings.

The aristocrat of Hikarimoyo is the metallic Sanke known as Yamatonishiki. This variety came on to the market in the 1960s from two distinct sources, the first breeder being Seikichi Hoshino, who took 15 years to develop it. The complex process involved an initial cross between an Asagi and a Kin Kabuto and subsequent introductions of Sakura Ogon blood. A similar fish — Koshi-nishiki — was bred in Yamakoshi by crossing a Yamabuki Doitsu with a Gin Showa. Both are now grouped together as Yamatonishiki.

Metallic skin in koi of Hikarimoyo can dull the underlying colors because the light is diffused through them. This results in sumi appearing dark gray rather than black, and red becoming more orange. However, in Yamatonishiki this is compensated for by the platinum skin and finnage, which may or may not carry Sanke-style sumi stripes. The head of this variety is preferably adorned with hi markings in the manner of a normal Sanke.

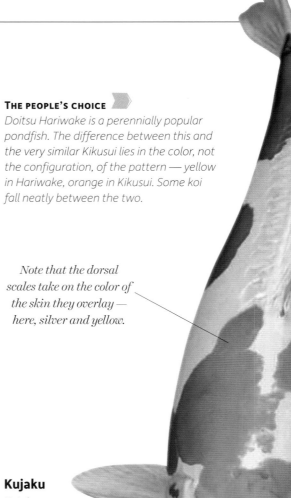

Note that the dorsal scales take on the color of the skin they overlay — here, silver and yellow.

Kujaku

Kujaku, or Kujaku Ogon as they are still sometimes known, are highly regarded by the Japanese, as the patterning on a good specimen can rival that of Go Sanke. Like Goshiki, they are said to be five-colored koi, but this sometimes stretches credulity — not all modern examples display white, black, red, brown and yellow markings. The first ones were bred in Ojiya in1960 by Toshio Hirasawa from a female Shusui and a male Kin Matsuba and Hariwake.

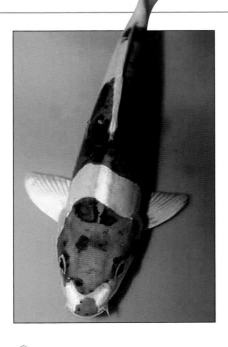

BANDED BEAUTY
Clear-cut color contrasts make this Doitsu Yamatonishiki (metallic Sanke) a showstopper. The large, lustrous pectoral fins line up with the silver band behind the head, with striking effectiveness.

The head of all metallic koi should have a deep luster.

PERFECT PECS
Fully scaled Hariwake are subtler than their Doitsu equivalent. This one has a Kohaku-like pattern, and the white area on the face lends it balance. There are no head blemishes, and the pectoral fins are imposing.

❖ KEEP A CLEAR HEAD ❖

Dark "spectacles" are a common fault in metallic koi.

KOI DEFINITIONS

Asagi ~ Koi showing a bluish back with reticulated scale pattern. Some red on cheeks, flanks and pectoral fins

Doitsu ~ Koi with no scales other than enlarged scales along the lateral line and two lines running either side of the dorsal fin

Gin Kabuto ~ Black koi with silver edges to scales

Gin Matsuba ~ Metallic silver with pinecone scalation

Gin Showa ~ Metallic Showa with a silver luster

Go Sanke ~ Koi from the Kohaku, Sanke and Showa classes

Goshiki ~ Koi with five-color pattern made up from red, white, black, light blue and dark blue

Hikarimoyo ~ Class for all multicolored metallic koi except Utsuri and Showa

Hikarimuji ~ Class for single-colored metallic koi

Hikari Utsuri ~ Class for metallic Utsuri and Showa

Kin Kabuto ~ Black koi with gold edges to scales

Kin Matsuba ~ Metallic gold koi with pinecone scalation

Koshi-nishiki ~ Cross between Yamabuki Doitsu and Gin Showa

Kujaku (Ogon) ~ Metallic koi with red pattern on a white base and matsuba scalation

Matsuba ~ Black center to scale, giving a pinecone appearance

Ogon ~ Single-colored metallic koi

Sakura Ogon ~ Metallic Kohaku

Sanke ~ White koi with red and black markings

(Koi are normally spawned in trios, with one female and two males. It is therefore impossible to establish the exact parentage of the first Kujaku.) The result was a metallic platinum fish with black Matsuba scalation overlaying a hi pattern, a clear red head, and some blue derived from the original female parent koi. Many of these first Kujaku (the word literally means "peacock") were Doitsu, again the result of the Shusui influence.

Doitsu Kujaku are sometimes mistaken for Ginsui and Kinsui (these days not popular varieties). However, in the German-scaled Kujaku, the hi overlaid with black forms a distinct pattern along the dorsal surface and lateral lines, whereas in Ginsui, if much hi appears at all, it is in typical Shusui configuration, that is, on the cheeks and flanks, and the platinum skin tends to have a bluish tint. Judging standards for modern Kujaku have become quite flexible. For instance, "interesting" head patterning (provided there is no black intruding) is just as acceptable as plain red or platinum. A subvariety, the Beni Kujaku, is predominantly red.

Sakura Ogon

Kohaku of the Hikarimoyo are known either as Platinum Kohaku or Sakura Ogon. The distinction between them used to be drawn on the basis that in the latter, the hi patterning resembled that of a Kanoko Kohaku (namely dappled), whereas Platinum Kohaku displayed more traditional hi. A more accurate assessment would be that Sakura Ogon show a more flowery pattern — small (but cohesive and stable) patches of red scales. In both varieties, the hi overlaying platinum skin is actually more of an orange color.

The Doitsu version of the Sakura Ogon is known as a Kikusui ("water chrysanthemum"), a platinum fish with orange overlay running in wavy lines either side of the dorsal fin or else placed in traditional Kohaku manner. "Orenji

PROUD AS A PEACOCK
This koi shows you why Kujaku are held in high esteem by the Japanese. The more you look at it, the better it gets — the head marking resembles an island, whereas the body has a strong Matsuba scalation over a subtle color combination.

PROMISING YOUNGSTER
A young Doitsu Kujaku. The German scales are not very even, but the overall coloration is stunning. This koi should eventually "grow into" its presently rather oversized pectoral fins.

Hariwake Doitsu" is an old-fashioned term for this koi, but describes exactly what it is.

A Shochikubai is a metallic Ai Goromo, a variety not often seen. The higher the metallic luster, the more likely the reticulated hi is to appear brown, but this only lends a dignified appearance to this rare fish.

Gin Bekko (not to be confused with Gin-Rin Bekko) is simply a cross between a Shiro Bekko and a Platinum Ogon. The sumi markings tend to be subdued by the bright skin. Kin Showa are benched in another class, namely Hikari Utsuri.

ORANGE EQUALS KIKUSUI
Kikusui are always Doitsu. This one has a rather flowery Kohaku-style pattern, with a charming nose spot, but it is orange (as opposed to yellow) markings that make it Kikusui and not Doitsu Hariwake.

KOI DEFINITIONS

Ai Goromo ~ White koi with red Kohaku pattern. Each red scale is reticulated in black or dark blue

Beni Kujaku ~ Predominantly red subvariety of Kujaku

Doitsu ~ Koi with no scales other than enlarged scales along the lateral line and two lines running either side of the dorsal fin

Ginsui ~ Metallic Shusui with a silver luster

Hariwake ~ Two-colored koi with platinum base overlaid with orange or gold

Hikarimoyo ~ Class for all multicolored metallic koi except Utsuri and Showa

Kanoko Kohaku ~ Kohaku with dappled red pattern

Kikusui ~ Platinum koi with metallic orange markings and always Doitsu

Kinsui ~ Metallic Shusui with a gold luster

Kohaku ~ White koi with red markings

Matsuba ~ Black center to scale, giving a pinecone appearance

Orenji ~ Orange

Sakura Ogon ~ Metallic Kohaku

Shochikubai ~ Metallic Ai Goromo

Shusui ~ Doitsu Asagi

Sumi ~ Black

Tora, or Tiger Ogon ~ Metallic equivalent of Ki Bekko

Yamabuki ~ Yellow-gold

Yamatonishiki ~ Metallic Sanke

Hariwake

Hariwake are derived from Ogon or Ogon/Matsuba lineage and display two metallic colors — a platinum base overlaid with either yellow-gold (Yamabuki) or orange (Orenji) markings. These immensely bright and showy koi, much loved by beginners, are relatively easy to produce. The Doitsu versions are particularly popular. A Doitsu Orenji Hariwake is properly known as a Kikusui.

Ideally, fully scaled Yamabuki and Orenji Hariwake should have clear platinum heads, although if the second color intrudes it is not a disaster. The nicest examples show a lot of metallic white on the body, but others only have small areas of this platinum skin. As in Hikarimuji, the scales should convey a three-dimensional impression.

Doitsu Hariwake often fall down on the positioning of the mirror scales, which, as in all other Doitsu koi, should be bilaterally symmetrical and evenly spaced. Many examples show coarse scalation all over the caudal peduncle, whereas in others, the scales are overly large, with an armored appearance. Look beyond the overt appeal of these fish to be sure of acquiring a good specimen.

Fully scaled Hariwake Matsuba are virtually indistinguishable from Kujaku. The dark pinecone insertion point to each scale is toned down because of the metallic overlay. Hariwake Matsuba Doitsu are another matter, because the dark scales

RARE AND SUBTLE

A very subtly marked Shochikubai (metallic Ai Goromo). Hikarimoyo need not be brash to be good, and the pattern and skin quality of this fish put it right in among the best Go Sanke. The robing over the hi will develop further with age.

KOI DEFINITIONS

Bekko ~ Black Sanke-type markings on a white, red or yellow base

Beni ~ Red

Gin Bekko ~ Cross between a Shiro Bekko and a Platinum Ogon

Gin-Rin ~ Koi with reflective silver scales

Hariwake ~ Two-colored koi with platinum base overlaid with orange or gold

Heisei-Nishiki ~ Doitsu Yamatonishiki-type koi, but with Showa-style sumi

Hikarimuji ~ Class for single-colored metallic koi

Hikari Utsuri ~ Class for metallic Utsuri and Showa

Ki Bekko ~ Lemon-yellow with black sanke-type markings

Kikokuryu ~ Metallic Kumonryu

Kin ~ Gold

Kin Showa ~ Metallic Showa with gold luster

Kujaku (Ogon) ~ Metallic koi with red pattern on a white base and matsuba scalation

Kumonryu ~ Black doitsu koi with some white on head, fins and body

Shiro Bekko ~ White koi with black Sanke-type markings

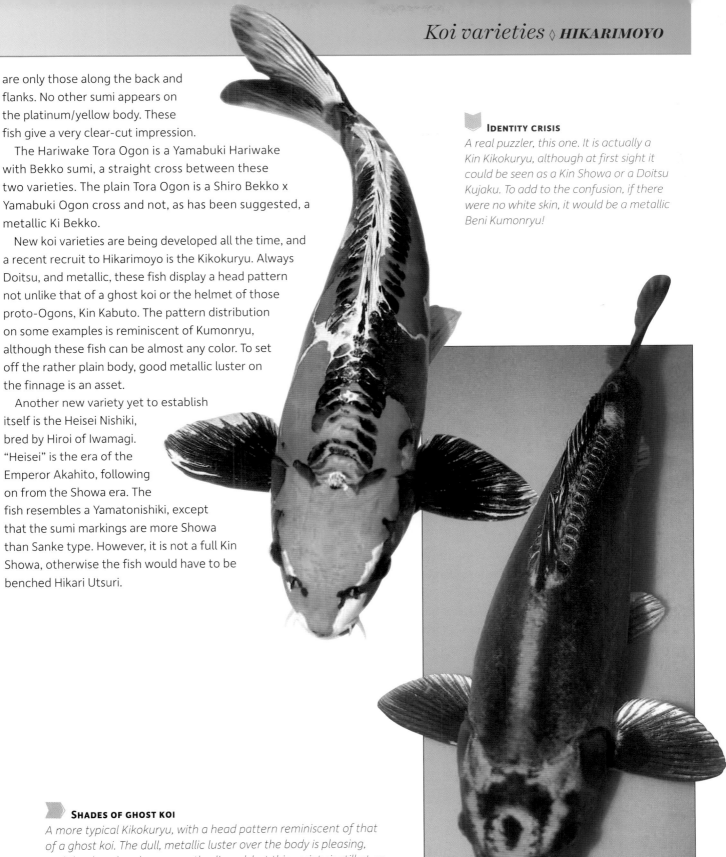

are only those along the back and flanks. No other sumi appears on the platinum/yellow body. These fish give a very clear-cut impression.

The Hariwake Tora Ogon is a Yamabuki Hariwake with Bekko sumi, a straight cross between these two varieties. The plain Tora Ogon is a Shiro Bekko x Yamabuki Ogon cross and not, as has been suggested, a metallic Ki Bekko.

New koi varieties are being developed all the time, and a recent recruit to Hikarimoyo is the Kikokuryu. Always Doitsu, and metallic, these fish display a head pattern not unlike that of a ghost koi or the helmet of those proto-Ogons, Kin Kabuto. The pattern distribution on some examples is reminiscent of Kumonryu, although these fish can be almost any color. To set off the rather plain body, good metallic luster on the finnage is an asset.

Another new variety yet to establish itself is the Heisei Nishiki, bred by Hiroi of Iwamagi. "Heisei" is the era of the Emperor Akahito, following on from the Showa era. The fish resembles a Yamatonishiki, except that the sumi markings are more Showa than Sanke type. However, it is not a full Kin Showa, otherwise the fish would have to be benched Hikari Utsuri.

IDENTITY CRISIS
A real puzzler, this one. It is actually a Kin Kikokuryu, although at first sight it could be seen as a Kin Showa or a Doitsu Kujaku. To add to the confusion, if there were no white skin, it would be a metallic Beni Kumonryu!

SHADES OF GHOST KOI
A more typical Kikokuryu, with a head pattern reminiscent of that of a ghost koi. The dull, metallic luster over the body is pleasing, and the dorsal scales are neatly aligned, but this variety is still at an early stage of development and will improve further.

Hikari Utsuri

Koi classified in Hikari Utsuri are basically metallic Showa and Utsurimono, the result of crossing Showa and Utsurimono with Ogon. Fish in this classification are nowhere near as popular as they once were and are underrepresented at shows. The reason is probably twofold. First, subtle appreciation of the finer points of koi is spreading from Japan to other parts of the world, and serious hobbyists are moving away from the "flashier" varieties. Second, although the metallic luster of Hikari Utsuri is a plus point, it can tone down hi and sumi, so although these koi sparkle in the pond, their patterning is not always clear-cut. This makes koi that overcome this potential drawback very valuable, and efforts have indeed been made to improve the overall quality of Hikari Utsuri by back-crossing to the original, nonmetallic half of the partnership.

All metallic Showa are known as Kin Showa. Kin and Gin Matsuba are recognized varieties in Hikarimuji, as they are either gold or silver, but there is no such thing as a Gin Showa, whatever the prevailing skin color may be.

The first point to appreciate is that under the metallic luster there should be a good Showa in its own right. All the key elements should be there, such as wraparound sumi, motoguro in the pectoral fins and the classic intrusion of an interesting black pattern into the head and face. Hi and sumi should be as strong and well-placed toward the rear of the body as in the area ahead of the dorsal fin, and there must be no congenital deformities.

Ideally, the hi should be crimson, but is typically more brownish, reminiscent of that on nonmetallic Showa when they were first developed. However, Showa sumi is particularly strong and can usually hold its own against the toning down effect of the metallic skin, as shown on the fish on page 232. Metallic Kindai Showa (those with much white on the body) are particularly striking.

A metallic Shiro Utsuri is known as a Gin Shiro (Gin Bekko are benched Hikarimoyo). The sharp contrast between the black and white areas of the parent Shiro Utsuri is not

A GIANT ACHIEVEMENT
An imposing 85 cm (33 in) Kin Ki Utsuri that won "best in variety" in the 2001 All-Japan Show. What makes it a winner are the imposing full body, even metallic luster, dark sumi in a pleasing arrangement, and the indefinable quality known as "presence." To grow this variety to its present size is an achievement in itself.

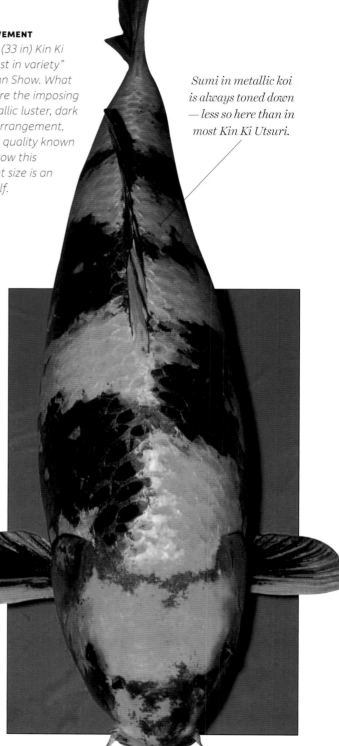

Sumi in metallic koi is always toned down — less so here than in most Kin Ki Utsuri.

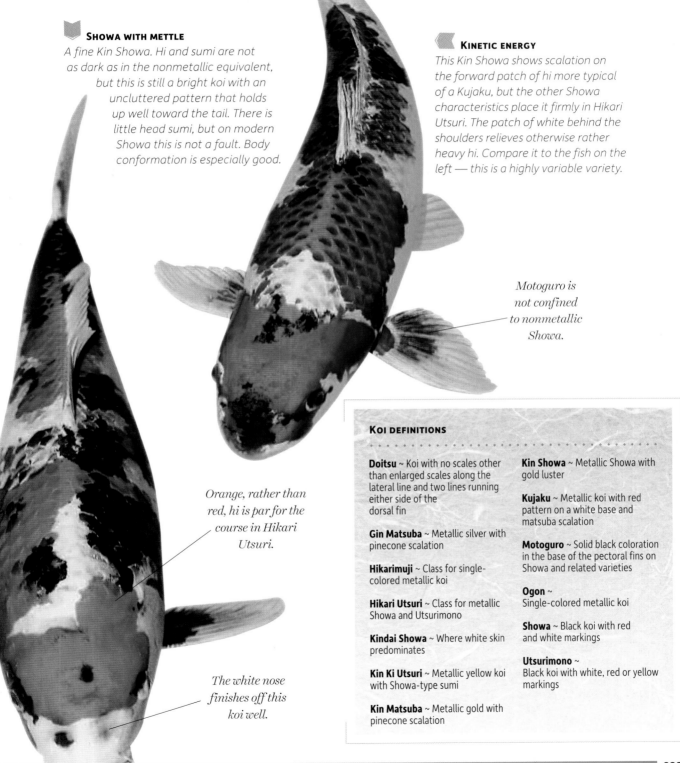

SHOWA WITH METTLE
A fine Kin Showa. Hi and sumi are not as dark as in the nonmetallic equivalent, but this is still a bright koi with an uncluttered pattern that holds up well toward the tail. There is little head sumi, but on modern Showa this is not a fault. Body conformation is especially good.

KINETIC ENERGY
This Kin Showa shows scalation on the forward patch of hi more typical of a Kujaku, but the other Showa characteristics place it firmly in Hikari Utsuri. The patch of white behind the shoulders relieves otherwise rather heavy hi. Compare it to the fish on the left — this is a highly variable variety.

Motoguro is not confined to nonmetallic Showa.

Orange, rather than red, hi is par for the course in Hikari Utsuri.

The white nose finishes off this koi well.

KOI DEFINITIONS

Doitsu ~ Koi with no scales other than enlarged scales along the lateral line and two lines running either side of the dorsal fin

Gin Matsuba ~ Metallic silver with pinecone scalation

Hikarimuji ~ Class for single-colored metallic koi

Hikari Utsuri ~ Class for metallic Showa and Utsurimono

Kindai Showa ~ Where white skin predominates

Kin Ki Utsuri ~ Metallic yellow koi with Showa-type sumi

Kin Matsuba ~ Metallic gold with pinecone scalation

Kin Showa ~ Metallic Showa with gold luster

Kujaku ~ Metallic koi with red pattern on a white base and matsuba scalation

Motoguro ~ Solid black coloration in the base of the pectoral fins on Showa and related varieties

Ogon ~ Single-colored metallic koi

Showa ~ Black koi with red and white markings

Utsurimono ~ Black koi with white, red or yellow markings

KOI DEFINITIONS

Gin Bekko ~ Cross between a Shiro Bekko and a Platinum Ogon

Gin Shiro ~ Metallic Shiro Utsuri

Hikarimoyo ~ Class for all multicolored metallic koi except Utsuri and Showa

Hi ~ Red

Hi Utsuri ~ Black koi with red or orange markings

Kage ~ Shadowy black reticulated marking over white (or red on Hi Utsuri)

Kindai Showa ~ White skin predominates

Kin-Gin-Rin/Gin-Rin ~ Koi with highly reflective gold and/or silver scales

Kin Hi Utsuri ~ Metallic black koi with red or orange markings

Kin Ki Utsuri ~ Metallic yellow koi with Showa-type sumi

Ki Utsuri ~ Black koi with yellow markings

Shimi ~ Undesirable individual dark brown or black scales on areas of ground color

Shiro Utsuri ~ Black koi with white markings

Yamabuki ~ Yellow-gold

Yamatonishiki ~ Metallic Sanke

QUALITY SHOWA SUMI

There is not much sumi on this Kin Ki Utsuri, but what there is, is pleasingly dark. However, the head could be said to be a little "untidy."

present, but the subtle sheen on these koi makes up for this. They look best if bred to the modern taste for limited areas of sumi. All-white pectoral fins, or those with neat motoguro, set off the rest of the fish better than dark fins, which do not contrast so effectively with the metallic luster.

Kin Hi Utsuri are arguably the most successful Utsurimono/Hikarimuji mix. The red in good specimens is bright crimson, and although the sumi may be toned down, this does mean that any shimis — normally the plague of Hi Utsuri — are less obvious. The pectoral fins — candy-striped black and white with a golden overlay — can practically glow. Head sumi is not generally as well-defined as in Shiro Utsuri, and dark nostrils on an otherwise all-red head are a common fault.

The final fish in this classification is the Kin Ki Utsuri — a metallic yellow koi with wraparound sumi. Whether this is a cross between Ki Utsuri and Ogon — is doubtful — a more likely parentage would be Yamabuki Ogon/Shiro Utsuri, since matt-scaled Ki Utsuri, although a very old variety, are hardly ever seen in the hobby nowadays. The yellow on these koi is a bright gold, and body sumi on good specimens gives each scale an almost tricolored appearance — dark where it enters the skin, blackish-gold in the center and dark again at the rim.

❖ **KITH AND KIN** ❖

Kin Showa can be Kindai (as here) or the traditional type.

Yamatonishiki (metallic Sanke) such as this can be confused with Kindai Kin Showa.

When in doubt, check sumi placement and type.

Head sumi on Kin Ki Utsuri is highly variable.

Three metallic colors complement one another on a scaleless head.

Subvarieties of this classification can be Doitsu or Kin-Gin-Rin; the latter look as though they are wearing a rich coat of mail with the double reflective qualities of metallic and sparkling scales. Kage patterning is also recognized, but does not affect how they are benched.

JET-BLACK ON SILVER
Metallic Shiro Utsuri are known simply as Gin Shiro. This is another koi with remarkably dark sumi, and this time the head pattern is as good as that on the body.

Kin-Gin-Rin

In 1929, Japanese koi enthusiast Eizaburo Hoshino first discovered individual sparkling scales on koi he had bred and named them "Gingoke." These mutant scales were later termed "Dia," but today the accepted word outside Japan is "Kin-Gin-Rin" — often shortened to plain "Gin-Rin."

Gin-Rin scales are quite different from those on the three groupings of metallic koi. Instead of an overall flat gleam, caused by the reflective pigment guanine, Kin-Gin-Rin scales have a sparkling deposit over all or part of their surface and, depending on the type, may be flat or raised. The color they appear is determined by the pigment they overlay — silver (Gin) in the case of sumi or white, and golden (Kin) over hi (red).

Subvarieties of Kin-Gin-Rin

Gin-Rin can be divided into four subvarieties. In Beta-Gin the whole surface of the scale is reflective, whereas Kado-Gin describes scales where only the leading edge carries this pigment. The latest type to appear — Diamond, or Hiroshima, Gin-Rin — originated in 1969 on the Konishi koi farm in southern Japan. Here, the reflective element radiates out from the insertion point of the scales in a fan shape. The Japanese like this type of Gin-Rin least of all, as it makes the koi appear flashy and unrefined and can blur the edges of hi and sumi patterns. Additionally, the leading edge of these scales is often ragged, coming to a series of small points, rather than being pleasantly rounded.

▶ **SPARKLING CHAGOI**
This rather plain Gin-Rin Chagoi is "lifted" by the sparkling coat of scales that overlay the entire body. But it is also a fine Chagoi in its own right, with a well-filled-out body, pectoral fins in proportion and the requisite clear head. It is more difficult to justify Gin-Rin scalation on Go Sanke, which some would argue do not require any further embellishment. And Gin-Rin can lend a misleading impression of quality to otherwise mediocre koi.

In Japan, this fish would be shown in the Gin-Rin B class (koi other than Go Sanke).

❖ *STYLES OF REFLECTION* ❖

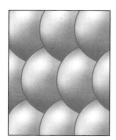

Beta-Gin, or fully reflective, scales.

Diamond Gin-Rin, the most recent form to appear.

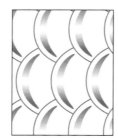

Kado-Gin, where only the scale edges are reflective.

Pearl Gin-Rin, with a slightly raised central area to each scale.

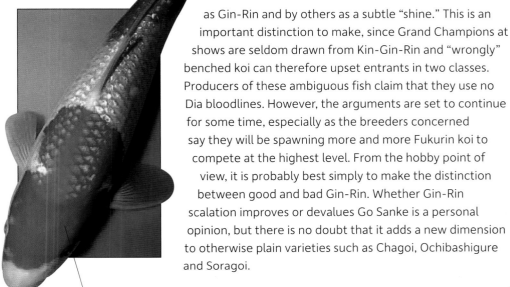

Where the sparkling deposit is heavy, the surface of the scales becomes slightly raised; this is Pearl Gin-Rin, also known as Tsubu- or Tama-Gin. More than one type of Gin-Rin scale can appear on the same fish. Beta-Gin is usually found on the abdomen, along the lateral line or in individual rows toward the dorsal surface. Diamond and Kado-Gin tend to cover the back of the koi. Most hobbyists today do not differentiate between the types of Gin-Rin, but accept them as enhancing already beautiful koi.

Already a fine two-step Kohaku, the Gin-Rin scales serve to make this fish still more impressive.

Metallic Kin-Gin-Rin

Even metallic fish are now being bred with this scalation and a good Gin-Rin Ogon is an unforgettable sight. To qualify as Gin-Rin, a koi should have more of these scales than it is possible to count as it swims past the observer — about 20 is the accepted minimum. Individual Gin-Rin scales on otherwise matt-scaled koi can look very attractive and do not detract from their value.

In the West, only Gin-Rin Go Sanke are benched Kin-Gin-Rin, although many other koi varieties have this type of scalation. In Japan, Kin-Gin-Rin "A" includes Go Sanke, whereas Kin-Gin-Rin "B" covers the rest.

A shimmering coat of reflective scales can lead the novice to fall for koi of otherwise limited attributes. Show judges in the Kin-Gin-Rin class, looking at a Gin-Rin Kohaku, will first ask themselves, "Is this a good Kohaku in its own right?" Only if they are satisfied that it is would they mark it highly.

Gin-Rin versus Fukurin

Some controversy exists over the status of Go Sanke said to possess "Fukurin" scalation, which is perceived by some as Gin-Rin and by others as a subtle "shine." This is an important distinction to make, since Grand Champions at shows are seldom drawn from Kin-Gin-Rin and "wrongly" benched koi can therefore upset entrants in two classes. Producers of these ambiguous fish claim that they use no Dia bloodlines. However, the arguments are set to continue for some time, especially as the breeders concerned say they will be spawning more and more Fukurin koi to compete at the highest level. From the hobby point of view, it is probably best simply to make the distinction between good and bad Gin-Rin. Whether Gin-Rin scalation improves or devalues Go Sanke is a personal opinion, but there is no doubt that it adds a new dimension to otherwise plain varieties such as Chagoi, Ochibashigure and Soragoi.

KOI DEFINITIONS

Chagoi ~ Nonmetallic brown koi

Dia ~ Mutant scales that appear gold over red and silver over white areas of skin

Fukurin ~ Reticulated effect created by lustrous skin around the scales of (usually) metallic koi

Gin ~ Silver

Go Sanke ~ Koi from the Kohaku, Sanke and Showa classes

Kin ~ Gold

Kin-Gin-Rin/Gin-Rin ~ Koi with highly reflective gold and/ or silver scales

Kohaku ~ White koi with red markings

Ochiba/Ochiba Shigure ~ Blue-gray koi with a brown pattern

Ogon ~ Single-colored metallic koi

Pearl Gin-Rin ~ Reflective, slightly convex silver scales

Showa ~ Black koi with red and white markings

Sanke ~ White koi with red and black markings

Soragoi ~ Plain blue-gray koi

Tancho

Tancho are very much koi for the purist, and the Tancho Kohaku, in particular, appeals to the Japanese for its extreme simplicity of pattern and the symbolism it evokes. In Japan, the national bird is the rare Tancho, or dancing, crane *(Grus japonensis)*, which sports a round, red head marking. This reminds the people of the Japanese flag, as does the head hi of Tancho koi.

Virtually any koi variety can display a symmetrical head marking in isolation, but only Go Sanke with this characteristic — Kohaku, Sanke and Showa — are benched Tancho. These can be in normal, Doitsu or Gin-Rin form, whereas a "Tancho" Goshiki in the West would go into the Koromo classification. For benching purposes (in Go Sanke only), Tancho overrides Gin-Rin. But for Go Sanke (Gin-Rin or otherwise) to qualify for Tancho status, the head hi has to be the only patch of that color on the fish. Those with separated head hi and red patterning elsewhere on the body are termed Maruten Kohaku, Sanke, etc.

The classic Tancho is the Tancho Kohaku, a pure white fish with only its head hi to set off the snowy skin. Traditionally, this hi is circular, of an even crimson, and placed centrally between the eyes. All other factors, such as skin quality and body shape, being equal, then the more perfect the circle, the more valuable the koi becomes.

PURE SIMPLICITY

Classic Tancho Kohaku, with a near-perfect circular head marking placed centrally between the eyes. A fine example of this, the simplest of varieties, is possibly the hardest to achieve, and a fish such as this would command an astronomical price.

In Tancho Kohaku, a good head is nothing without an equally flawless, snowy white body to set it off.

KOI DEFINITIONS

Doitsu ~ Koi with no scales other than enlarged scales along the lateral line and two lines running either side of the dorsal fin

Gin-Rin ~ Koi with reflective silver scales

Go Sanke ~ Koi from the Kohaku, Sanke and Showa classes

Goshiki ~ Koi with five-color pattern made up from red, white, black, light blue and dark blue

Hi ~ Red

Kohaku ~ White koi with red markings

Koromo ~ "Robed." Red coloration overlaid with blue or black

Maruten ~ Self-contained head marking, plus red elsewhere on the body

Sanke ~ White koi with red and black markings

Showa ~ Black koi with red and white markings

Sumi ~ Black

HIGH-CLASS TANCHO SANKE

A hi-deficient Sanke or a Shiro Bekko with an added element? There is no such thing as a Tancho Bekko, of course. This is a Tancho Sanke of the highest quality, with subtle tortoiseshell sumi markings.

HEAD-TURNING DISPLAY

In Tancho Showa, sumi intruding into the head hi is not seen as a fault. This fish would be a very passable Shiro Utsuri, but for the patch of red. The V-shaped head sumi is typically Showa, as are the evenly marked pectoral fins.

VARIATION ON A THEME

Unique Tancho markings deviate considerably from the plain circular spot, and this crown-shaped adornment falls into that category. However, from what can be seen of the koi, the body could do with more volume.

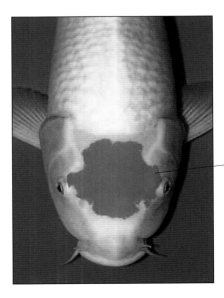

Do not confuse a stable, unique marking such as this with fading hi.

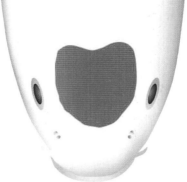

Heart-shaped head hi on a fish for a loved one, perhaps?

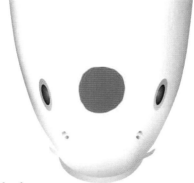

Right shape, wrong size. This Tancho mark is not imposing.

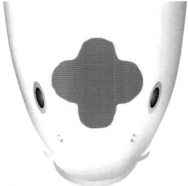

A flowery shaped Tancho mark is an acceptable variation.

If there is more than one hi marking, the koi is not a true Tancho.

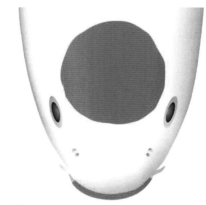

Red lips (Kuchibeni) technically disqualify this koi from Tancho status.

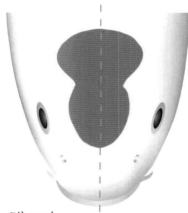

Bilateral symmetry is a plus point in this unusual Tancho marking.

Standards have been relaxed to a degree, so that Tancho Kohaku with oval, crown-shaped, heart-shaped or otherwise interestingly configured hi are also held in esteem. However, symmetry, although not normally adjudged to be essential to the pattern of a koi, is important in the case of Tancho. If an imaginary line is drawn down the center of the head, the hi on either side should match up and not, for example, slip down over one eye.

Good examples of Tancho Kohaku are very expensive because, of course, it is impossible to selectively breed fish with head hi only with any regularity. Many worthless Shiro Muji result from spawnings, and for every classic Tancho produced there will be hundreds more in which the head

pattern is disappointing. More frustrating still, a near-perfect head can be accompanied by one or more small areas of body hi. The fish then falls between two stools and is neither a good Tancho nor an acceptably patterned Kohaku.

In Tancho Sanke, the head hi is complemented by sumi markings on the body and in some or all of the fins. The fish is essentially a Tancho Bekko, but this term is not recognized because Shiro Bekko never have any red. Although sumi occasionally intrudes into the head of a normal Sanke, a Tancho Sanke's hi should sit on a clear white ground, with the first sumi markings appearing on the shoulders. Many Bekko are thrown from spawnings of this tricky variety, but at least these fish — unlike Shiro Muji — have some commercial value.

The third type of Tancho koi is basically a Shiro Utsuri with head hi only. But once again, the latter variety should not display any red, which is why "Tancho Showa" is the only acceptable term for these koi. They are interesting in that the head hi is usually cut through by the sumi, either in menware or V-shaped configuration. The classic wraparound Utsurimono sumi and motoguro on the pectoral fins are bold features in their own right, so that rather than seeing these koi as Showa lacking hi, it makes more sense to view them as Shiro Utsuri with that bit extra.

Because good examples of all three types of Tancho koi are so rare, it has been known for fish to be "doctored" in their country of origin to heighten their value. Head hi is bleached or treated cryogenically to make it more symmetrical, while individual red body scales are removed the same way. If hi is lacking where it is wanted it can even be tattooed in — something for buyers to watch out for!

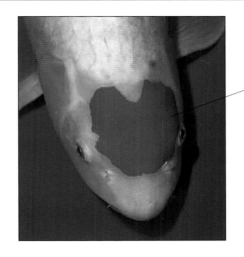

This heart-shaped Tancho mark is natural, but a few koi undergo the equivalent of cosmetic surgery to enhance what attributes they already have.

KOI DEFINITIONS

Bekko ~ Black markings on a white, red or yellow base

Hi ~ Red

Kohaku ~ White koi with red markings

Kuchibeni ~ Red lips — literally "lipstick"

Menware ~ Strike-through sumi pattern on head of Showa, Utsurimono or Hikariutsuri

Motoguro ~ Solid black coloration in the base of the pectoral fins on Showa and related varieties

Sanke ~ White koi with red and black markings

Shiro Bekko ~ White koi with black markings

Shiro Muji ~ White, nonmetallic koi

Shiro Utsuri ~ Black koi with white markings

Showa ~ Black koi with red and white markings

Sumi ~ Black

Tancho ~ Circular red spot on the head. No other red on the body

Tancho Sanke ~ Red on the head of a Sanke. No other red on the body

Tancho Showa ~ Red on the head of a Showa. No other red on the body

Utsurimono ~ Black koi with white, red or yellow markings

❖ **HEAD MARKINGS** ❖

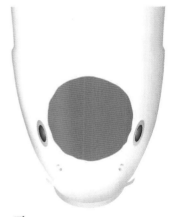

The near-unattainable, although ideal, Tancho Kohaku head.

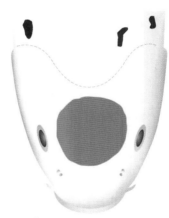

Tancho Sanke — sumi stays well away from the head area.

Menware sumi through the head hi of a Tancho Showa is quite acceptable.

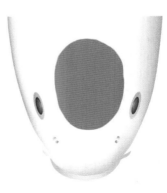

Oval Tancho marks are almost as valued as a perfect circle.

Doitsu

"Doitsu" (German-scaled fish) describes koi with no scales other than enlarged scales along the lateral line and two lines running either side of the dorsal fin. In Japan, the Doitsu classification applies only to Go Sanke, whereas in Western shows there is no separate category for any German-scaled fish, with the exception of Shusui. However, the growing popularity of these virtually naked-skinned koi suggests that some revision may be necessary, so that Doitsu scalation can be recognized for what it is — an intriguing and challenging variation on the endless theme of Nishikigoi.

Even when grouped together with Asagi, Shusui are underrepresented at shows, yet other classes are crammed full of koi so diverse that judging one against another becomes very difficult. How do you compare a Kumonryu with a fully scaled Chagoi in Kawarimono, for example? Putting all Doitsu koi together in Western shows would not require any extra classifications, as Shusui could be included and Asagi could move to Kawarimono (from which Doitsu koi would now be excluded), joining several other old varieties — such as Soragoi and Kigoi — whose virtue lies in their simplicity. The crowded Hikarimuji and Hikarimoyo classes would benefit similarly from having their Doitsu representatives benched elsewhere.

Doitsu koi with their own names, such as Midorigoi and Kinsui, would rub shoulders nicely with most other koi of German table carp lineage. (Strictly speaking, the suffix "Doitsu" is added at the end of the variety, e.g., Kin Matsuba Doitsu, Hariwake Doitsu. But most koi-keepers turn that round, i.e., Doitsu Hariwake. It is of no real consequence either way).

Separating Doitsu fish from their fully scaled counterparts would be especially appropriate in cases where the two fish appear very dissimilar. For example, Kin Matsuba Doitsu lack the overall pinecone reticulation, which appears only on the Doitsu scales, whereas Ai Goromo Doitsu have clear hi, and only the blue/black dorsal and lateral scales give a real clue to their lineage. And, given that the Japanese have wisely assigned Doitsu Go Sanke their own classification, would it not make sense to do this in other countries? At top show

▶ **NAKED PERFECTION**
This Doitsu Sanke has attributes in abundance — a wonderful Kohaku-type pattern, well-distributed yet subtle sumi markings and superb skin. The shoulder sumi is particularly well-placed to draw attention to the flawless, striped pectoral fins of what is probably a female fish — and one with plenty more growing still to do.

This sumi overlaps both hi and white skin, a bringing together of the three colors of the koi.

The nose spot balances what would otherwise be a rather plain head.

SNAPPY DRESSER

This Doitsu Goshiki is a very clean-cut koi, which could be mistaken at first glance for a Sumi Goromo. It will be interesting to see if the pure white saddle remains that way as the fish grows, and whether the pattern breaks further.

Less is more — this white skin is the canvas on which the pattern is drawn.

INTEREST ALL DOWN THE LINE

A Doitsu Showa, whose sumi is delicately placed to draw the eye all down the fish. The somewhat one-sided head marking does not matter a bit, only serving to emphasize the pure white skin on the nose and shoulder. Perfectly balanced pectoral fins emphasize a full, but not over-plump, body.

KOI DEFINITIONS

Asagi ~ Koi showing a bluish back with reticulated scale pattern. Some red on cheeks, flanks and pectoral fins

Chagoi ~ Nonmetallic brown koi

Goshiki ~ Koi with five-color pattern, made up from red, white, black, light blue and dark blue

Hariwake ~ Two-colored koi with platinum base overlaid with orange or gold

Hikarimoyo ~ Class for all multicolored metallic koi except Utsuri and Showa

Hikarimuji ~ Class for single-colored metallic koi

Kigoi ~ Nonmetallic lemon-yellow koi

Kin Matsuba ~ Metallic yellow with pinecone scalation

Kinsui ~ Metallic Shusui with a gold luster

Kumonryu ~ Black doitsu koi with some white on head, fins and body

Midorigoi ~ Greenish-yellow koi with mirror scales

Sanke ~ White koi with red and black markings

Shusui ~ Doitsu Asagi

Soragoi ~ Plain blue-gray koi

A REGULAR BEAUTY

*A Doitsu Hariwake with very
regular markings and the
requisite clear head. The variety
is probably the most popular
Doitsu metallic, and the dorsal
scales of this one are regular and
highly reflective.*

KOI DEFINITIONS

Ai Goromo ~ White koi with red
Kohaku pattern. Each red scale is
reticulated in black or dark blue

Doitsu ~ Koi with no scales other
than enlarged scales along the
lateral line and two lines running
either side of the dorsal fin

Go Sanke ~ Koi from the Kohaku,
Sanke and Showa classes

Hariwake ~ Two-colored koi
with platinum base overlaid with
orange or gold

Hi ~ Red

Kawarimono ~ Class for all
nonmetallic koi not included in
any other group

Kin-gin-rin/Gin-Rin ~
Koi with highly reflective gold
and/or silver scales

Kiwa ~ Border of red and white at
the rear edge of hi patterns

Kohaku ~ White koi with
red markings

Maruten ~ Self-contained head
marking, plus red elsewhere on
the body

Shiro Utsuri ~
Black koi with white markings

Sashi ~ Overlap of red and white
scales at the forward
edge of hi patterns

Showa ~ Black koi with red
and white marking

Sumi ~ Black

Yamatonishiki ~ Metallic Sanke

level, a Doitsu Kohaku would never beat a fully scaled koi
of the same quality, but that does not make it any the less
impressive a fish. Doitsu "A" for Go Sanke and Doitsu "B" for
the rest would be one way round the dilemma.

All patterned Doitsu koi should have clearly defined
markings. What they may lack is "refinement." The Japanese
still regard them as somewhat two-dimensional, and
therefore vulgar, compared to their scaled counterparts. Yet
without scales to diffuse the light, colors appear bright and
sharp: a good Doitsu Showa, for example, almost seems
lit from within.

The koi-buying public have no reservations about
Doitsu koi, especially in Kawarimono, where their sales
are increasing year-on-year. When you consider that any
koi, except for Kin-Gin-Rin, can be produced in a Doitsu
version, that is hardly surprising.

❖ **NOW YOU SEE THEM** ❖

These lateral mirror scales are not present in all Doitsu koi.

Not all Doitsu scalation extends over the shoulders, as here.

 HEADING IN THE RIGHT DIRECTION
This Doitsu Yamatonishiki could do with more hi down its left flank, but the Maruten head pattern is first-rate.

 NO SCALES, NO PROBLEM!
Doitsu Shiro Utsuri are rather rare, but with no kiwa and sashi to blur the sumi, this fish manages to combine the best of both elements in a clean-cut, but still subtle, pattern. All the sumi appears to be through in this mature example.

General Index

Page numbers in **bold** indicate major entries, *italics* refer to captions and annotations; plain type indicates other text entries.

Varieties Index

Page numbers in **bold** indicate major entries, *italics* refer to captions and annotations; plain type indicates other text entries.

CREDITS

Unless otherwise credited, practical photographs by Geoffrey Rogers © Interpet Publishing.

For copyright information regarding the diagnostic photographs featured on pages 94–95 and 114–115, refer to the specific A–Z entries themselves.

The publishers would like to thank the following photographers for providing images, credited by page number and position: (B)Bottom, T(Top), C(Center), BL(Bottom Left), etc.

Paul Allen: 124
Aqua Press (M-P & C Piednoir): 15(BR), 117(R), 134(T, Peter Cole)
Shunzo Baba (Kinsai Publishers Co. Ltd., Tokyo): 8(BR), 11(TL,C),
 163(BL,R), 180, 185, 200, 205, 226, 232, 236
Dave Bevan: 72, 73, 113(TR)
Bernice Brewster: 96(BL), 103(T), 106(B), 107(BR), 112(T), 113(CR),
 127(CR, BR), 131(T), 137(CL,CR), 143(C)
Bridgeman Art Library: 8(BC)
David Brown: 44, 168(TR, C)
David Bucke: 78(C, BC)
Nigel Caddock, Nishikigoi International: 171(CL, BC), 174, 177(C),
 179(L, R), 181, 183(R), 184, 186, 187, 189(R), 190, 191(R), 192, 193,
 194, 195, 196, 198, 199(R), 202(R), 208, 209(L), 211, 212(L, R),
 213(L, R), 214, 215, 216, 217(L, R), 221, 222, 223(C, R), 224, 227(T, C),
 228(C, BR), 229, 230, 231(C, R), 233(L), 234(L, R), 237, 238, 239, (BL,
 C, R), 242, 243(L, R), 244, 245(T, B)
Derek Cattani: Copyright page, 6–7, 14, 17(R), 18(BL), 27(BL), 32, 33,
 45, 51(T, BR), 52, 53(L, TR, BR), 77, 79, 118(TL, TR, CL, CR), 143(BC,
 BR),146(T), 150(T, B), 155, 156, 157(T), 158(BL, BR), 159, 161(BL)
Lee Cole: 136, 137(T)
Christina Guthrie: 160(TL, CR)
Steve Hickling: 9(TL, TR), 54(TL, C), 64, 165(TL, TR)
Keith Holmes: 97(C, BL, BR),
Andrew McGill: Half-title page, 12, 175, 176, 177(TL), 182, 183(L),
 189(L), 191(L), 199(BL), 202(L), 203, 204, 207, 209(TR), 219(L, R),
 220(BL, BR), 225(T, B), 233(TC), 241
Stan McMahon: 101
Will Moody: 161(CR)
Tony Pitham (Koi Water Barn): 10, 13, 15(TL), 28(TL), 144, 145(T),
 162(TL, TR, C), 164, 166 (TL, TR, C), 167
Graham Quick: 49
Rinko magazine: 96(BR), 97(T), 100, 104(R), 105, 117(L), 120, 121, 123,
 126, 129, 141
Alec Scaresbrook: Title page, 30(TR)
Sue Scott: 17(TL)
Neil Sutherland © Interpet Publishing: 80, 81, 82, 83, 84, 86, 87(T),
 88, 89, 90, 91, 92, 93, 98–99, 102(B), 103(BL, BR), 107(CL, BC),
 112(B), 116, 119, 122, 125, 127(TL), 128, 132(T), 133, 134(B), 135,
 139, 140
William Wildgoose: 131(B)
Chris Williams, Environment Agency: 99, 102(C), 103(C), 104(L),
 106–107(T), 108(B), 109, 111, 130, 132(B), 138
Steve Worcester: 65(C, CR, BL, BR), 67(TL, TR, CL, BR)

Computer graphics by Phil Holmes and Stuart Watkinson © Interpet Publishing.

ACKNOWLEDGMENTS

The publishers would like to thank World of Koi, Oakley Road, Bromley, Kent for their generous assistance with practical photography, both at head office and at various pond-building sites. In particular, thanks are due to Steve Hickling for his expertise and unbounded enthusiasm for the project, to Mick Martin for writing and holding the fort while Steve finished his sections, to Billy Stone for his expert advice, to Matt Bird for taking on site photographs and providing technical information, and to Kirk Jepson for demonstrating various practical techniques.

The following companies and individuals also helped during the preparation of this book: Tony Pitham and staff at Koi Water Barn, Chelsfield Village, Kent; NT Laboratories Ltd., Wateringbury, Kent; Tetra UK, Eastleigh, Hampshire; Tropical Marine Centre Ltd., Chorley Wood, Hertfordshire; Andrew Chatten and Chris Giles at Selective Koi Sales, Norwich; Andy Dixon of DKS, Lincoln; Mike Shaw at Evolution Aqua Ltd., Wigan, Lancashire; James Allison of Aquapic Solutions, Cheltenham, Gloucestershire; Steve Worcester for allowing photographic access to his emerging pond; Spencer Bell; Alan McDougal; Christina Guthrie, *Koi Carp* Magazine; Angela Rivers, *Koi Ponds and Gardens* Magazine; Geoff Kemp and Connoisseur Koi; Derek Henderson; George Rooney; John Peterson; Sally Wilson; Raymond Sawyer; Mario and Pauline Cavozzi; Pat Meecham; Ron Parlour; Denis Carter; Richard Barker for providing visuals for some of the graphics.

The authors would like to thank and express their appreciation of the following people and companies:
The late John Pitham; Sakai fish Farm (Hiroshima); Narita Koi Farm (Nagoya); Ogawa fish farm; Nakamori and Co; Michael Capot (Koi Ichi Ban); Martin Plows; Ornamental Aquatic Trade Association (OATA), Lisa Holmes.

Note to the Reader
While every effort has been made to ensure that the content of this book is accurate and up-to-date at the time of going to press, it must be accepted that knowledge of fish diseases, the side effects of treatments (on both fish and humans) and other aspects covered, is an every-changing science. Moreover, the manner in which the information container herein is utilized is beyond the control of the authors and publisher, although every effort has been made to warn of known dangers. For these reasons, no responsibility can be accepted by the authors and publisher for any loss, injury or other problem whatsoever experienced by any person using this book.

Always seek the advice of a veterinarian or a qualified koi health specialist before applying the treatments described in this book.